A Child's Story of America

—Second Edition—

Ad maiorem

Dei gloriam

CHRISTIAN LIBERTY PRESS
ARLINGTON HEIGHTS, ILLINOIS

A publication of
Christian Liberty Press
502 West Euclid Avenue
Arlington Heights, Illinois 60004

www.christianlibertypress.com

Scripture references are conformed to The Holy Bible, New King James Version ©1982, Thomas Nelson, Inc., so that modern readers may gain greater comprehension of the Word of God.

Writers:
    Charles Morris
    Michael J. McHugh
    Edward J. Shewan
Layout & Design:
    Robert Fine
Graphics:
    Christopher Kou
    Robert Fine
Editors:
    Edward J. Shewan
    Lars R. Johnson
Executive Editor:
    Michael J. McHugh

Printed in the United States of America

—Contents—

ABOUT THE HISTORY OF OUR COUNTRY

If any of the readers of this book should have the opportunity to ride in a train or car over the vast expanse of the United States, from the Atlantic to the Pacific Ocean, from the Great Lakes to the Gulf of Mexico, they would see a wonderful display of cities and towns, of factories and farms, and a great multitude of men and women actively at work. They would behold, spread out on every side, one of the busiest and happiest lands that the sun shines upon. Here and there, among the many farms, they might see a forest, here and there a wild beast, here and there an American Indian, a descendant of the first people who came to America; but these may be almost lost in the wonderful beauty of the intriguing scenery.

If our young traveler knew nothing of history he might think that it had always been this way, or that it had taken thousands of years for all those cities to be built and these great fields to be cleared and cultivated. Yet if he had been here only three hundred years ago, he would have seen a very different sight. He could not have gone over the country by airplane or railroad, for such things had never been invented. He could not have gone by highway, for there was not a modern road in the whole length and breadth of the land. Nowhere in this vast country would he have seen a large city or town; nowhere a ploughed field, a farmhouse, or a barn. Instead of great cities he would have seen only clusters of small dwellings; instead of fertile farms, only vast reaches of forest; instead of tame cattle, only wild and dangerous beasts.

Just think of it! All that we see around us is the work of about three hundred years! Great forests have fallen, great fields have been cleared and planted, great cities have risen, and myriads of men, women, and children have inhabited the wild expanse which the Indians used to roam, and all within a period not longer than three times the oldest person now living. Is this not as wonderful as the most marvelous tale of fiction? Is it not better to read the true tale of how this was done rather than certain imaginary stories?

The story of this great work is called the "History of the United States." This story you have before you in the book you now hold. You do not need to sit and dream about how the wonderful work of building our noble nation was done, for you can read it all here in language simple enough even the youngest child can understand. Here you are told how brave explorers came over the seas and found beyond the waves a land none of them had ever seen before. You are told how they settled on these shores, cut down the trees and built villages and towns, met the Indians and learned to cultivate the land, and made themselves homes in the midst of fertile fields. You are told how others came, how they spread wider and wider over the land, how log cabins grew into mansions, and villages into cities, and how at length they fought for and gained their liberty.

Read on and you will learn of more wonderful things still. The history of the past two hundred years is a story of a God-blessed land. In it you will learn of how the steamboat was first made and in time came to be seen on all our rivers and lakes; of how the locomotive was invented and railroads were built, until they are now long enough in our country to go eight times round the earth; of the marvels of the telegraph and telephone—the talking wire; of the machines that rumble and roar in a thousand factories and work away like living things, and of a multitude of computer-driven marvels which I cannot begin to speak of here. You will also learn how men kept on coming, and wars were fought, and new land was gained, and bridges were built, and canals were dug, and our people increased and spread until we became one of the greatest nations on the earth. All this and more you may learn from the pages of this book. It is written for the boys and girls of our great land, but many of their fathers and mothers may also find it pleasant and useful to read.

There are thousands of young people who do not have time to read large histories, which try to tell all that has taken place. For these people, this little history will be of great service, in showing them how, from a few half-starved settlers on a wild coast, this great nation has grown up. I need say no more, however, for the book has its own story to tell. I only lay this introduction before you as a handy stepping-stone into the history of this great nation. By its aid, you may cross the brook and wander on through the broad story which lies before you.

Michael J. McHugh
2005

Columbus, The Great Sailor 1

If you lived in Chicago over one hundred years ago, you would have heard about a wonderful display in that city. In 1893, dozens of great white buildings rose on the shore of Lake Michigan, as beautiful as kings' palaces, and filled with the finest of goods of all kinds, which millions of people came to see.

Do you know what this was? It was a World's Fair in honor of a wonderful event that had taken place four hundred years before the fair was built.

Some of you may think that white men have always lived in this country. I hope you do not all think so, for this is not the case. A little more than five hundred years ago very few white men had ever seen this country, and few knew that there was such a place on the face of the earth.

It was in the year 1492 that a brave sailor named Christopher Columbus crossed a wide ocean and came to this new and wonderful land. Since then, people have come here by the millions, and the mighty republic of the United States has grown up with its thousands of towns and cities. In one of these, which bears the name of Chicago, the grand World's Columbian Exposition was held in honor of the discovery of America by the great navigator who came here more than five hundred years ago.

Leif Ericson and the Norsemen

This is what I have set out to tell you about. I am sure you will all be glad to know how this broad and noble land, once the home of the Indians, was discovered and made a home for settlers from throughout much of Europe. Some of you may have been told that America was actually discovered more than four hundred and fifty years before Columbus was born, and so it was. At that time some of the daring sailors from the northern countries of Europe, who made the stormy ocean their home and loved the

Part of the World's Columbian Exposition of 1893, held in Chicago, Illinois

roll of the waves, had come to the frozen island of Iceland. In addition, a ship from Iceland had been driven by the winds to a land in the far west which no explorer from Europe had ever seen before. Wasn't this America?

Soon after, in the year of our Lord 1000, one of these Norsemen named Leif Ericson set sail for this new land. There he found wild grapes growing, and from them he named it Vineland. He also called it "Wineland the Good."

After him came others, and there was fighting with the Native Americans whom they called "Skrellings." In the end, the Norsemen left the country, and over the course of many years this new land was forgotten. Only lately the story has been found again in some old writings. Time, therefore, went on for nearly five hundred years more, and nothing was known in Europe about the land beyond the seas.

Young Christopher Columbus, watching the ships come into his home town port.

Young Christopher Columbus

Now let us go from the north to the south of Europe. Here there is a country called Italy, which runs down into the Mediterranean Sea almost in the shape of a boot. On the western shore of this nation is a famous old city named Genoa, in which many sailors have dwelt; and here, long ago, lived a man named Columbus, a poor man, who earned his living by making wool clothing.

This poor weaver had four children, one of whom (born in 1451) he named Christopher. Almost everybody who has ever studied history knows the name of this little Italian boy, for he became one of the most famous of men. What do you think that young Christopher did when he was a boy?

The known world at the dawn of the Age of Exploration

THE WORLD THAT COLUMBUS KNEW AS A BOY.

Like many young boys, Christopher had to help his father in his shop. The great Benjamin Franklin began work by pouring melted wax into molds to make candles. In the same way, little Columbus had to comb wool for his father and very likely got as tired of wool as Franklin did of candles.

The city he lived in was full of sailors, and no doubt he talked to many of them about life on the wild waters and heard so many stories of danger and adventure that he took an interest in going to sea himself.

At any rate, we are told that he became a sailor when only fourteen years old and made long and daring voyages while he was still young. Some of those were in Portuguese ships down the coast of the wild and mysterious continent of Africa. The young Columbus went north, too; some think as far as Iceland.

Columbus spent some time on the island of Madeira, far out in the Atlantic Ocean, and there the people told him of strange things they had seen. Among them were pieces of carved wood, and barrels so long that they would hold forty gallons of wine between their joints. Moreover, the dead bodies of two men had also come ashore, whose skin was the color of bronze or copper. These things had drifted over the seas before the west winds and landed on their island shores.

These stories set Columbus thinking. He was now a man and had read many books about travel. He also had studied all that was then known of geography. For a time he lived by making maps, charts, and globes for ship captains. This was in the city of Lisbon, in Portugal, where he married and settled down and had a little boy of his own.

"I could feel His hand upon me."

I prayed to the most merciful Lord about my heart's great desire, and He gave me the spirit and the intelligence for the task.... It was the Lord who put into my mind (I could feel His hand upon me) to sail to the Indies. All who heard of my project rejected it with laughter, ridiculing me. There is no question that the inspiration was from the Holy Spirit, because He comforted me with rays of marvelous illumination from the Holy Scriptures ... encouraging me continually to press forward, and without ceasing for a moment they now encourage me to make haste.

Our Lord Jesus desired to perform a very obvious miracle in the voyage to the Indies, to comfort me and the whole people of God. I spent seven years in the royal court ... and in the end they concluded that it was all foolishness, so they gave it up. But since things generally came to pass that were predicted by our Savior Jesus Christ, we should also believe that this particular prophecy will come to pass. In support of this, I offer the gospel text, Matthew 24:35, in which Jesus said that all things would pass away, but not his marvelous Word. He also affirmed that it was necessary that all things be fulfilled that were prophesied by Himself and by the prophets.

I said that I would state my reasons: I hold alone to the sacred and Holy Scriptures, and to the interpretations of prophecy given by certain devout persons.

The Holy Scripture testifies in the Old Testament by the prophets and in the New Testament by our Redeemer Jesus Christ, that this world must come to an end. The signs of when this must happen are given by Matthew, Mark, and Luke. The prophets also predicted many things about it.

Our Redeemer Jesus Christ said that before the end of the world, all things must come to pass that had been written by the prophets. Isaiah goes into great detail in describing future events and in calling all people to our holy catholic faith.... For the execution of the journey to the Indies I did not make use of intelligence, mathematics, or maps. It is simply the fulfillment of what Isaiah prophesied....

These are great and wonderful things for the earth, and the signs are that the Lord is hastening the end. The fact that the gospel must still be preached to so many lands in such a short time—this is what convinces me.

Christopher Columbus, *Book of Prophecies*

Discouraging Days

Columbus thought a great deal about the importance of taking the message of Christianity to new lands in the East. He sincerely believed that God had destined him to be the one to spread the Christian faith to people who were lost in pagan darkness. The desire that Columbus had for glory and worldly wealth was never as strong as his desire to promote the cause of Christ. Columbus wrote in his journal: "For this was the alpha and omega of the enterprise that it should be for the increase and glory of the Christian religion."

It is sad, however, to realize that few powerful leaders living during these times shared the concerns of Columbus regarding the spread of Christianity. More often than not, the kings or queens of Europe were more interested in obtaining worldly riches and fame. At this time in history, the people of Europe wanted to develop an easier way to bring silk, spices, and other riches from China and India. The businessmen in Europe were tired of traveling thousands of miles by way of overland caravans to obtain goods from the East. Christopher Columbus thought he could help by finding a way to sail west across the ocean to these far countries, just as a fly may walk around the surface of an orange and come back to where it started.

The more Columbus thought about this, the more certain he became that he was right. He was so sure of it that he set out to try and make other people think the same way. He wanted ships with which to sail across the unknown seas to the west, but he had no money of his own to buy them.

Ah! What a task poor Columbus now had. For years and years he wandered about among the kings and princes of Europe, but no one would believe his story and many laughed at him and mocked him.

First he tried Genoa, the city where he was born, but the people there told him he was a fool for thinking of such a voyage.

Then Columbus went to the king of Portugal. This king was a rascal and tried to cheat him. The king stole his plans from him and sent out a vessel in secret, hoping to get the honor of the discovery for himself. The captain he sent, however, was a coward and was scared by the rolling waves. He soon came back and told the king that there was nothing to be found but water and storm. King John of Portugal was very sorry afterward that he had tried to rob Columbus of his honor.

Columbus was very angry when he heard what the king had done. He left Portugal for Spain and tried to get the king and queen of that country to let him have ships and sailors. They were at war, however, with a heathen people called the Moors and had no money to spare for risky sailing ventures.

Columbus stayed there for seven long

A Most Unworthy Sinner

I am a most unworthy sinner, but I have cried out to the Lord for grace and mercy and they have covered me completely. I have found the sweetest consolation since I made it my whole purpose to enjoy His marvelous presence. No one should fear to undertake any task in the name of our Savior, if it is just and if the intention is purely for His holy service. The working out of all things has been assigned to each person by our Lord, but it all happens according to His sovereign will, even though He gives advice. He lacks nothing that it is in the power of God to give men. O what a gracious Lord, who desires that people should perform for Him those things for which He holds Himself responsible! Day and night, moment by moment, everyone should express to Him their most devoted gratitude.

Christopher Columbus,
Book of Prophecies

years. He talked to many powerful people, but some made fun of him. "If the earth is round," they said, "and you sail west, your ships will go downhill, and they will have to sail uphill to come back. No ship that was ever made can do that. Besides, you may come to places where the waters boil with the great heat of the sun, and frightful monsters may rise out of the sea and swallow your ships and your men." Even the boys in the street started laughing at him and mocking him as a man who had lost his mind.

After many years, Columbus got tired of trying in Spain. He then traveled to France to see what the king of that country would do. He sent one of his brothers to England to see its king and ask him for aid.

Columbus stands before Queen Isabella's court.

Queen Isabella Helps

He was now so poor that he had to travel along the dusty roads on foot, his little son going with him. One day, he stopped at a monastery called La Rabida to beg some bread for his son, who was very hungry.

The monks gave bread to the boy, and while he was eating it the director of the monastery came out and talked with Columbus, asking him his business. Columbus told him his story. He told it so well that the man believed in it. He asked him to stay there with his son and said he would write to Isabella, the queen of Spain, whom he knew very well.

Columbus decided to stay, and the director wrote a letter to the queen. In the end, the wandering sailor was asked to return to the king's court in Spain.

Queen Isabella was of great help and encouragement to Columbus. The king would not listen to the wandering sailor, but the queen offered to pledge her jewels to raise the money he needed for ships and sailors.

Columbus had won. After years and years of toil, hunger, and disappointment, he was to have ships and sailors and supplies. He was given a chance to prove whether it was he or the powerful men who were the fools.

What horrible ships they gave him, though! Why, you can see far better ones regularly moving down your local rivers. Two of them did not even have decks but were like open boats. With this small fleet Columbus set sail from Palos, a little port in Spain, on the third of August 1492, on one of the most wonderful voyages in world history.

Away they went far out into the "Sea of Darkness," as the Atlantic Ocean was then called. Mile after mile, league after league, day after day, on and on they went, seeing nothing but endless waves, while the wind drove them steadily into the unknown west.

These sailors never expected to see their

wives and children again. They were frightened when they started, and every day they grew more scared. They looked with starving eyes for the bleak fogs or the frightful monsters which they had been told to expect. At one place they came upon clumps of seaweed and thought they were in shallow water and would be wrecked on banks of mud. Then the compass, in which they trusted, ceased to point due north, and they were more frightened than ever. Soon there was hardly a strong heart in the fleet except that of Columbus.

The time came when the sailors grew half mad with fear. Some of them made a plot to throw Columbus overboard and sail home again. They would tell the people there that he had fallen into the sea and been drowned.

It was a terrible thing to think of, was it not? Desperate men, however, will do dreadful things. They thought one man had better die rather than all of them. Only God's grace preserved the life of the great sea captain.

"Land! Land!"

One day a glad sailor called his shipmates and pointed over the side. A branch of a green bush was floating by with fresh berries on it. It looked as if it had just been broken off a bush. Another day, one of them picked from the water a stick which had been carved with a knife. Land birds were seen flying over the ships. Hope came back to their hearts. They were sure that land must be near.

The day of October eleventh came. When night fell dozens of men were on the lookout. Each wanted to be the first to see land. About ten o'clock that night, Columbus, who was looking out over the waves, saw a light far off.

It moved up and down like a lantern carried in a man's hand.

Hope now grew strong. Every eye looked out into the darkness. About two o'clock in the morning came the glad cry of "Land! Land!" A gun was fired from the leading vessel. One of its sailors had seen what looked like land in the moonlight. You may be sure no one slept any more that night.

When daylight came the joyful sailors saw before them a low, green shore, on which the sunlight lay in beauty; men and women stood on it, looking in wonder at the ships, which they thought must be great white-winged birds. They had never

The month of March of the next year came before the little fleet was able to return to Europe. Columbus sailed again into the port of Palos. The people hailed them with shouts of joy, for they had mourned their friends as dead.

The news spread fast. When Columbus entered Barcelona, Spain, where the king and queen were, bringing with him new plants, birds and animals, strange weapons, golden ornaments, and a few Native Americans, he was received as if he had been a king. He was seated beside the king; he rode by his side in the street; he was made a grandee of Spain; all the honors of the kingdom were showered on him.

Columbus solves the riddle of the egg before the king's court.

Columbus and the Egg

A dinner was given in Columbus's honor and many great men were there. The attention Columbus received made some people jealous. One of them with a sneer asked Columbus if he did not think anyone else could have discovered the Indies. In response Columbus took an egg from a dish on the table and handing it to the questioner asked him to make it stand on end.

After trying several times the man gave up. Columbus, took the egg in his hand, tapped it gently on one end against the top of the table so as to break the shell slightly so it would balance.

"Anyone could do that," said the man. "So anyone can discover the Indies after I have shown him the way," replied Columbus.

It was his day of pride and triumph. The successful explorer, however, was soon to find

seen such things before. We can hardly imagine what we would have done under similar circumstances.

When the boats from the ships came to the shore and Columbus landed, clad in shining armor and bearing the great banner of Spain, the simple natives fell to the ground on their faces. They thought a god had come from heaven to visit them.

Some of the red-skinned natives wore ornaments of gold. They were asked by signs where they had got this gold and pointed south. Soon all were on board again, the ships once more spread their sails, and swiftly they flew southward before the wind.

Day by day, as they went on, new islands appeared, some small, some large, all green and beautiful. Columbus thought this must be India, which he had set out to find, and he called the people Indians. He never knew that it was a new continent he had discovered.

out how Spain treated its heroes. Three times again he sailed to the New World, and once a rude Spanish governor sent him back to Spain with chains upon his legs. After Columbus was released, he kept the chains hanging in his home till he died and asked that they should be buried with him.

COLUMBUS'S FIRST VOYAGE OF DISCOVERY ~ ~ ~ 1492

They who had once given him every honor now treated him with shameful neglect. He who had ridden beside the king and dined with the highest nobles of Spain became poor, sad, and lonely.

He died in 1506, fourteen years after his great discovery. Then Spain, which had treated him so badly, began to honor his memory. It came too late, however, for poor Columbus, who had been allowed to die almost like a pauper, after he had made Spain the richest country in Europe.

Chapter 1 Review Questions

1. What wonderful event took place in the city of Chicago in the year 1893?

2. In what year did the sailor named Columbus cross the Atlantic ocean and discover the New World?

3. Who do historians believe was the first explorer to visit America in the year 1000?

4. Who finally helped Columbus raise the money he needed to buy ships and sailors?

5. Why did many people think that Columbus would never be able to sail across the "Sea of Darkness" and return safely?

6. In what year did Columbus die?

Three Great Discoverers 2

Very likely some of the readers of this book have asked their fathers or mothers how Spain came to own the islands of Cuba and Puerto Rico. If you should ask me that question, I would say that these were some of the islands which Columbus found when he sailed into those sunny seas five centuries ago. They were settled by Spaniards, who conquered these islands and controlled them until the opening of the twentieth century. There they raised sugar cane, tobacco, coffee, oranges, bananas, and all kinds of fine fruits.

The Spaniards might have kept on owning these islands and raising these fruits for many years to come, if they had not been so cruel to the people that they revolted. With the assistance of the United States government, the islands were taken from Spain in 1898.

After Columbus told the nobles and people of Spain of his wonderful discovery and showed them the plants and animals, the gold, and other things he had found on these far-off islands, it started a great excitement in that country.

You may have heard how the finding of gold in California and Alaska sent thousands of our own people to these lands in search of the shining yellow metal. In the same way, desire for the gold which Columbus brought back sent thousands of Spaniards across the wide seas to the warm and beautiful islands where they hoped to find gold like stones in the streets.

John and Sebastian Cabot

Dozens of ships soon set sail from Spain, carrying thousands of people to the fair lands of the west. They hoped to come back laden with riches. At the

Sebastian Cabot

same time, two brave sailors from England, John Cabot and his son Sebastian, crossed the ocean farther north and, in 1497, found the land the Norsemen had found five hundred years before. In the seas the Cabots sailed, great fish were so plentiful that the ships could hardly sail through them, and bears swam out in the water and caught the fish in their mouths. The Cabots must have enjoyed seeing the bears' strange way of fishing.

When the Cabots came back and told what they had seen, you may be sure the needy fishermen of Europe did not stay long at home. Soon numbers of their stout little vessels were crossing the ocean, and most of them came back so full of great codfish that the water almost ran over their decks. Fishing soon developed into an important business off the Canadian and New England coasts, as was whaling for a time. One French official in Canada emphasized the importance of the fisheries off the coast of Canada when he wrote to the king that "They are our true mines...." The Grand Banks, which are off the coast of Newfoundland, Canada, still attract fishermen from around the world today.

Do you not think these fishermen were wiser than the Spaniards, who went everywhere seeking for gold and finding very little of it? Gold is only good to buy food and other things; but if these can be had without buying they are better still. At any rate, the hardy fishermen thought so, and they were more blessed in finding fish than the Spaniards were in finding gold.

Thus the years passed on, and more and more Spaniards came to the islands of Cuba and Hispaniola (which now contains the countries of Haiti and the Dominican Republic). Some of them soon began to sail farther west in search of new lands. Columbus, in his last voyage, reached the coasts of South America and Central America and other Spanish ships followed to those new shores.

Balboa, The Poor Explorer

I will tell you some wonderful things about these daring Spanish men. There was one of them named Balboa whose story you will be glad to hear, for it is full of strange events. This man had gone to the island of Hispaniola to make his fortune, but he found there only trouble. He had to work on a farm, and in time he became so poor and owed so much money

> ### Sebastian Cabot's "Rules of the Ship"
>
> ... No blaspheming of God or detestable swearing be used ... nor communication of ribaldrie [i.e., coarse or vulgar joking], filthy tales or ungodly talk to be suffered in the company ... neither dicing [i.e., gambling with dice], carding, tabling, or devilish games to be frequented, whereby ensueth not only poverty to the players but also strife, variance, brawling ... and provoking of God's most just wrath and sword of vengeance....

that it seemed as if he could never get out of debt. In fact, he was in sad straits.

No doubt the people who had lent him money often asked him to pay it back again.

Balboa, who slid into a worse state every day, at length took an odd way to rid himself of his troubles. A ship was about to set sail for the west, and the poor debtor managed to get carried aboard it in a barrel. This barrel came from his farm and was supposed to contain provisions, and it was not till they were far away from land that it was opened and a living man was found in it instead of salt beef or pork.

When the captain saw him, he was very much surprised. He had paid for a barrel of provisions, and he found something which he could not eat. He grew so angry at being

The captain was furious when he found Balboa in the barrel.

cheated that he threatened to leave Balboa on a desert island, but the poor fellow fell on his knees and begged so hard for his life that the captain finally forgave him. He made him work, however, to pay his way and very likely used the rope's end to stir him up.

Of course, you have learned from your geography where the Isthmus of Panama is, that narrow strip of land that is like a string tying together the great continents of North and South America. It was to the town of Darien, on this isthmus, that the ship made its way, and here

Balboa crossed the Isthmus of Panama and discovered the Pacific Ocean.

Balboa made a surprising discovery. Some of the Indian chiefs told him of a mighty ocean which lay on the other side of the isthmus, and that behind that ocean was the wonderful land of gold which the Spaniards wished to find.

What would you have done if you had been in Balboa's place and wanted gold to pay your debts? Some of you, I think, would have done what he did. You would have made your way into the thick forest and climbed the rugged mountains of the isthmus, until, like Balboa, you reached the top of the highest peak. Moreover, like him, you would have been filled with joy when you saw in the far distance the vast Pacific Ocean, its waves glittering in the summer sun.

Here was glory; here was fortune. The poor debtor had become a great discoverer. Before his eyes spread a mighty ocean, its waves beating on the shore. He hurried with his men down the mountainsides to this shining sea and raised on its shores the great banner of Spain. Soon after, he set sail on its waters for Peru, the land of gold. He did not, however, get very far, for the stormy weather drove him back.

Poor Balboa! He was to win fame but not fortune, and his debts were never to be paid. A jealous Spanish governor seized him, condemned him as a traitor, and had his head cut off in the market place. This is how Balboa's dream of gold and glory ended. I will now tell you of other wonderful adventures in these new lands.

There is the story of Cortez, who found the great kingdom of Mexico and conquered it with a few hundred Spaniards in armor of steel. Furthermore, there is Pizarro, who sailed to Peru, Balboa's land of gold, won it for Spain, and sent home tons of silver and gold. These stories, however, have nothing to do with the history of the United States, so we must pass them by and go back to the early days of the country in which we live.

Ponce de Leon searches for the Fountain of Youth.

Ponce de Leon

The first Spaniard to set foot on the shores of North America was an old man named Ponce de Leon, who was governor of the island of Puerto Rico. At that time there was a fable which many believed, which said that somewhere in Asia was a wonderful Fountain of Youth. Everybody who drank of or bathed in its waters would grow young again. An old man in a moment would become as fresh and strong as a boy. De Leon wanted youth more than he did gold, and like all men at that time he thought the land he was in was part of Asia and might contain the Fountain of Youth. He asked the Indians if they knew of such a magic spring. The Indians, who wanted to get rid of the Spaniards, by whom they had been cruelly treated, pointed to the northwest.

In the year 1513, old Ponce de Leon boarded a ship and sailed away in search of the magic spring. A few days later, on Easter Sunday, he saw before him a land so bright with flowers that he named it "Flowery Easter." Even today, it is still called Florida, the Spanish word for *flowery*.

I am sure none of my young readers believe in such a Fountain of Youth, and that none of you would have hunted for it as old

Saint Augustine, Florida

Saint Augustine is the oldest city in the United States. It is located on Matanzas Bay, five miles from the Atlantic Ocean, in northeastern Florida. Ponce de Leon landed there in 1513, claiming it for Spain.

More than fifty years later, French Huguenots established a colony there. In 1565, however, the Spanish destroyed it and then founded the present city of Saint Augustine. In 1672, they started building a fort, now called Castillo de San Marcos—the oldest fort in America, to protect their settlement. It took thirteen years to complete this fort with its thirteen-foot wide and thirty-foot high walls. The city is named after Saint Augustine, one of the foremost Christian thinkers of the early church.

De Leon did. Up and down that flowery land he wandered, seeking its wonderful waters. He found many sparkling springs and eagerly drank of and bathed in their cool waves, but out of them all, he came with white hair and wrinkled face. In the end, he gave up the search and sailed away, a sad old man. Some years afterwards, he came back again. This time, however, the Indians fought with the white men, and De Leon was struck with an arrow and hurt so badly that he soon died; therefore, he found death instead of youth. Many people go to Florida in our own day in search of health, but Ponce de Leon is the only man who ever went there to find the mythical Fountain of Youth.

Fernando de Soto

About twenty-five years afterwards, another Spaniard came to Florida. It was gold and glory for which he was searching, not youth. This man, Fernando de Soto, had been in Peru with Pizarro, and helped him conquer that land of gold. He now hoped to find a rich empire for himself in the north.

With nine ships and six hundred brave young men, he sailed away from his native land of Spain. They were a happy and hopeful band, while their bright banners floated proudly from the mastheads and waved in the western winds. Little did they dream of what a terrible future lay before them.

I think you will say that De Soto deserved little heavenly mercy, when I tell you that he brought bloodhounds to hunt the poor Indians and chains to fasten on their hands and feet. That was the way the Spaniards often treated the poor Native Americans. He also brought two hundred horses for his armed men to ride and hogs to serve them for fresh meat. Moreover, in the ships were large iron chests, which he hoped to take back full of gold and other precious things.

For two long years, De Soto and his band traveled through the country, fighting the Indians, burning their houses, and robbing them of their food. The Indians, however, were brave warriors, and in one terrible battle, the Spaniards lost eighty of their horses and many of their men.

In vain De Soto sought for gold and glory. Not an ounce of the yellow metal was found; no mighty empire was reached. He did make one great discovery, that of the vast Mississippi River. He never returned home, however, to tell of it, for he died on its banks, worn out by his battles and marches, and was buried under its waters. His men built boats and floated down the great river to the Gulf of Mexico. Here, at length, they built Spanish settlements. Of that brave and gallant band, however, half were dead, and the rest were so nearly starved that they were like living skeletons.

We must not forget that humble Italian traveler and explorer, Amerigo Vespucci, who in 1499 saw the part of South America where lies the island of Trinidad. Many years after, when maps were made of the part he visited, some one called it *America* and others seemed to be pleased and used that name too—so what should have been called Columbia has been called America.

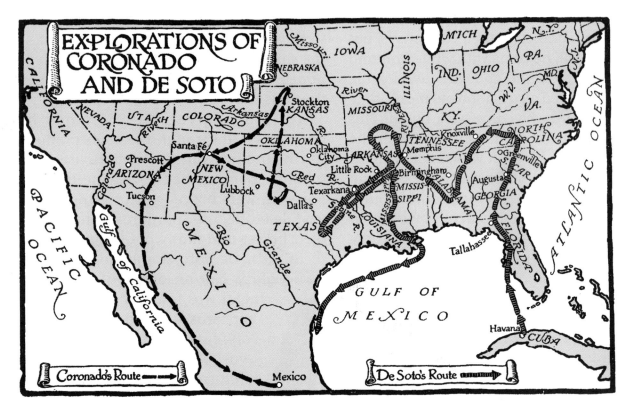

In 1539, De Soto, with about 600 men, 200 horses, and a number of bloodhounds, landed on the west coast of Florida in search of a new kingdom of gold. They found, instead, fighting, fever, and famine.

Chapter 2 Review Questions

1. What country in Europe first owned the islands of Cuba and Puerto Rico?

2. What two English sailors, father and son, sailed to the New World and discovered new lands in North America?

3. The explorer Fernando de Soto sailed from what nation?

4. What was the old sailor named Ponce de Leon searching for when he traveled throughout the land we now call Florida?

5. The land called America was named after what Italian explorer?

Heroic English Settlers 3

Captain John Smith

What do you think of Captain John Smith, the explorer of Virginia? Why, I feel half ashamed to say anything about him, for every one of you must know his story. I am sure all those who love adventure have read about him in some book.

John Smith was not the kind of man to work at a trade. He foolishly ran away from home when a boy and became a wanderer over the earth. He had a hard life. At one place he was robbed, and at another place was shipwrecked. Once he leaped overboard from a ship and swam ashore. At another time, he fought with three Turks and killed all of them without help. Then he was taken prisoner and sold as a slave to a cruel Turk, who put a ring around his neck and made him work very hard.

One day his master came out where he was at work and struck him with his whip. He soon found that John Smith was the wrong man to whip. He hit the Turk a hard blow with the shovel he was using and killed him on the spot. Then he ran away to Russia but, in time, made his way back to England. England, however, was too quiet a place for him. A ship was about to cross the sea to America and he volunteered to go on it. He still had a hunger and thirst for adventure. Some people think that Captain Smith bragged a little and did not do all he said. Well, that may be so. It is certain, however, that he was a brave and bold man, and just the man to help settle a new country where there were dangers of every kind.

The English were in no hurry in sending out settlers to the New World which Columbus had discovered. While the Spaniards were seeking gold and empires in the south, and the French were catching fish and exploring the rivers and lakes in the north, all the English did was to rob the Spanish ships and settlements.

The time came, however, a hundred years after North America was rediscovered by Columbus, when some of the English tried to form a settlement on the coast of North Carolina. Poor settlers! When the next ship came out they were all gone. Not a soul of them could be found. Nothing was left but some letters they had cut into the bark of a tree. What became of them nobody ever knew. Likely enough, they wandered away and were killed by Native Americans.

Nothing more was done until the year 1607, when the ship in which Captain John Smith had taken passage sailed up a bright and beautiful river in Virginia. It was the month of May, and the banks were covered with flowers.

The colonists thought that this was a very good place to live in, so they landed and began to look around. The river they called the James, and the place they named Jamestown. Instead of building a town and preparing for the future, as sensible men would have done, they began to seek for gold and soon were in no end of trouble. In a short time, their food was all eaten; then some of them got sick and died. Others were killed by the Indians. It looked as if this colony would be destroyed as the former one had been.

The settlers probably would have been wiped out if it had not been for Captain Smith. He was only one man among a hundred, but he was worth more than all the rest of the hundred. He could not keep still but hustled about, here, there, and everywhere. Smith could be seen exploring the country, sailing up the rivers or up the broad Chesapeake Bay. On other occasions, he could be found talking with the Native Americans, getting food from them for the starving colonists. John Smith was doing his best to make the men build houses and dig and plant the ground. You can see that this leader had enough to keep him busy. He had many adventures with the Indians. At one time, he was taken prisoner by them and was in terrible danger of being killed. He showed them, however, his pocket compass. When they saw the needle always pointing north, they thought there must be magic in it. They were still more surprised when he sent one of them with a letter to his friends. They did not understand how a piece of paper could talk, as his paper seemed to do.

All this, however, was not enough to save his life. The great chief Powhatan looked on him as the leader of these white strangers who had settled in his land. He wanted to get rid of them and thought that if he killed the man with the magic needle and the talking paper they would certainly be scared and go away.

On New Year's Day, 1607, the first colony, consisting of 150 men, set sail from London. In May, they sailed up the James River in Virginia and made a settlement.

Captain Smith was tied hand and foot and laid on the ground with his head on a log. A powerful Indian stood nearby with a large war club in his hand. Only a sign from Powhatan was needed, and that club would come down on the white man's head—it would be all over for the brave and bold John Smith.

Alas! Poor Captain Smith! There was no

pity in Powhatan's eyes. The burly Indian twisted his fingers about the club and lifted it in the air. One minute more and it might be all over for the man who had killed three Turks in one fight. Before that minute was over, however, a strange thing took place. A young Indian girl came running wildly into the hut, with her hair flying and her eyes wet with tears; she flung herself on the ground and laid her head on that of the bound prisoner and begged the chief to give him his life.

It was Pocahontas, the pretty young daughter of Powhatan. She pleaded so pitifully that the chief's heart was touched, and he consented that the captive should live and told them to take the bonds from his limbs.

Do you not think that this is a very amazing story? Some say that it is not true, but I think very likely it is. Afterwards, this compassionate Indian princess converted to the Christian faith and married one of the settlers named John Rolfe. A short time later, this couple traveled to London and were presented to the Queen. I am sorry to have to say that the poor woman became sick and died there and never saw her native land again.

Captain Smith went back to Jamestown.

Pocahontas

Pocahontas was an American Indian princess who allegedly saved the life of Captain John Smith and received the people of Jamestown with open arms. She was the daughter of Chief Powhatan and, supposedly, was as bright as she was beautiful.

In 1608, Captain John Smith, who helped settle Jamestown Colony, was captured by the Indians and brought to Pocahontas's village, which was about fifteen miles away from the English settlement. Smith was placed before a stone altar, but just before he was about to be killed, thirteen-year-old Pocahontas threw herself over his body and saved his life.

Pocahontas then became a messenger between Captain Smith and Powhatan, her father, who was a powerful Indian chief over thirty or more tribes. Supposedly, she persuaded her father to help the starving colonists by sending them food.

In 1613, Pocahontas was captured by Captain Samuel Argall and brought to Jamestown. Later she was taken to a new settlement called Henrico, where Reverend Alexander Whitaker taught her the basics of Christianity, and she became a convert. One year later, with her father's permission, she married John Rolfe. Their marriage brought peace to the region until Powhatan died. In 1615 they were blessed with a little baby boy named Thomas. The following year, the Rolfe family set sail for England. Pocahontas, now known as Lady Rebecca Rolfe, captivated the people of London. She even became a guest of the royal family at Whitehall. Sadly, however, Pocahontas took ill and died before she was able to return to her native land.

His troubles, however, were not at an end, for the colonists were as hard to deal with as the Native Americans. Some of them had found a kind of yellow stuff which they were sure was gold. They loaded a ship with this and sent it to England, thinking that they would all be rich. The yellow stuff, however, proved to be what is known as "fools' gold" and worth no more than so much sand. Instead of becoming rich, they were laughed at as great fools.

After a while, Smith was made governor, and he now tried a new plan to make the men work. He told them that if they did not work they should not eat. None of them wanted to starve, and they knew that John Smith meant just what he said, so they began to build houses and to dig the ground and plant crops. Some of them, however, grumbled and some of them swore. It was anything but a happy family.

Captain Smith did not like this swearing, so he developed an interesting plan to stop it. When the men came home at night, each one who had sworn had a can of cold water poured down his sleeve for every time he had done so. Did any of my readers ever try that? If they did, they would know why the men soon quit grumbling and swearing. All was beginning to go well in the colony when Captain Smith was hurt by some gunpowder that started burning and went off. He was hurt so badly that he had to go back to England. After that, all went downhill for the Jamestown settlement.

As soon as their governor was gone, the lazy men quit working. The profane men swore worse than before. They ate up all their food in a hurry, and the Indians would bring them no more. Sickness and hunger came and carried many of them to the grave. Some of them meddled with the Indians and were killed. There were five hundred of them when winter set in, but when spring came only sixty of them were alive. All this took place because one wise man, Captain John Smith, was hurt and had to go home. Those foolish people not only forsook Captain Smith, but they also forsook God. No wonder the Bible states that those who hate God love death.

The whole colony would have broken up if ships had not come out with more men and plenty of food. Soon after that, the people began to plant the ground and raise tobacco, which sold well in England. Many of them became rich, and the little settlement at Jamestown in time grew into the great colony of Virginia. This ends the story of the hero of Jamestown. Now let us say something about a hero of Plymouth.

Captain Miles Standish

In the year 1620, thirteen years after Smith and his companions sailed up the James River, a shipload of men and women came to a place they called Plymouth, on the rocky coast of New England. It was named after a town in England known as Plymouth. A portion of the rock on which they first stepped is still preserved and surrounded by a fence.

These people are known as the Pilgrims. They had been badly treated at home because they did not believe in some of the doctrines of the Church of England, and they had come across the stormy sea to find a place where they could worship God according to the Bible, without fear of being put in prison.

Shortly after arriving at Plymouth, the Pilgrims signed the "Mayflower Compact." This agreement stated that each person would do their best to do God's will and protect the rights of others. This document secured the right of all people to worship God and live in peace with their neighbors. Plymouth was the birthplace of true liberty. Liberty is not the right to live as we please, but the power to live as God requires!

With them came a soldier. He was named Captain Miles Standish. He was a little man, but he carried a big sword and had a stout heart and a hot temper. While the Pilgrims came to work and to pray, Captain Standish came to fight. He was a different man from Captain Smith and would not have been able to deal with the lazy folks at Jamestown. The Pilgrims, however, were different also. They ex-

Plymouth Plantation

[The people of Plymouth Plantation] cherished a great hope and inward zeal of laying good foundations, or at least making some ways toward it, for the propagation and advancement of the gospel of the kingdom of Christ in the remote parts of the world, even though they should be but stepping stones to others in the performance of so great a work.

Thus out of small beginnings greater things have been produced by His hand that made all things of nothing, and gives being to all things that are; and, as one small candle may light a thousand, so the light here kindled hath shone unto many, yea in some sort to our whole nation; let the glorious name of Jehovah have all the praise.

Governor Bradford

pected to work and live by their labor. They no sooner landed on Plymouth Rock than they began to hunt and fish, while the sound of the hammer rang merrily all day long as they built houses and prepared for the cold winter. For all their labor and carefulness, however, sickness and hunger came, as they had at Jamestown, and by the time spring came, half the

Mayflower Compact

In ye name of God, Amen. We whose names are underwriten, the loyall subjects of our dread soveraigne Lord, King James, by ye grace of God, of Great Britaine, France, & Ireland, king, defender of ye faith, etc., having undertaken, for ye glorie of God, and advancemente of ye Christian faith, and honour of our king & countrie, a voyage to plant ye first colonie in ye Northerne parts of Virginia, doe by these presents solemnly & mutually in ye presence of God, and one of another, covenant & combine our selves togeather into a civill body politick, for our better ordering & preservation & furtherance of ye ends aforesaid; and by vertue hearof to enacte, constitute, and frame such just & equall lawes, ordinances, acts, constitutions & offices, from time to time, as shall be thought most meete & convenient for ye generall good of ye Colonie, unto which we promise all due submission and obedience.

In witnes wherof we have hereunder subscribed our names at Cap-Codd ye 11. of November, in ye year of ye raigne of our soveraigne Lord, King James, of England, France, & Ireland ye eighteenth, and by Scotland ye fiftie fourth. Ano:Dom. 1620.

Before landing, the Pilgrims signed the Mayflower Compact, which established biblical law in the colony.

poor Pilgrims were dead.

The Native Americans soon became afraid of Captain Standish. They were afraid of the Pilgrims, too, for they found that these religious men could fight as well as pray. One Indian chief, named Canonicus, sent them a bundle of arrows with a snake's skin tied round it. This was their way of saying that they were going to fight the Pilgrims and drive them from the country. The leader of the Pilgrims, Governor William Bradford, however, filled the snake skin with powder and bullets and sent it back. When Canonicus saw this, he became very scared, for he knew well what it meant. He had heard the white men's guns and thought they had the power of using thunder and lightning, so he made up his mind to let the white strangers alone. Governor Bradford was an important spiritual leader of the Pilgrims as well. He encouraged the people to follow the laws of God contained in the Holy Bible.

The Pilgrims, however, did not trust the Native Americans. They put cannons on the roof of their log church. They walked to church on Sunday like so many soldiers on the march, with guns in their hands and Captain Standish at their head. Furthermore, while they were listening to the sermon one man stood outside on the lookout for danger.

At one time, some of the Indians made a plot to kill the English. A friendly Indian told Captain Standish about it, and he made up his mind to teach them a lesson they would remember. He went to the Indian camp with a few men and walked boldly into the hut where the plotting chiefs were talk-

ing over their plans. When they saw him and the men with him, they tried to frighten them. One of them showed the Captain his knife and talked very boldly about it.

A big Indian looked with scorn on the little Captain. "Poh, you are only a little fellow, if you are a captain," he said. "I am not a chief, but I am stronger and brave."

Captain Standish was very angry, but he said nothing then. He waited until the next day, when he met the chiefs again. Then there was a quarrel and a fight, and the little captain killed the big Indian with his own knife. More of the Indians were slain, and the others ran for the woods. That put an end to the plot. Captain Miles Standish was eventually able to help establish peaceful relations with the local Indians.

Miles Standish lived to be seventy years old and to have a farm of his own with a house on a high hill near Plymouth. This is called Captain's Hill, and on it there is now a stone shaft one hundred feet high with a statue of bold Captain Standish on its top. America owes a great debt of gratitude to the Pilgrims and their brave leaders.

The Pilgrims were quickly followed by other people, who settled at Boston and other places around Massachusetts Bay until there were a great many of them. These were called Puritans. They came across the seas for the same reason as the Pilgrims, to worship God as the Bible requires.

John Winthrop

We have now our third hero to speak of, John Winthrop. He was not a captain like the others, but a political leader. He was a brave man and showed, in his own way, just as much courage as either of the captains.

Winthrop sailed from his native land of England and landed in the town of Salem, Massachusetts, in June 1630. The tiny colony of Massachusetts was in a very sad condition. Many of the Puritan settlers had died the previous winter, and most of the people who remained were sick or hungry.

It was during this difficult time that Winthrop began to lead by example and gave up nearly all of his worldly possessions to help feed the poor and establish shelter for the homeless. The people soon began to see that this godly man was fit to lead their tiny colony.

Winthrop was one of several godly Christian leaders who helped to establish the laws and government for the New England colonies. This leader believed that Church and State were to cooperate in the goal of establishing a just and peaceful society. Winthrop believed that all civil leaders were ultimately responsible to Almighty God for how well they obeyed the Holy Scriptures.

John Winthrop was elected as the governor of the colony of Massachusetts a total of eleven times. During his time in office, he helped to establish a Christ-honoring system of civil government in Massachusetts. Winthrop understood very well the Bible verse that states, "Blessed is the nation whose God is the Lord."

At this same time in history, there were wars going on in Europe about religion, and everybody who did not believe in the religion of the state was punished. Many people like John Winthrop traveled to America to find freedom to worship God and to secure that same liberty for others. The Massachusetts Bay Colony became a blessed haven for the God-fearing Puritans and for many persecuted refugees.

Do you not think John Winthrop was as brave a man as John Smith or Miles Standish, and as much a hero? He did not kill anyone. He was not that kind of hero. He did much, however, to make men happy and good and to do justice to all men, and I think that is the best kind of hero. It is because of the sacrifices of brave men like Governor Winthrop that all Americans have the great blessing of religious freedom.

Chapter 3 Review Questions

1. Captain John Smith became governor of what town?

2. Where did the Pilgrims settle in the year 1620?

3. The Pilgrims signed an agreement among themselves before they left their ship. What was the name of this agreement?

4. Who was the brave military leader and protector of the Pilgrims?

5. Who was one of the early governors of the Pilgrims?

6. Who was elected eleven times as governor of the Puritans in the Massachusetts Bay Colony?

More Settlers Come to America 4

I wonder how many of my readers have ever seen the great city of New York. I wonder even more how many of them know that it is one of the largest cities in the world.

Why, if you should go back to the 1660s, you would barely find a city of New York. All you would see would be a sort of large village on Manhattan Island, at the mouth of the Hudson River. Furthermore, if you went back to the early seventeenth century (1600–1625), I think you would see nothing on that island but trees, with Indian wigwams beneath them. Not a single white man or a single house would you see.

Henry Hudson

In the year 1609, just two years after Captain Smith sailed into the James River, a strange-looking Dutch vessel came across the ocean and began to prowl up and down the coast. It was named the *Half Moon*. It came from Holland, the land of the Dutch, but its captain was an Englishman named Henry Hudson, who had done so many daring things that men called him "the bold Englishman."

What Captain Hudson would have liked to do was to sail across the continent of North America and come out into the Pacific Ocean, and so make his way to the rich countries of Asia. We now know that this idea is silly. To think that he could sail across three thousand miles of land and across great mountain ranges!

You must not think, however, that Captain Hudson was crazy. Nobody then knew how wide America was. For all they knew, it might be fifty miles wide. Captain John Smith tried to get across it by sailing up the James River. The bold Captain Hudson thought he might find a stream that led from one ocean to the other.

On he went, up and down the coast, looking for an opening for this great river. After a while, the *Half Moon* sailed into a broad and beautiful bay, where great trees came down to the edge of the water and Indians paddled about

in their canoes. Captain Hudson was delighted to see it. "It was," he said, "as pleasant with grass and flowers as I have ever seen, and very sweet smells."

This body of water was what we now call Long Island Sound. A broad and swift river runs into it, which is now called the Hudson River, after Henry Hudson. The bold captain thought that this was the stream to go up if he wished to reach the Pacific Ocean; so, after talking as well as he could with the Indians in their canoes, and trading beads for corn, he started up the splendid river. Some of the Indians came on board the *Half Moon*.

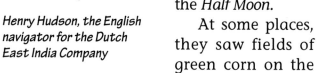

Henry Hudson, the English navigator for the Dutch East India Company

At some places, they saw fields of green corn on the water's edge. Farther on were groves of tall trees, and for miles great cliffs of rock rose like towers. It was all very grand and beautiful. "It was a very good land to come to," said Captain Hudson, "and a pleasant land to see."

They sailed on and on till they came to mountains which rose on both sides of the river. After passing the mountains, the captain went ashore to visit an old chief who lived in a round house built of bark. The Indians here had great heaps of corn and beans. What they liked best, however, was roast dog. They roasted a dog for Captain Hudson and asked him to eat it, but I do not know whether he did so or not. Later on, they broke their arrows and threw them into the fire, to show that they did not mean to harm the white men.

After leaving the good old chief, the Dutch explorers went on up the river till they reached a place about 150 miles to the north, where the city of Albany now stands. Here the river became so narrow and shallow that Captain

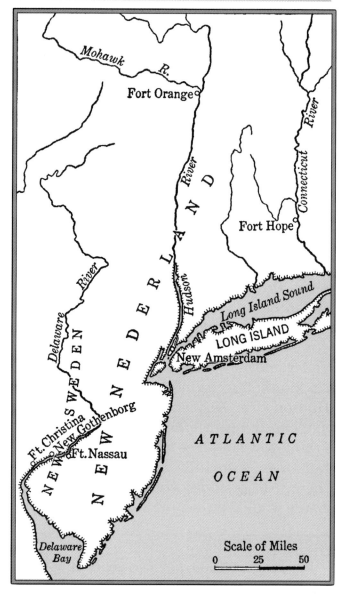

Hudson saw he could not reach the Pacific by that route, so he turned and sailed back to the sea again.

A sad event soon happened to Captain Hudson, "the bold Englishman." The next year he came back to America. This time, however, he went far to the north and entered the great body of water which we call Hudson Bay. He thought this would lead to the Pacific, and he would not turn back, although the sailors' food was nearly all gone. At last, the crew got desperate, put the captain and some others into an open boat on the wide waters, and returned home again. Nothing more was ever heard of Captain Hudson, and he must have died on that cold, lonely bay.

New Amsterdam

Earlier, however, he had told the Dutch people all about the Hudson River, and that the Native Americans had many fine furs which they would be glad to trade for beads, knives, and other cheap things. The Dutch were fond of trading and liked to make a good bargain, so they soon began to send ships to America. They built a fort and some log huts on Manhattan Island, and a number of them stayed there to trade with the Indians. They paid the Indians for the island with some cheap goods. I do not think any of you could guess how many billions of dollars that island is worth now. For the great city of New York stands where the log huts of the Dutch traders once stood, and a few beads would hardly buy as much land as you could cover with your hand.

The country around New York City is now a mixture of farm land, housing developments, businesses, and factories. Back then it was all woodland for hundreds of miles away. In these woods lived many foxes and beavers and other fur-bearing animals. These the Indians hunted and killed in order to sell their furs to the Dutch, so that there was soon a good trade for both the Indians and the Dutch. The Dutch were glad to get the furs, and the Indians were as glad to get the knives and beads. More and more people came from Holland, and the town grew larger and larger. Soon strong brick houses took the place of the log huts, and in time there was quite a town.

Men were sent from Holland to govern the people. Some of these men were not fit to govern themselves, and the settlers did not like to have such men over them. One of them was a stubborn old fellow named Peter Stuyvesant. Since he had lost one of his legs and wore a wooden leg with bands of silver round it, he was called "Old Silver Leg."

While he was governor an important event took place. The English had a settlement in Virginia and another in New England, and they said that all the coast lands belonged to them, because the Cabots had been the first to see them. The Cabots came from Italy, but they had settled in England, and sailed in an English ship.

In 1664, a small fleet of English vessels came into the bay, and a letter was sent to shore which said that all this land belonged to England and must be given up to them. The Dutch might stay there, but they would be under an English governor. Old Peter tore up the letter and stamped about in a great rage on his silver leg. He had treated the people so badly, however, that they would not fight for him, so he had to give up the town.

The English called it New York, after the Duke of York, the king's brother. It grew and grew until it became a great and rich city and sent ships to all parts of the world. Most of the Dutch stayed there, and their descendants are among the people of New York today. Not long after these English ships came to New York Bay, other English ships came to a fine body of water, about 100 miles farther south, now called the Delaware Bay. Into this runs a great stream of fresh water, called the Delaware River, as wide as the Hudson. I think you will like to learn what brought the English settlers to this area.

Quakers Settle in America

The Englishmen who came to this part of the country were called Quakers. Did any of my young readers ever see a Quaker? In old times, you would have known them, for they dressed in a different way from other people. They wore very plain clothes and broad brimmed hats, which they would not take off to do honor to king or noble. Today they dress like the people around them.

The Quakers were treated badly in Boston, and they were treated worse in England. Thieves were given as bad a time as the poor Quakers. Some of them were put in jail and kept there for years. Some were whipped or put in the stocks, where nasty people called them vile names and threw mud at them. Indeed, these quiet people, who did no harm to anyone but were kind to others, had a very hard time. They were treated more cruelly than the Pilgrims and the Puritans who also came from England.

Among them was the son of a brave English admiral, who was a friend of the king and his brother, the Duke of York. Since the admiral's son was a Quaker, he was put in prison for preaching the Quaker doctrines and wearing his hat in court.

This prisoner was William Penn after whom Pennsylvania was named. You may well think that the son of a rich admiral, who was also a friend of royalty, did not like being treated as though he was a thief because he chose to wear a hat with a broad brim and to say "thee" and "thou," and because he would not go to the king's church.

What is more, the king owed William Penn money, which he could not or would not pay. He had owed this money to Admiral Penn, and after the admiral died he owed it to his son.

William Penn thought it would be wise to do as the Pilgrims and Puritans had done. There was plenty of land in America, and it would be easy there to make a home for the poor Quakers where they could live in peace and worship God in the way they thought right. This they could not do in England.

Penn went to the king and told him how he could pay his debt. If the king would give him a piece of land on the west side of the Delaware River, he would give him a receipt in full for the money owing to his father.

King Charles, who never had money enough for his own use, was very glad to pay his debts in this easy way. He told Penn that he could have all the land he wanted and offered him a piece that was nearly as large as the whole of England! This land belonged to the Indians, but that did not trouble King Charles. It is easy to pay debts with other people's property. All Penn was asked to pay the king was two beaver skins every year and one-fifth of all gold and silver that should be mined. As no gold or silver was ever mined, the king received nothing but his beaver skins, which were a kind of rent.

What do any of my young readers know about the Delaware River? Have any of you seen the wide, swift stream which flows between the states of Pennsylvania and New Jersey and runs into the broad body of water known as Delaware Bay? On its banks stands the great city of Philadelphia, in which live more than one and a half million people, and where there are many busy factories and well-filled stores. This large and fine city came from the way the king paid his debt. King Charles was not a good man, but he did one good thing

William Penn

by paying his debt to William Penn.

There were other settlers from Europe living west of the Delaware River before the Quakers came. Many years earlier a number of people from Sweden had come and settled along the river. Then the Dutch from New York said the land was theirs, and took possession of the forts of the Swedes. The English of New York next claimed the land as theirs. Later Quakers came and settled in New Jersey. Finally came William Penn, in a ship called the *Welcome,* and after that the land belonged to the Quakers. The Swedes decided to stay in this land as well. They lived in peace with the Quakers.

We have something very pleasant to say about good William Penn. He knew very well that King Charles did not own the land and had no right to sell it or give it away, so he called the Native Americans together under a great elm tree on the river bank and had a long talk with them. He told them he would pay them for the land he wanted. This pleased the Indians very much, and from that time on, they loved William Penn. The Native Americans were blessed because Penn followed the golden rule of the Bible, "Do unto others as you would have them do unto you."

Do you not think it must have been an interesting scene when Penn and the Quakers met the Indian chiefs under the great tree—the Indians in their colored blankets and the Quakers in their great hats? That tree stood for more than a hundred years afterwards, and when the British army was in Philadelphia during the War for American Independence, their general put a guard around Penn's tree so that the soldiers would not cut it down for firewood. The tree is gone now, but a stone monument marks where it stood. A city was laid out along the river, which Penn named Philadelphia, or "Brotherly Love." I suppose there is some brotherly love there still, but not nearly so much as there should be.

Streets were made through the woods, and the names of the trees were given to these

The Log Cabin

The log cabin is one of the most familiar images from the American frontier. It has been symbolic in American history for pioneer life and humble beginnings. Abraham Lincoln was born in a log cabin in Kentucky in 1809, and William Henry Harrison used the log cabin as a campaign symbol when he campaigned for President of the United States in 1840. Yet, in spite of the log cabin's familiarity, few are aware of its beginnings in America.

It is thought that Swedish settlers in the New World—who had come from a heavily forested region of Europe—were the first to introduce log cabins. They had come to America to found the colony of New Sweden near the mouth of the Delaware River, in present-day Delaware, New Jersey, and Pennsylvania. The first settlement, Fort Christina, was established in 1638.

New Sweden did not last long, however. Although other settlements were established, the colony did not grow very large; Sweden was too far away to adequately support the colony. The Swedes were able to keep the peace with the local Native American tribes, but had trouble with the Dutch of New Netherlands. The Dutch considered the Swedes to be trespassers on their claims. The Dutch decided to bring an end to the Swedish colony, and, so after seventeen years of existence, New Sweden was conquered by the Dutch in 1655. While New Sweden disappeared from history, the contribution of the log cabin by the Swedish settlers went on to have an important impact on American frontier life.

streets, which are still known as Chestnut, Walnut, Pine, Cherry, and the like. People soon came in numbers, and it is wonderful how fast the city grew. Soon there were hundreds of comfortable houses, and in time there was a large city.

The Native Americans looked on in wonder to see large houses springing up where they had hunted deer, and to see great ships where they had paddled their canoes. The white men spread more and more into the land, and the Native Americans were pushed back, and in time, few of them were left in Penn's woodland colony. This was long after William Penn had died.

By the time William Penn was growing old and poor, Pennsylvania was growing large and rich. He spent a great deal of money on his province and received very little back. At last, he became so poor that he was put in prison for debt, as was the custom in those days. In the end, he died and left the province to his widow and sons. The Indians sent home beautiful furs to Penn's widow in memory of their great and good brother. They said these furs could help to make her a cloak "to protect her while she was passing through the stormy wilderness of life without her guide."

Under the spreading branches of an Elm tree, William Penn made a treaty of peace with the Indians. By this treaty, he paid them fairly for the land and gave them presents.

Chapter 4 Review Questions

1. What was the name of Henry Hudson's ship?
2. How did Captain Hudson die?
3. Who founded and established the area of land we now call Pennsylvania?
4. What were some of the unusual habits of the people called Quakers?
5. How did William Penn treat the Indians?

The Colonies of the South 5

Virginia has often been called the Cavalier colony. Do any of you know who the Cavaliers were? Perhaps I had better tell you. They were the lords and the proud people of England. Many of them were loyal to the interests of the English kings and queens and often sought to establish royal power in the southern colonies. There were plenty of God-fearing people in the southern colonies, but there were many Cavalier leaders who were too proud to work and expected others to work for them, simply because they were friends of the King of England.

These were the kind of men who had come over with John Smith, and that is why he had so much trouble with them. The Puritans, however, had come from the working people of England, and nobody had to starve them to keep them from swearing or being lazy. They worked hard for the glory of their Lord and Savior Jesus Christ.

The Colony of Maryland

The first to come after John Smith and the Jamestown people were Englishmen who followed the Roman Catholic religion. You should know that the Catholics were treated in England even worse than the Puritans and the Quakers. The law said they must go to the English Church instead of to their own. If they did not, they would have to pay a large sum of money or go to prison. This was very harsh and unjust to say the least.

The Catholics were not all poor people. There were rich men and nobles among them. One of these nobles, named Lord Baltimore, asked the king for some land in America where he and his friends might dwell in peace and have churches of their own. This was many years before William Penn asked for the same thing. The king was a friend of Lord Baltimore and told him he might have as much land as he could use, so he picked out a large piece just north of Virginia. The king named it Maryland, after his wife, Queen Mary, who was a Catholic. All Lord Baltimore had to pay for this land was two Indian arrows every year and a part of the gold and silver, if any were found. This was done to show that the king still kept some claim to Maryland and did not give away all his power over the colonies.

Lord Baltimore

I will now tell you a story, much the same as I have told you several times before. A shipload of Catholics and other people came across the ocean to the new continent which Columbus had discovered many years before. These sailed up the broad Chesapeake Bay. You may easily find this bay on your maps. They landed at a place they called St. Mary's, where there was a small Indian town. As it happened, the Native Americans in this town had been so much troubled by fighting tribes farther north that they were just going to move somewhere else. They were very glad to sell their town to the strangers from England.

All they wanted for their houses and their fields were some hatchets, knives, beads, and other things they could use. Gold and silver would have been of no value to them for they had never seen these metals. The only money the Indians used was round pieces of seashell with holes bored through them. Before these people left their town, they showed the white men how to hunt in the woods and how to plant corn, and their wives taught the white women how to make food out of corn and how to bake muffins. The people of Maryland, therefore, did not suffer from hunger like those of Virginia and New England. They had plenty to eat and were happy from the start.

This was in the year 1634, just about the time John Winthrop went to Massachusetts. Lord Baltimore did the same thing that John Winthrop did; he gave the people religious liberty. Every Christian who came to Maryland had the right to worship God as he believed the Bible dictated.

It was not long before other people came to Maryland, and they began to plant tobacco, as the people were doing in Virginia. Tobacco was a good crop to raise. It could be sold for a high price in England so the Maryland planters did very well. Many of them became rich. Liberty, however, did not last there very long, and the Catholics were not much better off than they had been in England. All the poor people who had come with Lord Baltimore were Protestants. Only the rich ones were Catholics. Many other Protestants soon came, some of them being Puritans from England, who rarely enjoyed religious liberty. Rich people began to fight with poor people over the subject of religion.

The Southern Colonies

There was much fighting between the Catholics and the Protestants. First one party had control, and then the other. In the end the province was taken from Lord Baltimore's son. When a new king, named King William, came to the throne, he said that Maryland was his property and that the Catholics should not have a church of their own or worship in their own way in that province. It did not seem right, after Lord Baltimore had given religious liberty to all men, for others to come and take it away. The custom in those days, however, was that all men must be made to think the same way, or be punished. This seems strange today, when every man has the right to worship as he pleases. It is even more strange, however, to see how many people in America today fail to understand the importance of religious liberty.

After 1616, raising tobacco became the main source of wealth in the Southern colonies.

In time there was born a Lord Baltimore who became a Protestant, and the province was given back to him. It grew rich and full of people, and large towns were built. One of these was named Baltimore, after Lord Baltimore, and is now a great city. Washington, D.C., the capital of the United States, stands on land that was once part of Maryland. St. Mary's, the first town built, however, has gone, and there is hardly a mark to show where it stood.

The Carolinas

Maryland, as I have said, lies north of Virginia. The Potomac River runs between them. South of Virginia was another great piece of land, extending all the way to Florida, which the Spaniards then owned. Some French Protestants called Huguenots tried to settle there, but they had been cruelly murdered by the Spaniards, and no one else came there for many years.

About 1660, people began to settle in what was then called "the Carolinas," but is now called North Carolina and South Carolina. Some of these came from Virginia and some from England, and small settlements were made here and there along the coast. One of these was called Charleston (Charles Town). By about 1700, approximately 5,000 settlers were living in the area of Charles Town. A number of these settlers were exiled French

Slavery in the Colonies

Slavery has existed throughout history, from ancient times into the twentieth century—it is even found in the Bible. Slaves were the property of their owners and had to do whatever they were told to do. In America, slaves usually worked in their masters' homes or in their fields.

Slavery existed among some Indian tribes in North America, but widespread slavery did not exist in the New World until the arrival of the Europeans. African slaves were first brought to the New World by the Spanish and Portuguese in the 1500s to replace the Indians who had originally been forced to work in their plantations but had largely died from hard labor. The Dutch, English, and French also used African slaves on their sugar plantations on the islands of the West Indies. Slaves first came to the English colonies of North America when a Dutch ship brought about twenty black African slaves to Jamestown, Virginia, in 1619.

The African slave trade was profitable for European and African traders, but hard on the slaves. Local African traders would bring captives to coastal trading stations and sell them to European slavers. The slavers would put as many slaves as possible into the holds of ships and send them to the Americas under very difficult condi-

Slaves being shipped to the colonies

tions during what is called the Middle Passage. Sick, dead, and dying slaves on such voyages would simply be thrown overboard into the ocean; British slavers themselves are thought to have thrown more than 250,000 slaves into the Atlantic Ocean by 1776. Once the slave ships arrived at their destinations, the Africans would be sold to their new masters and put to work. The exact number of slaves stolen from Africa and sent to the Americas is unknown. It has been estimated, however, that at least six million were shipped by 1776, with about 270,000 being sent to the British colonies in North America.

Slavery spread throughout all of the thirteen colonies, but it was far more common south of Pennsylvania. It became an important part of the Southern economy. There were attempts to restrict slavery in the colonial period, but they proved to be of limited success. Some of the southern colonies tried to restrict the slave trade, but were forbidden to do so by the English kings. It was not until 1808 that the United States ended the external slave trade. Slavery was slowly outlawed in the North, beginning with Rhode Island in 1774, but it was not abolished throughout the entire nation until 1865.

Huguenots, religious dissenters from New England, and groups of African slaves.

There were some noblemen in England who thought that this region might be worth much money, so they asked the king, Charles II, to give it to them. This was the same king who gave the Dutch settlement to the Duke of York and who afterwards gave Pennsylvania to William Penn. He was very ready to give away what did not belong to him, and told these noblemen that they were welcome to the Carolinas. There were eight of these men, and they made up their minds that they would have a very nice form of government for their new province. They went to a well-known philosopher named John Locke and asked him to draw up a form of government for them.

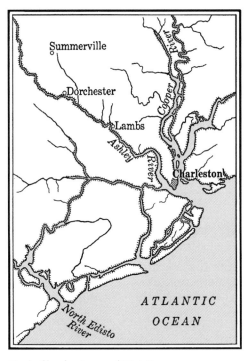

Early Charleston and Vicinity

John Locke drew up a plan of government which they thought very fine, but which everybody now thinks was very foolish. He knew more about philosophy than he knew about government. He called it the "Grand Model," and the noble lords thought they had a wonderful government indeed. There were to be earls and barons and lords—the same as in Europe. The poorer people were to be like so many slaves. They could not even leave one plantation for another without asking permission from the lord or baron who owned it.

What do you think the people did? You must not imagine they came across the ocean to become slaves. No, indeed! They cared no more for the "Grand Model" than if it was a piece of tissue paper. They settled where they pleased and would not work for the earls and barons. In fact, they fought with their governors and refused to pay the heavy taxes which

the eight noble owners asked.

In time, these noblemen got so sick of the whole business that they gave their province back to the king. It was then divided into two colonies, known as North Carolina and South Carolina. As for the lords and barons, nobody heard from them anymore.

The people of the Carolinas had other things beside the "Grand Model" government to trouble them. There were Indians back in the country who attacked them and killed many of them. In addition, there were pirates along the coast who attacked ships and killed all on board. In the face of such hardships, they still were able to plant rice and indigo—and afterwards, cotton. The people worked hard and a lot of tar and turpentine were harvested from the pine trees in North Carolina. As the years advanced, these colonies became rich and prosperous, and the people began to be happy.

Georgia, The Penal Colony

I hope none of my young readers are tired of reading about kings and colonies. I am sure you must have enjoyed reading about John Smith, Miles Standish, William Penn, and the rest of the great leaders. At any rate, there is only one more colony to talk about, and then we will be through with this part of our story. This is the colony of Georgia, which lies in the section of land between South Carolina and Florida.

I am sure that when you are done reading this book you will be glad that you did not live three or four hundred years ago. Why, in those days, every man who owed money and could not pay it back might be put in prison and kept there for years. He could not work there and earn money to pay his debts, and if his friends did not pay them, he might stay there till he died. As I have told you, even the good William Penn was put in prison for debt and kept there till his friends paid the money.

There were as many poor debtors in prison as there were thieves and villains. Some of them became sick and died, and some were starved to death by cruel jailors, who would not give them anything to eat if they had no money to pay for food. One great and good man, named General James Oglethorpe, visited the prisons and felt sorry for the debtors he saw there. He decided to help them and asked the king to give him a piece of land in America where he could take some of these suffering people.

General James Oglethorpe

There was now not much land left to give. Settlements had been made all along the coast except south of the Carolinas, and the king told General Oglethorpe that he could have the land which lay there, and could take as many debtors out of prison as he chose. He thought it would be a good thing to take them somewhere where they could work and pay their debts. The king who was then on the throne was named King George, so Oglethorpe called his new colony Georgia.

It was now the year 1733, a hundred years after Lord Baltimore had come to Maryland. General Oglethorpe took many of the debtors out of prison, and they were very glad to get out, you may be sure. They landed on the banks of a fine river down South, where he laid out a town which he named Savannah.

Early Christianity in Georgia

The Christians who came to Georgia were from many different kinds of churches. All that we know about the first 116 people who came to the colony is that they were debtors who had served time in British prisons. They claimed that they were Protestants, so they were allowed to go. Under the leadership of General James Oglethorpe, they settled in Savannah, where he served as Georgia's first governor from 1733 to 1743. In addition, a small colony of 175 Scottish Christians was established on the southern frontier.

Reformed Christians also came to the colony from the continent of Europe. Some came in small groups from France and Switzerland; others came in larger numbers from the German Palatinate—most of whom came as servants who worked for the colony for a certain length of time and then were free to settle in Georgia. The largest body of German Protestants to come, however, were from the province of Salzburg; they had been driven from their homes by the Catholic Archbishop, so they sought safety in Georgia. They first began to arrive in 1733 and

continued to come for the next ten years, until more than 200 had settled in and around Ebenezer, Georgia. Some Moravians from the great estate of Count Zinzendorf in Saxony also began to arrive in 1734.

Georgia became a royal colony in 1752, with a royal Governor who was appointed by King George II. Almost at once, some people tried, like others did in the southern colonies, to make the Church of England (or the Anglican Church) the official church of Georgia. In 1758, a law was passed to establish the Church of England in Georgia. The Anglican Church, however, remained weak in Georgia throughout colonial times, with rarely more than two ministers in the colony at the same time. The dissenters (Christians who belonged to churches other than the Anglican Church) continued to increase as people pushed in from the northern colonies. Soon the combined membership of the dissenters—Congregationalists, Presbyterians, Baptists, Quakers, Lutherans, and Catholics—far outnumbered the members of the Church of England.

The happy debtors now found themselves in a broad and beautiful land, where they could prove whether they were ready to work or not. They were not long in doing this. Right away they began to cut down trees, build houses, and plant fields—and very soon, a pretty town was built for all to see.

General Oglethorpe knew, as well as William Penn, that the land did not belong to the king. He sent for the Indian chiefs, told them the land was theirs, and offered to pay them for it. They were quite willing to sell, and soon he had all the land he wanted, and what is more, he had the Native Americans for friends.

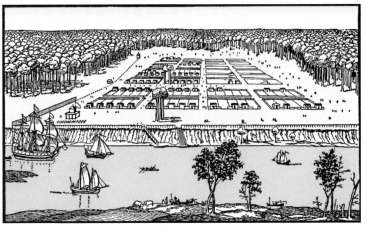
A painting of early Savannah, Georgia, in 1741

Even though the General had no trouble with the Native Americans, he had a good deal of it with the Spaniards of Florida. They said that Georgia was a part of Florida and that the English had no right to be there. The Spaniards sent an army and tried to drive them out.

I believe they did not know that Oglethorpe was an old soldier, but he soon showed them that he knew how to fight. He drove back their armies and took their ships, and they quickly made up their minds that they had better let the English alone. There was plenty of land for both, for the Spaniards had only one town in Florida. This was St. Augustine.

Before long, some Germans came from Europe and settled in the new colony. People came also from other parts of Europe. Corn was planted for food, and some of the colonists raised silkworms and made silk. After a few years, cotton came to be the chief crop of the colony.

General Oglethorpe lived to be a very old man. He did not die till long after the War for American Independence. Georgia was then a flourishing state, and the little town he had started on the banks of the Savannah River was a fine city with broad streets, fine mansions, and beautiful shade trees. I think this old man must have been very proud of this charming city, and of the great state which God allowed him to start.

Chapter 5 Review Questions

1. Who founded the colony called Maryland?

2. Do most people in America today understand the importance of religious liberty?

3. What was the name of the philosopher who drew up a plan of government for the Carolinas?

4. Who founded and established the colony called Georgia?

5. What people tried to drive the English from the colony of Georgia?

The Story of the Native Americans 6

Now that you have been told about the settlement of the colonies, it is good to recall how many of them there were. Let us see. There was the settlement in Plymouth by the Pilgrims, the Puritan settlements in New England, the Quaker one in Pennsylvania, the Catholic settlement in Maryland, the Dutch settlement in New York, the Cavalier ones in Virginia and the Carolinas, and the debtor settlement in Georgia. Then there were some smaller ones, making a total of thirteen English colonies.

These stretched all along the coast, from New France (Canada) in the north to Spanish Florida in the south. The British took a long time to settle these places, for nearly 250 years passed after the time of Columbus before General Oglethorpe came to Georgia.

While all this was going on, what was happening to the native people of America, the Indians? I am afraid they were having a very hard time of it. The Spaniards made slaves of them and forced them to work so terribly hard in the mines and fields that they died by the thousands. The French and the English fought with them and drove them away from their old homes, killing many of them.

This activity went on and on until the Native Americans, who once spread over all this country, were kept in a very small part of it. Today there are not as many Indians as there once were; some live on lands set aside by the government, while others live among us.

Indian Life in North America

What do you know about these Native Americans? I have been busy so far talking about the settlers from Europe, and what they did, and have not taken the time to tell you about the people they found on this continent and how they treated them. I think I must make this chapter about the Native Americans.

The Native Americans generally lived in a simple fashion. They spent much of their time in hunting, fishing, and planting. They raised some Indian corn and beans and were fond of tobacco. Most of their food came from wild animals killed in the woods. They were also as fond of fighting as they were of hunting. They were divided into tribes, some of which were nearly always at war with each

other. They had no weapons but stone hatchets, spears, and bows and arrows, but they were able with these to kill many of their enemies. Although it is true that Native Americans were often treated badly by the European settlers, they treated one another worse than the settlers ever did.

When they took a prisoner, they would tie him to a tree and build a fire around him and burn him to death. While he was burning they would torture him all they could. We cannot feel so much pity for the Native Americans when we think of all this. The European settlers did treat them very unjustly, but they have since stopped all these terrible cruelties, and that is something for which to be thankful. In this country, where once there was constant war and bloodshed, and torturing and burning of prisoners, now there is peace and a better system of law and justice. Even though evil has been done by settlers and Indians alike, good has come of it by the providence of God.

At the time of which I am speaking, forests covered much of this great continent called North America. They spread everywhere, and the Native Americans lived under their shade and had wonderful skills in following animals or enemies through their shady depths. They read the ground much as we read the pages of a book. A broken twig, a bit of torn moss, a footprint which we could not see, were full of meaning to them, and they would follow a trail for miles through the woods where we would not have been able to follow it a yard. Their eyes were trained to this kind of work, but in time, some of the explorers became as expert as the Indians and could follow a trail as well.

Different Groups of Indians

In the East, the American Indians lived mostly in little huts covered with skins or bark, which they called wigwams. Some of the tribes lived in villages where there were large bark houses. They did not often stay in their houses,

however, for they liked to be in the open air. They often liked to hunt deer in the woods, fish, paddle their bark canoes in the streams, and smoke their pipes in front of their huts while dancing their war dances.

The men did the hunting, clearing of fields, and fighting. The women had to do all other work, such as cooking, planting and gathering corn, building wigwams, and the like. They did some weaving of cloth, but most of their clothes were made from the skins of wild animals.

I have spoken of the tribes of the American Indians. Some of these tribes were quite large and were made up of a large number of men and women who lived together and spoke the same language. Each tribe was divided up into clans, or small family-like groups. Each clan had its "sachem," or chief. The sachems or chiefs governed the tribes and made such laws as they had.

Every clan had some animal which it called its totem, such as the wolf, bear, or fox. They were proud of their totems, and the form of the animal was tattooed on their breasts; that is, it was pricked into the skin with needles. Most of the Indians liked dancing, and their war dances were as fierce and wild as they could make them. Very few Native Americans during this time were aware of the true God of the Bible.

The tribes in the South were more peaceful than those in the North. They practiced

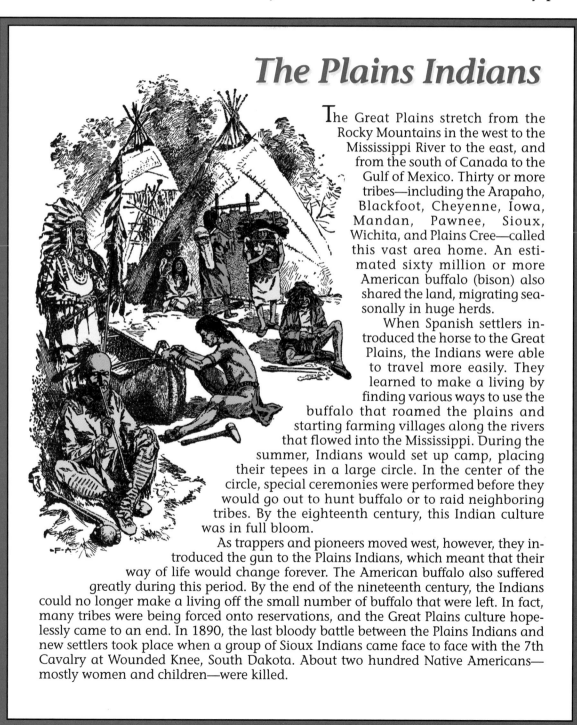

The Plains Indians

The Great Plains stretch from the Rocky Mountains in the west to the Mississippi River to the east, and from the south of Canada to the Gulf of Mexico. Thirty or more tribes—including the Arapaho, Blackfoot, Cheyenne, Iowa, Mandan, Pawnee, Sioux, Wichita, and Plains Cree—called this vast area home. An estimated sixty million or more American buffalo (bison) also shared the land, migrating seasonally in huge herds.

When Spanish settlers introduced the horse to the Great Plains, the Indians were able to travel more easily. They learned to make a living by finding various ways to use the buffalo that roamed the plains and starting farming villages along the rivers that flowed into the Mississippi. During the summer, Indians would set up camp, placing their tepees in a large circle. In the center of the circle, special ceremonies were performed before they would go out to hunt buffalo or to raid neighboring tribes. By the eighteenth century, this Indian culture was in full bloom.

As trappers and pioneers moved west, however, they introduced the gun to the Plains Indians, which meant that their way of life would change forever. The American buffalo also suffered greatly during this period. By the end of the nineteenth century, the Indians could no longer make a living off the small number of buffalo that were left. In fact, many tribes were being forced onto reservations, and the Great Plains culture hopelessly came to an end. In 1890, the last bloody battle between the Plains Indians and new settlers took place when a group of Sioux Indians came face to face with the 7th Cavalry at Wounded Knee, South Dakota. About two hundred Native Americans—mostly women and children—were killed.

more farming and had large and well-built villages. Some of them had temples and priests, and looked upon the sun as a god. They kept a fire always burning in the temple and seemed to think this fire was a part of their sun god. They had a great chief who ruled over the tribe, and also a war-chief, a high priest, and other rulers. In short, they were idol worshipers who lived in the darkness of sin. God would, however, not always leave them in total darkness. Christian missionaries would tell the American Indians about the gospel of Jesus Christ some years later.

In the Southwest, Indians built houses out of sun-dried bricks (adobe); these houses were almost like towns, for they had hundreds of rooms. A whole tribe could live in one of these great houses, sometimes as many as three thousand people. Other tribes lived in holes in the sides of steep rocks, where their enemies could not easily get at them. These are called cliff-dwellers. Then there were some who lived on top of high, steep hills, which were very hard to climb. These Indians raised large crops of corn and other plants.

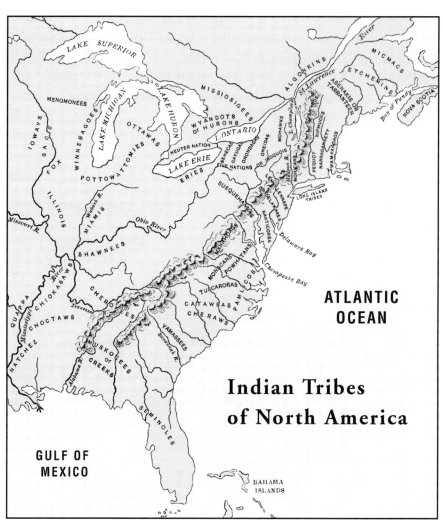

Indian Tribes
of North America

The Pequots Fight Back

Do you think, if you had been an Indian, you would have liked to see strange people coming in ships across the waters and settling down in your country as if they owned it? Many of the settlers did not pay for the land they took, although some people like William Penn and General Oglethorpe did. Most of them acted as if the country belonged to them, and it is no wonder the old owners of the coun-try did not like it, or that there was fierce fighting between the settlers and the Native Americans.

Do you remember the story of Canonicus and the snake skin, and that of Miles Standish and the chiefs? There was not much fighting then, but there was some a short time later in Connecticut, where a number of settlers had come from Massachusetts and England during the 1630s. Here there was a warlike tribe called the Pequots, who became very angry as they saw the strangers in their country.

They began to kill the settlers whenever they found them alone. Then the European settlers began to kill the Indians. Soon there was a deadly war. The Pequots had made a fort from trunks of trees, set close together in the ground. They thought they were safe in this fort, but the English made an attack on it, got into it, and set fire to the Indian wigwams inside. The fight was terrible in the smoke and flame until nearly 600 Pequots were killed. Only two settlers lost their lives.

King Philip's War

There was another Indian war in southern New England a number of years later, from 1675 to 1676. Many people on both sides were killed during these wars. The good chief Massasoit, who was an honorable leader of the Native Americans in New England, was a friend to the white men as long as he lived. After his death, however, his son Philip became one of their greatest enemies.

Philip's brother became sick and died after he had been to Plymouth, and the Indians thought that the people there had given him poison. Philip said that they would try to kill him next, and he made up his mind to fight them and drive them out of the country. The Indians had guns now and knew how to use them, and they began to shoot the settlers as they

John Eliot

John Eliot, a New England Puritan, has been called the "Apostle to the Indians" because he did much to spread the gospel among them. Although he came to America as a minister to the English settlers, he began to study the language of the Indians of Massachusetts and, in 1646, to preach to them. A year later, he began translating the Bible into the Algonquin language. This Bible was the first ever to be printed in the New World. Because of Eliot's work, Parliament established the Society for Propagation of the Gospel in New England in 1649. The outgrowth of his missionary efforts helped open the way for a century and a half of worldwide missionary endeavor.

went quietly along the roads.

Next they began to attack the villages of the settlers. They would creep up at night, set the houses on fire, and shoot the men as they came out. The war went on for a long time in this way, and there were many terrible fights.

At one place the people saw the Indians coming and ran to a strong building called a blockhouse. The Indians came whooping and yelling around this house, and tried to set it on fire by shooting arrows with blazing rags on their points. Once the roof caught fire, but some of the men ran up and threw water on the flames.

Then the Indians brought a cart and filled it with hay. Setting this on fire, they pushed it up against the house. It looked as if all the men, women, and children would be burned alive. The house caught fire and began to blaze. Just then a shower of rain came that put out the fire, and the people inside were saved once more. Before the Indians could do anything further, some soldiers came and the Indians all ran into the woods.

There were other wonderful escapes, but many of the settlers were killed, so Philip began to think he would be able to drive them out of the country, as he wished to do. The settlers knew more about war than the Indians, and, in the end, they began to drive them back. One of their forts was taken, and the wigwams in it were set on fire, like those of the Pequots. A great many of the poor Native American warriors perished in the flames.

The best fighter among the European settlers was Captain Church. He followed King Philip and his men to one hiding place after another, killing some and taking others prisoners. Among the prisoners were the wife and little son of the Indian king.

"It breaks my heart," said Philip, when he heard that his family were taken captive. "Now I am ready to die," said this warrior king.

He did not live much longer. Captain Church chased him from place to place till he came to Mount Hope in Rhode Island, where the famous leader Roger Williams had decided to set up his colony. Here King Philip was shot, and the war ended. It had lasted more than a year, and a large number had been killed on both sides. It is known in history as King Philip's War.

Other Indian Wars

There were wars with the Indians in many other parts of the country. In Virginia, the Indians made a plot to kill all the settlers there. They pretended to be very friendly and brought them meat and fish to sell. While they were talking quietly, the killers drew their tomahawks and began to kill the people. In that one morning, nearly three hundred and fifty were killed— men, women, and little children.

Hardly any of the settlers were left alive, except those in Jamestown, who were warned in time. They proceeded to attack the Indians, shooting down all they could find.

This was after the death of Powhatan, who had been a friend to the Virginia colony. About twenty years later, in 1644, another Indian massacre took place. After this, the Indians were driven far back into the country and did not give any more trouble for thirty years. The last war with them broke out in 1675 and ended a short time later.

The Dutch in New York also had their troubles with the Native Americans. They paid for all the

lands they took, but one of their governors was foolish enough to start a war that went on for two years. Worse trouble than that began in North Carolina, where there was a powerful tribe called the Tuscaroras. These warriors attacked the settlers and murdered numbers of them. In the end, however, they were driven out of the country. The only colonies in which the Indians stayed friendly for a long time were Pennsylvania and Georgia.

We know the reason for this. William Penn and General Oglethorpe were wise enough to make friends with the Indians from the start, and continued to treat them with justice and kindness. The Native Americans came to love these good men. The book of Proverbs states this point well in Chapter 16, "When a man's ways please the Lord, he maketh even his enemies to be at peace with him."

David Zeisberger

During the middle of the seventeenth century, John Eliot and Thomas Mayhew, Jr. (two pastors from Massachusetts), were the first ones to preach the gospel to the Native Americans. God blessed their work, and many Indians were converted to Christ and organized into "praying towns." In 1675, however, King Philip's War broke out, and all the Indians, including those who claimed the name of Christ, fell under suspicion. In fact, Indian believers were taken to Deer Island in Boston Harbor, where they had to stay until the end of

The French and Indian War, however, disturbed his work among the Iroquois Indians in the Wyoming Valley of northeastern Pennsylvania. He began, therefore, to minister among the Delaware Indians, and God blessed his efforts. Like Eliot, he formed the Indian believers into quiet, productive villages, but strife again interrupted the progress of the gospel. Whites accused the Indian converts of helping other Native Americans in their warfare against the settlers.

An old drawing of Moravians baptizing Indian converts

the war. As a result, many left the faith and returned to their people.

Moravian Christians from Germany, however, had greater success among the Native Americans. David Zeisberger (1721–1808) led the way in spreading the gospel to the American Indians. Although he worked for six long, difficult years, God blessed his labors and many were converted. Humanly speaking, part of his success may be attributed to his willingness to adapt to Indian ways more readily than missionaries from other churches did.

Zeisberger had to help the Delaware Indian believers to move several times as the white settlers took over more and more of their land. In 1772, he helped them settle in the territory of Ohio, where they were joined by other Indian converts. During the War for Independence, they were forced again to move to upstate New York and Ontario. Zeisberger finally brought them to a new settlement in Ontario, where they were able to live and worship in peace and safety for many years. He called this settlement Gnadenhütten, or "Guarded by Grace."

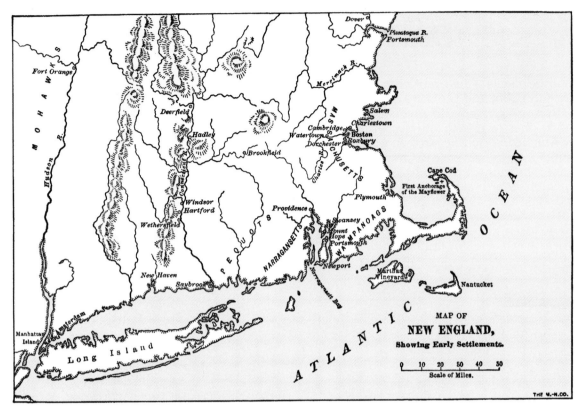

This map of New England, shows the Indian tribes that surrounded the early English settlements. Note the area inhabited by the Pequot Indians in what is now the state of Connecticut.

Chapter 6 Review Questions

1. Which Europeans had large areas of land in the eastern part of America during the 1600s and 1700s?

2. How often did the Native American tribes fight with each other before the settlers from Europe arrived in America?

3. What names did the different groups of Indians give to the homes that they lived in?

4. Who was the Indian chief that led a war against settlers in southern New England?

5. What two English colonies had little trouble with the American Indians?

Royal Governors, Loyal Captains

7

Do any of my young readers know what is meant by the word "charter"? A charter is a written or printed paper which grants certain rights or privileges to the party to whom it is given. It may come from a king or a congress or from any person in power, and it may be given to any other person who wishes the right to hold a certain property or to do some special thing.

Do you understand any better now? I am sorry I cannot put it in plainer words. I think the best way will be to tell you about some charters which belong to American history. You should know that all the people who crossed the ocean to make new settlements on the Atlantic coast had charters from the king of England; this was the case with the Pilgrims and the Puritans. Charters were also granted to individuals such as William Penn, Lord Baltimore, and others about whom I have spoken.

These charters were great written documents that gave these people the right to settle on and own certain lands, form certain kinds of government, and do a variety of things which in England no one could do but the king and the parliament.

The colonies in New England originally had the right to choose their own governors and make their own laws; they were self-governing colonies, but Massachusetts and New Hampshire eventually became royal colonies, with governors appointed by the king. The colonies of Connecticut and Rhode Island, however, were able to keep their original charters and choose their own governors.

King James vs. the Colonies

All kings, you should know, were not alike. Some let the colonies govern themselves, and others wanted to control the colonies. Some were willing for the people to have liberty, and some were not. The kings who gave the charters to New England were of the first kind. They were followed, however, by kings of the sec-

THE ENGLISH COLONIES ABOUT 1700.

represents the extent of early settlements.

ond kind, who thought that the people beyond the sea had too much liberty, and who wished to take away some of it.

Charles II, who gave some of these charters, was one who did not trouble himself about the people in the colonies, but James II, who came after him, was one of the bad kings. He acted like a tyrant, who wanted to make the laws himself and take the right to do this from the people. After trying to rob the people of England of their liberties, he thought he would do the same thing with the colonists in America. "Those folks across the seas are having too good a time," he thought. "They have too many rights and privileges, and I must take some of them away. I will let them know that I am their master."

Sir Edmund Andros

They had their charters which gave them these rights, however, the wicked king thought the first thing to do was to take their charters away from them. With their rights gone, he could then make for them a new set of laws and force them to do everything he wished. How would he do this, though?

What King James did was send a nobleman named Sir Edmund Andros to New England to rule as royal governor. He was the agent of the king and was to do all that the king ordered. One of the first things he was commanded to do was to rob the people of their charters. You see, even a tyrant king did not like to go against the charters, for a charter was a sacred pledge.

Clever Captain Wadsworth

Well, the new governor went about ordering the people to give him their charters. One of the places he went was Hartford, Connecticut. There he told the officers of the colony that they must deliver up their charter; the king had said so, and the king's word must be obeyed.

If any of you had lived in Connecticut in those days I know how you would have felt. The charter gave the people a great deal of liberty, and they did not wish to part with it. I know you and I would have felt the same way. What could they do, though? If they did not give it up peacefully, Governor Andros might come again with soldiers and take it from them by force, so the governor and the lawmakers were concerned about what they should do.

They asked Governor Andros to come to the Statehouse and talk over the matter. Some of them thought they could get him to leave them their charter, though they might have known better. There they sat—the governor in the lofty chair of the state, the others seated in a half circle before him. There was a broad table between them, and on this lay the great parchment of the charter. Some

King James sent Sir Edmund Andros to New England to rule as royal governor.

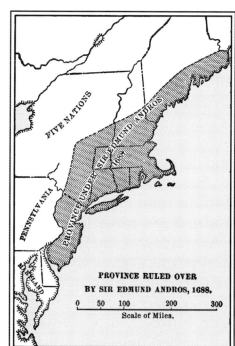

PROVINCE RULED OVER BY SIR EDMUND ANDROS, 1688.

0   50   100   200   300
Scale of Miles.

of those present did a great deal of talking. They told how King Charles had given them the charter, how happy they had been under it, and how loyal they were to King James; they begged Governor Andros not to take it from them. They might as well have talked to the walls, however. He had his orders from the king and was one of those men who do just what they are told.

While the talk was going on, a strange thing happened. It was night, and the room was lit up with tall candles. Of course you know that these were the best lights people had at that time; electric lights had not yet been invented. They did not even have matches during this time period. The only way to light a flame in those days was by use of the flint and steel, which was a very slow method indeed.

In 1856, the noble old tree, which stood in what is now Charter Oak Place, Hartford, was blown down. A marble tablet marks the spot.

Suddenly, while one of the Hartford men was talking and the governor was looking at him in a tired sort of way, all the lights in the room went out, and the room was in deep darkness. Everybody jumped up from their chairs, and there was no end of bustle and confusion—likely some pretty angry words were said. Then they had to hunt in the dark for a flint and work to make sparks on the tinder. As a result, it was some time before the candles were lit again.

When this was done, the governor opened his eyes very wide, for the table was empty, and the charter was gone! I am afraid that he swore a great deal when he saw that. No matter how much he swore, however, he could not bring the charter back with evil words. It was

gone, and nobody knew where. Everybody looked for it, right and left, in and out, in drawers and closets, but it was nowhere to be found. Very likely most of them did not want to find it. At any rate, the governor had to go away without the charter, and years passed before anybody saw it again.

Do you wish to know what became of it? We are told that it had been taken by a bold young soldier named Captain Wadsworth. While all the people in the room were looking at the one who was making his speech, the Captain quickly took off his cloak and gave it a quick fling over the candles, so that in a moment they were all put out. Then he snatched up the charter from the table and slipped quietly out of the room. While they were busy snapping the flint and steel, he was hurrying down the street towards a great oak tree which was more than a hundred years old. This tree was hollow in its heart, and there was a hole in its side which opened into the hollow. Into this hole Captain Wadsworth pushed the charter and it fell into the hollow space. I do not think any of us would have thought of looking there for it. I know nobody did at that time, and it lay there for years until the tyrant King James was driven from the throne and a new king had taken his place. Then it was joyfully brought out, and the people were very glad to see it again.

The old tree stood for many years in the main street of the town and became famous as the Charter Oak. The people loved and were proud of it as long as it stood. Many years ago,

---

Preamble to "The Fundamental Orders of Connecticut"

Forasmuch as it hath pleased the almighty God by the wise disposition of His divine providence so to Order and dispose of things that we the Inhabitants and Residents of Windsor, Harteford, and Wethersfield are now cohabiting and dwelling in and upon the river of Coneticotte and the Lands thereunto adjoining; And well knowing where a people are gathered together, the Word of God requires that to maintain the peace and union of such a people there should be an orderly and decent Government established according to God, to order and dispose of the affayres of the people at all seasons as occasion shall require; do therefore associate and conjoin our selves to be as one Public State or Commonwealth; and do, for our selves and our Successors and such as shall be adjoined to us at any time hereafter, enter into Combination and Confederation together, to maintain and preserve the liberty and purity of the gospel of our Lord Jesus which we now profess, as also the discipline of the Churches, which according to the truth of the said gospel is now practised amongst us; As also in our Civil Affairs to be guided and governed according to such Laws, Rules, Orders, and Decrees as shall be made, ordered, & decreed, as followeth:...

---

however, the old oak fell, and now only some of its wood is left. This has been made into chairs and boxes and other objects which are now of great value.

Wadsworth Fights with Drums

Do you not think Captain Wadsworth was a bold and daring man, and one who knew just what to do in times of trouble? If you do not, I think you will when I tell you another story about him.

This took place after the charter had been taken from the oak and brought to the Statehouse again. At this time, there was a governor in New York named Fletcher, who claimed that the king had given him the right to command the militia, or citizen soldiers, of Connecticut. He came to Hartford, where Captain Wadsworth was in command and where the people did not want any stranger to have power over them. Governor Fletcher told the captain why he had come and that he had a commission to read to the soldiers.

The militia were called out and drawn up in line in the public square of the town, and Governor Fletcher came before them, full of importance. He took out of his pocket the paper which he said gave him the right to command and began to read it in a very proud and haughty manner. He had not read ten words, however, when Captain Wadsworth told the drummers to beat their drums, and, before you could draw your breath, there was such a rattle and roll of noise that not a word could be heard.

"Silence!" cried Fletcher. "Stop those drums!" The drums stopped and he began to read again.

"Drum!" ordered Wadsworth in a loud tone, and such a noise began that a giant's voice would have been drowned out.

"Silence!" again shouted Fletcher. He was very red in the face by this time.

"Drum, I say!" roared the captain.

Then he turned to the governor and said, laying his hand on his sword, "I command these men, Governor Fletcher, and if you interrupt me again I will make the sun shine through you in a minute." Moreover, he looked as if he meant what he said. All the governor's pomp and courage were gone, and his face turned from red to pale. He quickly thrust the paper back into his pocket and soon left Hartford for New York. No doubt he thought that Connecticut was not a good place for royal governors.

Bacon's Rebellion

Suppose I now tell you the story of another royal governor and another bold captain. This was down in Virginia, but it was long after

Captain Smith was dead and after Virginia had become a large and prosperous colony.

The king sent there a governor named Berkeley, who acted as if he was master and all the people were his slaves. They did not like to be treated this way, but Berkeley had soldiers under his command, and the people were forced to obey. While this was going on, the Indians began to murder the settlers. The governor ought to have stopped them, but he was afraid to call out the people and he let the murders go on.

There was a young man named Nathaniel Bacon who asked Governor Berkeley to let him raise some men to fight the Indian warriors. The governor refused. This, however, did not stop brave young Bacon, for he called out a force of men and drove off the murdering Indians.

Governor Berkeley was very angry at this. He said that Bacon was a traitor and ought to be treated like one, and that the men with him were rebels. Bacon at once marched with his men against Jamestown, and the proud governor ran away as fast as he could.

While Bacon and his men were fighting the Indians again, however, Governor Berkeley came back and talked more than ever about rebels and traitors. This made Bacon and the people with him very angry. To be treated in this way, while they were saving the people from the Indian knife and tomahawk, was wrong in Bacon's mind. They

In 1676, Nathaniel Bacon, a young patriot, raised a force against the governor's orders and held back the Indians. When Berkeley objected to this "rebellion," Bacon drove him out of Jamestown and burned it to the ground.

marched against Jamestown again. This time the governor did not run away, but prepared to defend the place with soldiers and cannons.

They did not fire their guns, however. Bacon had captured some of the wives of the principal men, and he put them in front of his line as he advanced. The governor did not dare tell his soldiers to fire on these women, so he left the town again in a hurry, and it was taken by the Indian fighters.

Bacon made up his mind that Governor Berkeley should not come back to Jamestown again. He had the town set on fire and burned to the ground. Some of the men with him set fire to their own houses, so that they should not give shelter to the governor and his men. That was the end of Jamestown. It was never rebuilt. Only ashes remained of the first English town in America. Today there is a historical park to show where the town stood.

We cannot tell what might have happened if brave young Bacon had lived. As it was, he became sick and died. His men now had no leader and soon dispersed. Then the governor came back full of fury and began to hang all those who opposed him. He might have put a great many of them to death if King Charles had not stopped him and ordered him back to England. This was King Charles II, whose father had been put to death by Lord Oliver Cromwell for his tyrannical acts in England years before.

King Charles II was angry at what Governor Berkeley had done, and said, "That old fool has hung more men in the Virginia colony than I have in crowded England."

Chapter 7 Review Questions

1. What is a charter?
2. Why was Sir Edmund Andros sent to New England by King James?
3. Who was Captain Wadsworth?
4. What town did Nathaniel Bacon and his troops burn down?
5. Why was King Charles II of England angry with Governor Berkeley?

Old Times in the Colonies 8

What a wonderful change has come over this great country of ours since the days of our forefathers! Look at our great cities, with their grand buildings and their miles of streets, with swift speeding cars and trains, and great stores lit by brilliant electric lights, and huge companies filled with amazing computers and marvelous machines! Also look at our broad fields filled with cattle or covered by growing crops, and divided by splendid highways and railroads thousands of miles in length! Is it not all very wonderful?

"Has it not always been this way, though?" some young children may ask. "I have lived so many years and have never seen anything else."

My dear young friend, if you had lived fifty or sixty years, as many of us older folks have, you would have seen very different things. In addition, if we had lived as long ago as our great-grandfathers did, and then come back again today, I think our eyes would open wider than Governor Andros's did when he saw that the charter was gone.

The "Good Old Days"

In those days, as I told you, when anyone wanted to turn on lights, he could not flip a switch as we do. He had to hammer away with flint and steel, and then had nothing better than a homemade candle to light. Why, I am sure that many of you never even saw a pair of snuffers, which people then used to cut off the candle wick.

Some of you who live in old houses with dusty attics, full of old furniture, have perhaps found there odd-looking wooden frames and wheels, and strange old tools of various kinds. Sometimes these wheels are brought down stairs and set in the hall as

The Spinning Wheel

The spinning wheel was brought to America by the colonists. It had a spindle, or round tapered stick, that was attached horizontally and connected to a large wheel with a circular band. With the left hand, a spinner would feed the short fibers from the distaff, or stick, on which the cotton fibers were wound, into the spindle which was turned by the wheel with the right hand. As the fibers were being pulled onto the spindle, they would twist together, making thread long enough to weave into cloth or be used in sewing. The fiber spun into thread formed a skein, or coil, of yarn, which was removed from the spindle and ready to use. The spinning wheel made the spinning of cotton much easier than the old hand-spun method.

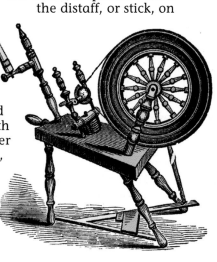

something of which to be proud. The old eight-day clocks stand there, too, with their loud "tick-tock," buzzing and ticking away today as if they had not done so for a hundred years.

The wheels I speak of are the old spinning wheels with which some of our great-great-great-grandmothers spun flax into thread. This thread they wove into homespun cloth on old-fashioned looms. All work of this kind used to be done at home, though now it is done in huge factories. We also buy our clothes in stores, instead of spinning, weaving, and sewing them in a great old kitchen before a huge fireplace.

Really, I am afraid many of you do not know how people lived in the old times. They are often spoken of as the "good old days." I believe you will hardly think so when I have told you something more about them. Would you think it very good to have to get up in a freezing cold room, go down and pump ice-cold water to wash your face, go out in the snow to get wood to make the fire, and shiver for an hour before the house began to warm up? That is only one of the things you would not like in the old days. I shall certainly have to stop here and tell you about how people lived in old times, and then you can say if you would like to go back to them.

Would any boy and girl among you care to live in a little one-story house, made of rough logs laid one on another and with a roof of thatch—that is, of straw or reeds, or anything that would keep out the rain? Houses, I mean, with only one or two rooms, and some of them with chimneys made of wood, plastered with clay on the inside so that they could not be set on fire. These were the oldest houses. Later on, people began to build larger houses, many of which were made of brick or stone. I am afraid, however, there was not much comfort in the best of them. They had no stoves and were heated by great stone fireplaces where big logs of wood were burned. They made a bright and cheerful blaze, it is true, but most of the heat went roaring up the wide chimney, and only a

little of it came out into the room. In the winter, the people lived in their kitchens with the blazing wood fire for heat and light and, at bedtime, went shivering off to ice-cold rooms. Do you think you would have enjoyed that?

They had very little furniture, and most of what they had was rude and rough, much of it chopped out of the trees by the farmer's axe. Some of the houses had glass windows, little diamond-shaped panes, set in lead frames, but most of them had nothing but oiled paper, which kept out as much light as it let in.

All the cooking was done on the great kitchen hearth, where the pots were hung on iron cranes and the pans set on the blazing coals. They did not have as much food to cook as we have. Mush and milk, or pork and beans, were their usual food, and their bread was mostly made of rye or cornmeal. The boys and girls, who had nice books they wanted to read, often had to do so by the light of the kitchen fire; but I can tell you that books were very scarce things in those days.

If any of us had lived then, I know how glad we would have been to see the bright springtime with its flowers and warm sunshine. We might have shivered again, however, when we thought of the next winter.

Of course, the people had some good times. They had Thanksgiving Day, when people came with grateful hearts unto God for all the good things they had to eat, and election day and harvest day, when they had outdoor sports. They also had quilting and husking parties, spinning bees, sleigh rides, picnics, and other amusements. A wedding was a happy time, and even a funeral was followed by a great dinner.

After all, however, there was much more hard work than holiday, and nearly everybody had to labor long and received little for it. They were making themselves homes in a new country, as you know, and it was a very hard task. Today, we are still being blessed by the work of these early Ameri-

The First Thanksgiving

I may not here omit how, notwithstand[ing] all their great pains and industry, and the great hopes of a large crop, the Lord seemed to blast, and take away the same, and to threaten further and more sore famine unto them. By a great drought which continued from the third week in May, till about the middle of July, without any rain and with great heat for the most part, insomuch as the corn began to wither away though it was set with fish, the moisture whereof helped it much. Yet at length it began to languish sore, and some of the drier grounds were parched like withered hay, part whereof was never recovered. Upon which they set apart a solemn day of humiliation, to seek the Lord by humble and fervent prayer, in this great distress. And he was pleased to give them a gracious and speedy answer, both to their own and the Indians' admiration that lived amongst them.

For all the morning, and the greater part of the day, it was clear weather and very hot, and not a cloud or any sign of rain to be seen; yet toward evening it began to overcast, and shortly after to rain with such sweet and gentle showers as gave them cause of rejoicing and blessing God. It came without either wind or thunder or any violence, and by degrees in that abundance as that the earth was thoroughly wet and soaked and therewith. Which did so apparently revive and quicken the decayed corn and other fruits, as was wonderful to see, and made the Indians astonished to behold.

And afterwards the Lord sent to them such seasonable showers, with interchange of fair warm weather as, through His blessing, caused a fruitful and liberal harvest, to their no small comfort and rejoicing. For which mercy, in time convenient, they also set apart a day of thanksgiving.

William Bradford, *Of Plymouth Plantation*

cans. We should always thank God for His wise and good plan for our nation.

Down South, people had more comfort. The weather was not nearly so cold, so they did not have to keep up blazing fires or shiver in their cold beds. Many of the rich planters built themselves large mansions of wood or brick. They also bought costly furniture from England and lived in great show, with gold and silverware on their tables. They had fine coaches drawn by handsome horses when they went to town.

In New York, the Dutch built quaint old houses like the ones they had in Holland. In Philadelphia, the Quakers lived in neat two-story houses with wide orchards and gardens round them where they raised plenty of fruit. When anyone opened a shop, he would hang out a basket, a wooden anchor, or some such sign to show what kind of goods he had to sell.

In New England, Sunday was kept in a very strict fashion, for the people loved God very much and obeyed Him. It was regarded as wicked to play or work on the Sabbath. Almost everybody liked to go to church. All who did not go were disciplined. What marvelous sermons they preached in those old churches, preaching away sometimes for three or four hours at a time! The boys and girls listened to them, as well as the men and women. It was only natural for these people to want to spend as much time as possible in fellowship with God. People today could learn something from these dedicated Christians, because they loved God and His law.

Now do you think those were the "good old days"? I imagine some of you will think they were the "hard old days." They were, however, not nearly so bad as you may think. You must bear in mind that the people knew nothing of many of the things we enjoy. They were used to hard work and plain food and coarse furniture and rough clothes and cold rooms, and were more hardy and could stand more than people who sleep in furnace-heated rooms and have their tables heaped with all kinds of fruits and vegetables and meats.

Life on the Frontier

There was one thing, however, that could not have been pleasant, and that was their constant fear of the Indians and having to carry muskets with them even when they went to church. All around them were the forests in which the Indians roamed; their cruel yell might be heard at any time or a sharp arrow might whiz out from the thick leaves.

The farm houses were built like forts, and in all the villages were strong buildings called blockhouses, to which everybody could run in times of danger. In these, the second story spread out over the first, and there were holes in the floor through which the men could fire down on the Indians below. It makes us tremble, however, to think that, at any time, the traveler or farmer might be shot down by a lurking Indian, or might be seized and burned alive. We can hardly wonder that the people grew to distrust the Native Americans

and to kill them or drive them away.

There were many animals in the woods, and the rivers were full of fish. Many of the people spent their time in hunting and fishing. They became as expert in this as the Indians themselves, and some of them could follow a trail as well as the most sharp-sighted of the Indian warriors.

Some of you may have read James Fenimore Cooper's novels of Indian life and know what a wonderful hunter and Indian trailer old Natty Bumpo was. We, however, do not need to go to novels to read about great hunters, for the life of Daniel Boone was as full of adventure as that of any of the heroes of Indian life.

Daniel Boone was the most famous hunter this country has ever known. He lived much later than the early times I am talking about, but the country he lived in was as wild as that found by the first settlers of the country. When he was only a little boy, he went into the deep woods and lived there by himself for several days, shooting game and making a fire by which to cook it. He made himself a little hut of sticks and sod and lived there like an American Indian, and there is where his father and friends found him when they came seeking him in the woods.

Years afterwards, he crossed the high mountains of North Carolina and went into the great forest of Kentucky where only Native Americans and wild animals lived. For a long time he stayed there by himself, with the Indians hunting and trying to kill him. He was too wide awake, however, for the smartest of them all.

One time, when they were close on his trail, he slipped away from them by catching hold of a loose grapevine and making a long swinging jump, and then running on. When the Indians got there, they lost the marks of his footprints and gave up the chase. At another time when he was taken prisoner, he got up,

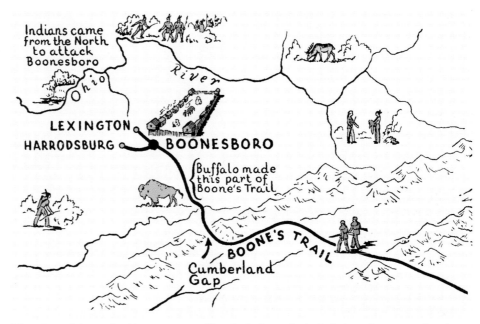

After Daniel Boone had been captured by the Indians, he heard that they were planning an attack on Boonesboro. He escaped and returned in time to warn his friends.

took one of their guns, and slipped away from them without any of them waking up.

Many years afterwards, when he and others had built a fort in Kentucky and brought out their wives and children, Boone's daughters and two other girls were carried off by Indians while they were out picking wildflowers.

Boone and other hunters were soon on their trail and followed it by the broken bushes and bits of torn dress which the smart girls had left behind them. In this way, they came up to the Indians while they were eating their supper, fired on them, and then ran up and rescued the girls. These young folks did not go out of the fort to pick wildflowers after that!

Once Daniel Boone was taken prisoner, and he would have been burned alive if an old woman had not taken him for her son. The Indians painted his face and made him wear Indian clothing and live with them as one of themselves. One day, however, he heard them talking and found that they were going to attack the fort where all his friends were, so he slipped out of the village and ran away. He had a long journey to make, and the American Indians followed him closely. He walked in the water to hide his footsteps and lived on roots and berries, for fear they would hear his gun if he shot any game. In the end, he made it back to the fort. He found it in bad condition, but he set the men to make it strong, and when the Indians came they were beaten off.

Daniel Boone lived to be a very old man and kept going farther west to get away from the new people who were coming into the Kentucky forest, eventually moving to Missouri. He said he wanted "elbowroom." He spent all the rest of his life hunting, and the Native Americans looked on him as the greatest woodsman and the most wonderful hunter the settlers ever had.

Chapter 8 Review Questions

1. Describe what it was like to live in a colonial home.

2. How did people cook their food during this time period?

3. How did the people living in New England at this time view worship on Sundays?

4. What was the name of the great hunter and woodsman who helped to settle the wilderness of Kentucky and other nearby states?

Jonathan Edwards, Town Crier for God 9

Revival Fires in New England

The townspeople of Enfield, Connecticut, crowded into their church meetinghouse on a sizzling July day in 1735. They had not as yet felt the heat of the New England revival fires that were flickering around their part of the country, but they were anxious to listen to the revival leader, Jonathan Edwards, who was a Congregational pastor from Northampton, Massachusetts.

As the preacher entered the room, he was greeted by an irreverent buzz of conversation punctuated by coarse laughter. Some smirked openly. He had been attending a presbytery meeting when he received the invitation to speak. It was given at such short notice that he had dipped into his saddle bags and chosen a sermon preached at Northampton a month before.

It was Edwards's custom to read his sermon. After he had spoken a few sentences in his solemn voice, the disorder subsided and a calm crept over the room. Hearers who had mocked the preacher sat riveted to their seats, mouths gaped, as they heard: "You hang by a slender thread, with the flames of divine wrath flashing about it, and ready every moment to singe and burn it asunder; and you have nothing to keep off the flames of wrath, nothing of your own, nothing that you have ever done, nothing that you can do, to induce God to spare you one moment."

The people clutched their pews and some shook uncontrollably. Before the two-hour sermon ended, many were sobbing with such intensity that the preacher had to request silence to be heard.

The people of Enfield turned to God that day— much as had the young and old, the poor and rich, of Edwards's hometown. They were caught up in a surge of revival that swept from New England south to the other colonies in following years. Hundreds of churches were built and thousands of converts became new members during this Great Awakening, led by Jonathan Edwards and advanced by the eloquent English preacher, George Whitefield.

Jonathan Edwards has become famous in history for his sermon, "Sinners in the Hands of an Angry God," but careful biographies more correctly describe him as a genius, an outstanding colonial leader, and devout Christian. Actually he could not be considered a "fire and brimstone" preacher. Only a few months before the Enfield sermon, revival had come to his home congregation when he gave an exposition from I Corinthians 13 on the love of Christ.

In addition to being a pioneer revivalist to early America, Jonathan Edwards was a diligent pastor, brilliant theologian, noted educator, respected philosopher, and prolific writer. From his early years, he had shown great promise.

The Early Years

When he was born on October 5, 1703, the colonies were tossing in the tides of endless European conflicts. The frontier was constantly in danger from invading Indian war parties. The political status of the colonies was uncertain. Puritan leaders

The Old Tennent Church

How the Great Awakening Began

The Great Awakening had its roots in the ministry of Theodore Frelinghuysen (1691–1747). He was born at Lingen in East Friesland, Germany. There he came under the strong influence of Puritan teaching which stressed the work of the Holy Spirit who gives men the ability to believe. In 1720, he came to America to pastor a Dutch Reformed Church in the colony of New Jersey. Having undergone spiritual revival himself, he became concerned by the lack of zeal for God that many of the colonial churches displayed. This concern so affected him that he began to boldly preach the gospel which stirred the whole area of the Raritan Valley in central New Jersey.

Gilbert Tennent (1703–1764), a nearby Presbyterian minister, was encouraged by what he saw happening in the Dutch Reformed churches; therefore, he began to preach the good news of Christ's death and resurrection. His message reflected the very heart of the gospel—salvation by grace through faith (Ephesians 2:8, 9). Tennent told his congregations that keeping the outer forms of religion did not make someone a Christian. A person must personally be changed by the power of

God, and Christ must take control of his whole life. As a result, many New Jersey Presbyterians were converted. Reports spread quickly of his "awakening" sermons that warned church members of their need to run to Jesus Christ for shelter from the coming wrath of God upon sinners.

In 1734, a truly great revival broke out in New England. This was the Great Awakening that was led by Jonathan Edwards—one of the most brilliant men America has produced. He was pastor of the Congregational Church in Northampton and had a profound faith in God. This revival took place while he was preaching a series of sermons on "Justification by Faith." As he described the results of sin and the horrors of hell, many of his listeners wept and hundreds placed their faith in Jesus Christ. In Northampton, virtually every person came under conviction.

Within a few years, after the revival in Northampton began, similar revivals occurred at various locations throughout New England. By 1740, mass conversions were being recorded throughout the region. Between 25,000 and 50,000 new Christians were added to the churches in a region whose total population was then about 300,000. The revival that swept New England vastly changed the moral and religious attitudes of the people there.

had been concentrating their attentions upon political problems, and the moral and religious life of the colonists had dropped to a low ebb. By the adoption of the "Halfway Covenant," unconverted persons were allowed to become "halfway" church members—thus filling the churches with a mixed multitude.

At the age of ten, Jonathan began writing detailed essays on insects and natural science. A curiosity that never slackened kept his notebook stuffed with questions. "Why, having two eyes, do we not see double? Why are distant mountains blue?" Botany, zoology, physiology, geology, and astronomical physics were a few of his numerous interests.

Science, however, seemed inadequate to the budding genius. It dealt with only segments of knowledge; it was superficial in that it could never satisfy all the queries of his mind. Edwards wanted to understand the true source of all wisdom and knowledge.

Turning to theology and philosophy, he came to conclude that the perfect order of the universe demands the "eternal existence of an all-comprehending Mind" and that "no happiness is solid and substantial but spiritual happiness." His first recorded interest in spiritual things came at age ten during a revival at his father's church. He and his playmates built a "prayer booth" in a swamp. Often he talked with God in the woods.

In his youth, he had several deep spiritual experiences. An outstanding one is traceable to his reading of I Timothy 1:17—"Now unto the King eternal, immortal, invisible, the only wise God, be honor and glory for ever and ever. Amen."

He wrote: "There came into my soul a sense of the glory of the Divine Being different from anything I had ever experienced before. I went to pray to God that I might enjoy Him, and prayed with a new sort of affection."

At thirteen years of age, he entered the Collegiate School of Connecticut, later renamed Yale, with a reading knowledge of Greek, Hebrew, and Latin. Four years later, he graduated as valedictorian of his class. He spent two additional years at Yale preparing for the ministry, then pastored a Presbyterian church in New York for eight months before returning to Yale as a tutor.

When he was twenty-four, his self-discipline and study was somewhat interrupted by a very special person. He had fallen in love with Sarah Pierrepont, the daughter of one of Yale's founders. It was at this time that the Congregational Church of Northampton, Massachusetts, the most prosperous inland community of the state, called him to assist his grandfa-

Results of the Great Awakening

The Great Awakening did much to help America. Many churches were established and many colonists were converted. Church members also took their faith more seriously. Much concern for the needs of people and practical righteousness resulted as well.

In addition, the Awakening greatly helped in the area of education. Christians realized that reading and writing were very important to the spread of the gospel. Training missionaries and pastors was also stressed. The need for general Bible knowledge and godly wisdom among the people was seen as a key to the growth of the nation that was about to be born. Up to this time, the churches had to have men trained in England; however, the desire now was to have their own schools in America. Because of this desire, many Christian colleges were started—including Princeton, Rutgers, Brown, and Dartmouth.

The revival also raised the concern for Christian freedom which resulted in the United States Constitution. Americans today who enjoy First Amendment freedoms—of religion, press, speech, and assembly—have been helped by people who were set free from the slavery of sin during the Great Awakening. Their zeal for religious freedom led to a desire for political freedom. The Great Awakening, therefore, helped the colonists to think and live according to biblical standards, which would help them as they began to establish a new nation under God.

ther, Solomon Stoddard, in the pastorate. Six months later he rode to New Haven to marry seventeen-year-old Sarah.

When his grandfather died in 1729, Jonathan assumed the duties of the pastorate at Northampton. Twice a day he prayed in private. Thirteen hours daily were spent in study. He exercised by walking, chopping wood, or riding horseback, meditating at the same time.

While rearing twelve children, Sarah sidetracked idlers who would interrupt her husband's study, nursed him when he was sick, watched his diet, and judiciously ran the household affairs. "She never had to shout at the children," an observer remembers. After Whitefield, a bachelor, visited the parsonage, he remarked: "A sweeter couple have I not seen."

David Brainerd, the missionary to the Indians, looked upon Jonathan Edwards as a father. When Brainerd came down with tuberculosis, he moved into the Edwards's household. There seventeen-year-old Jerusha Edwards took care of him until his death. Just before dying he whispered to her, "We shall spend a happy eternity together." Jerusha died shortly afterward and was buried beside David.

David Brainerd

In tribute to his intended son-in-law, David Brainerd, Jonathan Edwards wrote a book concerning the experiences of the missionary, a volume widely read today.

Edwards Takes a Stand

In his seventh year with the Northampton church, Edwards wrote: "The spirit of God began extraordinarily to work amongst us." Hardened sinners were converted, the town tavern was emptied, and the congregation became spiritually alive. During a six month period, almost half of the 620 members professed conversion. Then like a prairie fire the awakening spread until the entire Connecticut River Valley was ablaze.

Revival fires burned brightly for six months, then died down only to shoot up again at Northampton in 1740. The Great Awakening had been born and it was to become the colonies' most significant spiritual development. An estimated one-sixth of the total colonial population was converted. The moral fiber of the colonists was toughened for the coming battle for national independence.

In his twenty-fourth year at Northampton, trouble enveloped Edwards. Part of it arose from his blunt criticism of the "Halfway Covenant."

This firm conviction of Edwards clashed head-on with the views of leading members. "I cannot in good conscience receive another halfway member into the church," he told his wife. The "Halfway Covenant" had been practiced by his grandfather before him and enabled a person to belong to the church and receive all its benefits, except communion and voting privileges, without a testimony of faith in Christ.

Several who were disgruntled about Edwards's criticism of the young people seized upon his stand on the "Halfway Covenant" as an excuse to work for his dismissal. They accomplished it in 1750, thereby dismissing one of New England's greatest leaders.

"I am now thrown upon the wide ocean of the world and know not what will become of me and my numerous family," Edwards declared. After six unhappy months, he accepted a call to the church at the Indian village of

Stockbridge, Massachusetts, where he became pastor for the small colony of settlers and the missionary-teacher for illiterate Indians.

For eight years, the best educated man in the colonies ministered for a salary too low to feed his family. The Edwards children pitched in to help by making fans and lace to sell in Boston. The seeming setback proved to be a blessing in disguise for the following generations. With limited pastoral duties, he had time to write, so he was able to prepare his *Freedom of the Will, Doctrine of Original Sin,* and other theological books that have influenced theological thinking for more than two centuries.

In 1757, the trustees of the College of New Jersey, known today as Princeton, elected him president. He was installed the following year.

At this time, an epidemic of smallpox was raging on the campus. Edwards was inoculated, but complications came and provoked a fatal illness.

Edwards had served as college president only two months. He died at the height of his career. Yet his testimony was not finished. Standing like a spiritual giant, his life and influence had helped to mold the progress of the colonies, and his recorded experiences and written works formed a great spiritual heritage for the dynamic young nation that was soon to be born.

Isaac Backus

During the Great Awakening, many converts became uneasy with the close ties between the church and government in New England. They also believed that it was proper to baptize people only after they had been converted. Due to these and other issues, many decided to leave the established Congregational churches and join the independent Congregational movement that eventually became what we now call the Baptists. In such churches, the emphasis on evangelism and reform lasted long after the revival fires had cooled in the Congregational Churches.

During this time, Isaac Backus (1724–1806) led the ongoing work of the Baptists in New England. Backus was converted during the Great Awakening and later served as a pastor in an independent Congregational church for a while. He then became a minister in a church that was "open" to those of differing convictions about baptism, allowing them to become members. After several years, he organized a Baptist church in Massachusetts.

As an outgrowth of the Great Awakening, the Baptists multiplied rapidly. Their churches increased from a meager twenty-five in 1740 to more than 300 after the turn of the century.

Chapter 9 Review Questions

1. When was Jonathan Edwards born?

2. What was the most famous sermon preached by Edwards?

3. What did the "Halfway Covenant" permit people to do?

4. Who was the English preacher that helped to spread revival throughout New England and the other colonies?

5. What college did Jonathan Edwards serve as president?

6. Who was David Brainerd?

A Hero of the Colonies 10

Do you not think there are a good many interesting stories in American history? I have told you some, and I could tell you many more. I am going to tell you one now, about a brave young man who had a great deal to do with the making of our glorious country. To reach it, however, we will have to take a step backward two hundred and fifty years. That is a pretty long step, isn't it? It takes us way back to about the year 1750. People had been coming into this country for nearly a hundred and fifty years before that, and there were a great many men and women in America at that time who had come from Europe.

These people had come from Spain, France, Great Britain, Holland, Germany, Sweden, and other countries besides. The Spaniards had spread through many regions in the south; the French had gone west by way of the Great Lakes and then down the Mississippi River; but the British were settled close to the ocean, and the country back of them was still forest land, where only Native Americans and wild beasts lived. That is the way things were set at the time of the story which I now propose to tell.

A Brave Young Woodsman

The young man I am about to speak of knew almost as much about life in the deep woods as Daniel Boone, the great hunter of whom I have just told you. Why, when he was only sixteen years old, he and another boy went far back into the wild country of Virginia to survey or measure the lands there for a rich landholder.

The two boys crossed the rough mountains and went into the broad valley of the Shenandoah River, and for months they lived there alone in the broad forest. There were no roads through the woods and they had to make their own paths. When they were hungry they would shoot a wild turkey or a squirrel, or sometimes a deer. They would cook their meat by holding it on a stick over a fire of fallen twigs, and for plates they would cut large chips from a tree with their axe.

> ## Rules for Godly Living
>
> As a young man, George Washington held to high code of ethics that guided his life. Some of them are listed below:
>
> 1. When you speak of God, or His attributes, let it be seriously and with reverence.
>
> 2. Honor and obey your natural parents although they be poor.
>
> 3. Let your recreations be manful, not sinful.
>
> 4. Labor to keep alive in your [heart] that little spark of [heavenly] fire called conscience.

All day long they worked in the woods, measuring the land with a long chain. At night they would roll themselves in their blankets and go to sleep under the trees. If the weather was cold they gathered wood and made a fire. Very likely they enjoyed it all, for boys are fond of adventure. Sometimes a party of Indians would come up and be very curious to know what these boys were doing. The Indians, however, were peaceful then and did not try to harm them. One party amused the young surveyors by dancing a war dance before them. A fine time they had in the woods, and when they came back the land-holder was very pleased with their work.

Five years later, the backwoods boy-surveyor had become a young man twenty-one years of age. If we could take ourselves back to the year 1753 and plunge into the woods of western Pennsylvania, we might see this young man again in the deep forest, walking along with his rifle in hand and his pack on his back. He had with him an old frontiersman named Gill and an Indian who acted as their guide through the forest.

Their guide, however, turned out to be a treacherous fellow. One day, when they were not looking, he fired his gun at them from behind a tree, but he did not hit either of them. Some men would have shot him, but the two frontiersmen did not; they let him go away and walked on alone through the deep woods. They built a fire that night but did not sleep before it. They were afraid the Indian might come back and try to kill them while they were sleeping, so they left the fire burning and walked on a few miles and went to sleep without one.

Young George Washington

A few days after that they came to the banks of a wide river. You may find it on your map of Pennsylvania. It is called the Allegheny River and it runs into the Ohio River. It had been frozen, for it was winter time, but now the ice was broken and floated swiftly down the stream.

What were they to do? They had to get across that stream. The only plan they could think of was to build a raft out of logs and try to push it through the ice with long poles. They did and were soon out on the wild river among the floating ice. This was a long and difficult passage. The great cakes of ice came swirling along, striking like heavy hammers against the raft, almost hard enough to knock it to pieces. One of these heavy ice cakes struck the pole of the young traveler and gave him such a shock that he fell from the raft into the freezing cold water. He had a hard struggle to get back on the raft again.

After a while, they reached a little island in the stream and got ashore. There was no wood on it, and they could not make a fire, so they had to walk about all night to keep from freezing. The man was wet to the skin, but he was young and did not suffer as much as the older man with him. When morning came they found that the ice was frozen fast between the island and the other shore, so all they had to do was to walk across it.

These were not the only adventures they had, but they eventually made it back to Virginia, from which they had set out months before.

Do you want to know who this young traveler was? His name was George Washington. He had been sent on this journey by the governor of Virginia, and I shall have to tell you why.

England and France Disagree

First, however, you must go back with me to an earlier time. The time I mean is when the French were settling in Canada along the St. Lawrence River, going west over the lakes, and floating in canoes down the Mississippi River to the Gulf of Mexico. Wherever they went, they built forts and claimed the country for their king. At the same time, the English

English colonies and French claims in 1754

were settling along the Atlantic shores and pushing slowly west into the countryside.

You should know that the French and the English were not the best of friends. They had their wars in Europe, and every time they went to war there, they also began to fight in America. This made terrible times in the new country. The French had many of the Native Americans on their side, so the Indians marched through the woods and attacked some of the English towns. These warriors murdered many of the poor settlers who had done them no harm. There were three such wars, lasting for many years, and a great many innocent men, women, and children, who had nothing to do with the wars in Europe, lost their lives.

The biggest of all the wars between the French and the English was still to come. Between the French forts on the Mississippi and the English settlements

A French fort in the Ohio Territory

on the Atlantic, there was a vast forest land, and both the French and the English said it belonged to them. In fact, it did not belong to either of them, but to the Indians; but the men from Europe seldom troubled themselves about the rights of the old owners of the land.

While the English were talking, the French were acting. About 1750 they built two or three forts in the country south of Lake Erie. What they wanted was the Ohio River, with the rich and fertile lands which lay along that stream. Building those forts was the first step. The next step would be to send soldiers to the Ohio Valley and build forts there also.

When the English heard what the French were doing, they became very alarmed. If they did not do something quickly, they would lose all this great western country. The governor of Virginia wished to know what the French meant to do, so he picked out the young backwoods surveyor, George Washington, and sent him through the great forest to the French forts.

Washington was very young for so important a duty. He was tall and strong and quick-witted, however, and he was not afraid of any man or anything; he also knew all about life in the woods. Therefore, Washington was chosen, and far west he went over plain and mountain, first on horseback and then on foot. He followed the Indian trails through the forest until at last he came to the French forts and visited the soldiers there.

The French officers told him that they had come there to stay. They were not going to give up their forts to please the governor of Virginia. A few minutes later, Washington's quick eyes saw that they were getting canoes ready to go down the Ohio River the next spring. This was the news the young messenger was taking back to the governor when he had his adventures with the Indian and the ice.

If any of you know anything about how wars are started, you may well think there was soon going to be war in America. Both parties wanted the land, and both were ready to fight to get it. When people feel that way, fighting is not far off. War is most often caused by the sinful pride and greediness of human beings.

Washington Helps the British

Indeed, the spring of 1754 was not far advanced before both sides were on the move. Washington had picked out a beautiful spot for a fort. This was where the two rivers which form the Ohio come together. On that spot the city of Pittsburgh now stands, but then it was a very wild place.

As soon as the governor heard Washington's report, he sent a party of men in great haste to build a fort at that point. In a short time, however, a larger party of French came down the Allegheny River in canoes and drove the English workmen away. Then they finished the fort for themselves and called it Fort Duquesne.

Meanwhile, Washington was on his way back. A force of two hundred Virginians had been sent out under an officer named Colonel Frye. The Colonel, however, died on the march, and young Washington, then only twenty-two years old, found himself at the head of a regiment of soldiers and about to start a great war. Was it not a difficult position for so young a man? Not many men of that age would have known what to do, but George Washington was not an ordinary man. He trusted in God and as a man of prayer found strength and courage to press on in his duty.

An Old Indian Chief Remembers Washington

I am a chief and ruler over my tribes. My influence extends to the waters of the Great Lakes and to the far blue mountains.

I have traveled a long and weary path that I might see the young warrior [Washington] of the great battle [with Braddock]. It was on the day when the white man's blood mixed with the streams of our forests that I first beheld this [Washington].

I called to my young men and said, "Mark yonder tall and daring warrior? He is not of the red-coat tribe; he has an Indian's wisdom, and his warriors fight as we do—himself alone exposed."

"Quick, let your aim be certain, and he dies." Our rifles were leveled, rifles which, but for you, knew not how to miss. It was all in vain, though; a power mightier far than we shielded you. Seeing you were under the special safekeeping of the Great Spirit, we immediately ceased to fire at you.

I am old and soon shall be gathered to the great council fire of my fathers in the land of shades; but before I go, there is something bids me speak in the voice of prophecy:

Listen! The Great Spirit protects that man and guides his destinies. He will become the chief of nations, and a people yet unborn will hail him as the founder of a mighty empire. I am come to pay homage to the man who is the particular favorite of heaven and who can never die in battle.

While the Virginians were marching west, the French were marching south, and it was not long before they came together. A party of French soldiers hid in a thicket to watch the English. Washington, thinking they were there for no good, ordered his men to fire. They did so, and the leader of the French was killed. This was the first shot in the coming war.

The youthful commander, however, soon found that the French were too strong for him.

The French in the Ohio Valley

He built a sort of fort at a place called Great Meadows and named it Fort Necessity. It was hardly finished before the French and Indians came swarming all around it and a severe fight began.

The Virginians fought well, but the French were too strong and fired into the fort till Washington had to surrender. This took place on July 4, 1754, just twenty-two years before the American Declaration of Independence. Wash-

ington and his men were allowed to march home with their arms, and the young soldier was praised when he got home. During early 1755, Washington was promoted to the rank of colonel and appointed as the commander in chief of the Virginia Militia.

When the news of this battle crossed the ocean, there was great excitement in England and France, and both countries sent soldiers to America. Those from England were under a general named Braddock, a man who knew nothing about fighting in America; and what was worse, he would not let anyone help him. Washington generously tried to do so, but he was pointedly snubbed by the proud British general for his attempt to teach him.

After a while, General Braddock marched with his British soldiers in their fine redcoats. Washington went with him with a body of Virginians dressed in plain clothes. On and on they went, through the woods and over the mountains, cutting down trees and opening a road for their wagons, and bravely beating their drums and waving their flags. At length they came near Fort Duquesne—the drums still beating, the flags still flying, and the gun barrels glittering in the bright sunlight.

"Let me go ahead with my Virginians," said Washington. "They know all about Indian fighting."

"Forget your Indians!" said Braddock, snapping his fingers. "They will not stay in their hiding places long when my men come up."

Soon after, they came into a narrow place, with steep banks and thick bushes all around. Suddenly loud Indian war-whoops and the crack of guns came from those bushes. Not a man could be seen, but bullets flew like hailstones among the redcoats. The soldiers fired back, but they wasted their bullets on the bushes. Washington and his men ran into the woods and got behind trees like the Indians, but Braddock would not let his men do the same, and they were shot down like sheep. At length General Braddock fell wounded, and then his brave redcoats turned and ran for their lives. Very likely not a man of them would have escaped if Washington and his men had not kept back the French and American Indians.

This defeat was sad news for the poor settlers, for the Indians began murdering them on all sides, and during all the rest of the war, Washington was kept busy fighting with the Indians as well as the French. It took until 1758 before the English and the Virginians were able to take Fort Duquesne. Colonel Washington helped to capture this key French fort while fighting under an English general named Forbes. Late in 1758, Washington left the army and resigned his commission.

After Washington resigned his commision, he returned to Mount Vernon and soon afterward married Mrs. Martha Curtis, a rich young widow.

Chapter 10 Review Questions

1. What job did George Washington do for a rich landholder when he was a teenager?

2. What country did General Braddock serve during the war?

3. How did General Braddock die?

4. Did the Indians fight against the French army or the English army during this war?

5. What was the name of the old frontiersman who surveyed land in western Pennsylvania with George Washington?

The French and Indian War 11

ave any of my young readers read the beautiful poem called "Evangeline," written by the poet Longfellow? Very likely it is too old for you, though the time will come when you will read it and enjoy it very much. Evangeline was a pretty and godly woman who lived in a French settlement called Acadia, on the Atlantic coast. You will not find this name on any of your maps, because Acadia is now known as Nova Scotia. The story of Evangeline tells us about the cruel way in which the poor Acadians were treated by the English years ago. It is a sad story, as you will see after you have read it.

The Cruelty of War

It was one of the darkest results of the war between the French and the English. There were many cruel deeds in this war, and the people who suffered the most were those who had the least to do with the fighting. In one place, a quiet, happy family of father, mother, and children—living on a lonely farm and not dreaming of any danger—suddenly heard the wild war shout of the Indians, and soon they saw their doors broken open and their houses blazing. They were carried off into cruel captivity and some were killed on the spot. In another place, all the people of a village were driven from their comfortable homes by soldiers and forced to wander and beg for bread in distant lands. All this took place because the kings of England and France, three thousand miles away, were fighting about some lands which did not belong to either of them.

If those who brought on wars had to suffer for them, wars would soon come to an end. In real life, however, most people who start wars revel and feast in their splendid palaces while poor and innocent people do the suffering. The war that began in the wilds of western Pennsylvania—between the French and Indians and the English—lasted nine years, from 1754

to 1763. During that time, there were many terrible battles, and thousands of soldiers were killed. There was much suffering and slaughter among the people—houses were burned, property was destroyed, and horrors of all sorts were experienced.

It was called the "French and Indian War" because there were many Indians on the side of the French. There were, however, some on the side of the English as well. Indian warriors were very cruel in their way of fighting, as you already know. I shall have to tell you one instance of their love of bloodshed. One of the English forts, called Fort William Henry, which stood at the southern end of Lake George, had to surrender to the French and its soldiers were forced to march out and give up their guns.

There were a great many Indians with the French, and while the prisoners stood outside the fort without a gun in their hands, the Indian warriors attacked and began to kill them with knives and tomahawks. The French had promised to protect them, but they stood by and did nothing to stop this terrible slaughter; many of the helpless soldiers were murdered. Others were carried off by the Indians as prisoners. It was the most dreadful event of the whole cruel war.

I must now ask you to look at a map of the state of New York. There you will see that the Hudson River runs up north from the city of New York, past Albany, the capital of the state, and ends in a region of mountains. Near its upper waters is a long, narrow lake named Lake George, which is full of beautiful islands. North of that is a much larger lake named Lake Champlain, which reaches up into Canada.

The British had forts on the Hudson River and Lake George. The French had forts on Lake Champlain, and also between the two lakes, where the strong Fort Ticonderoga stood. It was around these forts and along these lakes that much of the fighting took place. For a long time the French had the best

of it. The British lost many battles and were driven back. They had the most soldiers, however, and in the end, began to defeat the French and drive them back; then Canada became the ground for war. Let me return, though, to the story of the Acadians.

The British Uproot the Acadians

Acadia was a country which had been settled by the French way back in 1604, before there was an English settlement in America. Captain John Smith, you know, came to Virginia in 1607, three years afterwards. Acadia was a very fertile country, and the settlers planted fields of grain and orchards of apples and other fruits and lived a very happy life, with neat houses and plenty of good food. In time, the whole country became a rich farming land.

The British, however, would not let these happy farmers alone. Every time there was trouble with the French, soldiers were sent to Acadia. It was captured by the British in 1690, but they gave it back to France in 1697, when that war ended. It was taken again by the British in another war that began in 1702, and this time it was not given back. Even its pretty name of Acadia was taken away, and it was called Nova Scotia.

Thus it was that when the French and Indian War began in 1754, Acadia was held as a province of Great Britain. To be sure, most of its people were descended from the old French settlers and did not like their British masters, but the Acadians could not help themselves and went on farming in their old fashion. They were simple-minded countrymen, who looked upon France as their country and were not willing to be British citizens.

That is the way with the French. It is the same today, even though Canada is an independent country. The descendants of the former French still speak their old language and love their old country. Now they "fight" the leaders of Canada with their votes as they once fought the British with their swords.

The British did not hold the whole of Acadia. The province of New Brunswick, which lies north of Nova Scotia, was part of it and was still held by the French. In 1755, the British government decided to attempt the capture of this territory and sent out soldiers for that purpose. Fighting began, but the French defended themselves bravely, and the British found they had a hard task to perform.

What made it worse for them was that some of the Acadians, who did not want to see the British succeed, acted as spies among them. These patriots told the French soldiers about their movements so that the French were everywhere ready for them. The Acadians also helped the French in other ways, which gave the British a great deal of trouble.

Everyone feels like helping his friends against his enemies, and that is what the Acadians did. You may be sure, though, that this made the British very angry, and in the end they cruelly decided to send all the Acadians away from their native land to distant, foreign countries. The Acadians, however, were told they might stay if they would swear to be true subjects of the king of England. This they would not do, for they were French at heart and looked on King Louis of France as their true and rightful ruler.

Since it was not easy to tell who was acting as a spy, the English government ordered all of them to be removed. There were hundreds of boys and girls like yourselves among these poor Acadians who had happy homes, loved to work and play in their pretty gardens and

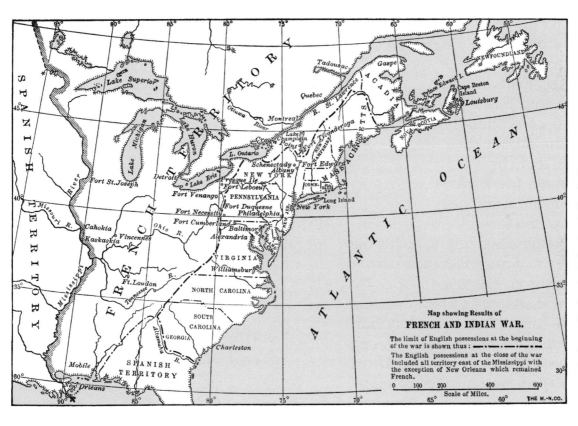

Can you find the province of Acadia on this map? Many of the Acadians were forced to move to New Orleans by the British. Try to find New Orleans on the map.

green fields, and whose fathers and mothers did no harm to anyone. Because a few spies gave news to the French, though, all of the people were to be torn from their comfortable homes and sent far away to wander in strange lands, where many of them would have to beg for bread. It was a heartless act, and the world has consistently said so. Among all the cruel things the British have done, the removal of the Acadians from their homes is looked upon as one of the worst.

When soldiers are sent to do a cruel thing, they are very apt to do it in the most brutal fashion. The Acadians did not know what was going to happen. It was kept secret for fear they might run away and hide. A large number of soldiers were sent out, and they spread like a net over a wide stretch of country. Then they marched together and drove the people before them. The poor farmers might be at dinner or working in their fields, but they were told that they must stop everything and leave their homes at once, for they were to be sent out of the country. Just think of it! What grief and terror they must have felt at this time.

They were hardly given time to gather the few things they could carry with them. On all sides, they were driven like so many sheep to the seaside town of Annapolis, where ships had been brought to carry them away. More than six thousand of these unhappy people—young men, women, and little ones—were gathered there; many of them weeping bitterly, many more with looks of despair on their faces.

Around them were soldiers to keep them from running away. They were made to get on the ships in such haste that families were often separated—husband and wife, or children and their mothers, being put on different ships and sent to different places. For fear that some Acadians might come back again, their houses were burned and their farms laid waste. Many of them went to French settlements in Louisiana, and others to different parts of America. Poor exiles! They were scat-

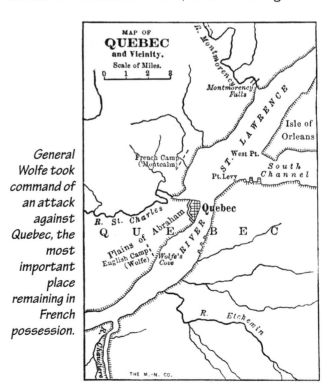

General James Wolfe

tered widely over the earth. Some of them in time came back to Acadia, but most of them never saw it again. It was this dreadful act about which Longfellow wrote in his poem "Evangeline."

The War Comes to an End

Now I must tell you how the French and Indian War ended. The French had two important cities in Canada—Montreal and Quebec. Quebec was built on a high, steep hill and was surrounded by strong walls, behind which were more than eight thousand soldiers. It was not an easy city to capture.

A large British fleet with an army of eight thousand men under the command of General Wolfe, was sent against

General Wolfe took command of an attack against Quebec, the most important place remaining in French possession.

MAP OF
QUEBEC
and Vicinity.
Scale of Miles.
0   1   2   8

R. Montmorency
Montmorency Falls
ST. LAWRENCE
Isle of Orleans
French Camp (Montcalm)
West Pt.
South Channel
Pt. Levy
Quebec
R. St. Charles
Q U E   B E C
Plains of Abraham
English Camp (Wolfe)
Wolfe's Cove
RIVER
R. Etchemin

THE M.-N. CO.

Quebec in 1759. For two or three months they fired at the city from the river below, but the French ignored them from their steep hilltop. At length General Wolfe was told of a narrow path by which he might climb the hill. One dark night he tried it, and by daybreak a large body of men had reached the hilltop and had dragged up a number of cannons with them.

When the French saw this they were frightened. They hurried out of the city, thinking they could drive the English over the cliff before any more of them got up. They were mistaken in this. The English met them boldly, and in the battle that followed, they gained the victory and Quebec fell into their hands.

General Wolfe was mortally wounded, but when he was told that the French were in flight, he said: "God be praised! I die happy."

Montcalm, the French general, also fell wounded. When he knew that he would die he said, "So much the better; I shall not live to see the surrender of Quebec."

The following year Montreal was captured by the British and the fighting ended. In the treaty of peace, France gave up all her colonies in America. England ruled Canada and the land east of the Mississippi River, and Spain ruled Louisiana. All of North America now belonged to two nations—England and Spain.

Marquis de Montcalm

With the fall of Quebec, the last stronghold of the French in America passed into the hands of the English.

Benjamin Franklin

Wise Mr. Franklin

Of these men, there is only one I shall say anything about. This man's name you should know and remember, for he was one of the wisest men that ever lived in this country. His name was Benjamin Franklin. Forty years before this time, he was a little boy at work in his father's shop in Boston, helping him make candles. Afterwards, he learned how to print; then, in 1732, he went to Philadelphia, where he soon had a shop and a newspaper office. After many years of hard work, Franklin became rich.

There was nothing happening in which

In 1732 Franklin began to publish "Poor Richard's Almanac," which he continued to publish for twenty years. It was full of witty sayings which people could apply to everyday living.

Franklin did not take part. In his shop, he bound books, made ink, and sold rags, soap, and coffee. He was not ashamed of honest work and would take off his coat and wheel his papers along the street in a wheelbarrow. He started many institutions in Philadelphia. Among these were a great university, a large hospital, and a fine library. No doubt you have read how he captured the power of lightning along the string of a kite, proving that lightning is the same thing as electricity. In addition, he took an active part in all the political movements of the time. That is why he was sent to Albany in 1754 as a member of the Albany Convention.

Franklin always did things in ways that started people thinking. When he went to Albany, he took with him copies of a strange picture which he had printed in his newspaper. This was a snake cut into several pieces. Under each piece was the first letter of the name of a colony, such as "P" for Pennsylvania. Beneath the whole were the words "Unite or Die."

That was like Franklin—he was always doing something interesting. The cut-up snake stood for the divided American colonies. What Franklin meant was that they could not exist alone. A snake is not very strong when it is chopped into bits, but it is a dangerous crea-

Franklin's picture of the colonies in 1754.

ture when it is whole. He proposed that there should be a grand council of all the colonies, a sort of Congress, meeting every year in Philadelphia, which was the most central large city. Over them all was to be a governor general appointed by the king. This council could make laws, decide on taxes, and perform other important duties.

That is enough to say about Franklin's plan, for it was not accepted. It was passed by the convention, it is true, but the king would not have it and the colonies did not want it, so the snake lay stretched out along the Atlantic in thirteen pieces. Then came the great war with the French of which I have told you. After that was over, things came to pass which in the end forced the colonies to unite. Franklin's plan, or something like it, was eventually carried out, but until then the country was in a terrible state. This is what I am now going to tell you about.

King George Angers the Colonists

You should know that the war with the French cost the king and the colonies a great deal of money. The king of England at that time was named George. He was a stubborn

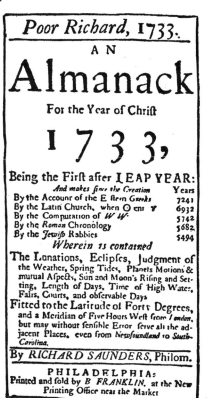

Front page of Franklin's "Poor Richard's Almanac"

man but not a very wise one, as you will see when you have learned more about him. One thing he wanted to do was to send soldiers to America to protect the colonists from Indian attacks and to keep the French from getting back what they had lost. Soldiers cost money and the king wanted the colonists to pay for them. He also wanted the colonists to send him money to pay the governors and judges whom he had chosen to rule over them. The English Parliament—a body of lawmakers like our Congress—began to pass a series of laws and taxes to pay the expenses of governing the British colonies in North America.

The colonists thought they could take care of themselves, and did not want British soldiers. They also preferred to pay the governors and judges themselves as they had always done, and did not want King George to do it for them. Ultimately, they did not want to pay the taxes he demanded.

Some of you may think this was very unkind and ungrateful of the Americans after all the British had done to help them in their war with the French. They knew very well, however, that King George could not be trusted. They thought that if they gave the king a dollar today, he might want five dollars tomorrow, and ten dollars the next day. They judged it best not to begin with the dollar. Kings, you should know, do not always make the best use of money that is given them by their people. The people knew that if King George gained the power to tax the colonies, he could destroy them.

That was not all. The people in the colonies did not like the way they had been treated by the English. They had mountains full of iron, but the king would not let them make this iron into tools. They had plenty of wool, but he would not let them weave it into cloth. They must buy these and other things in England, and must keep farming. The colonists were not allowed to sell their grain to England, but had to eat it all at home. They could not even send goods from one colony to another. Thus they were to be kept poor so that the English merchants and manufacturers might grow rich.

These were some of the things the American people had to complain about. At first, the colonists continued to express loyalty to Great Britain and the king. These problems, however, continued to get worse and eventually a good many of the Americans came to have very little love for the English king and people. They felt that they were in a sort of slavery, almost as if they had ropes on their hands and chains on their feet.

Taxation Without Representation

Do you know where the famous principle of "no taxation without representation" came from? It was the New York legislature's response to Parliament's first tax—the Sugar Act of 1764. This was the first time that the English Parliament has passed a law specifically designed to tax the colonies.

While most colonists disliked the Sugar Act tax, they really hated the Stamp Act of 1765. The stamp tax was considered unjust. The Americans were quite willing to pay taxes to their own colonial governments, but they were not willing to buy the stamps which the British government sent them in 1765. Why? Well, they had good reason for it, and the reason was that they had nothing to do with making the law. The English people would not pay any taxes unless they were made by the people whom they elected to Parliament, and the Americans said they had the same right. They were not allowed to send any members to Par-liament, so they said that Parliament had no right to tax them. Their own legislatures might vote to send the king money, but the English Parliament had no right to vote for them.

How do you think the colonists responded to the Stamp Act? Well, they refused to accept it. They would not pay the tax and forced the tax collectors to resign. Parliament had no choice but to repeal the tax in 1766.

For a while, things were quiet, but in 1767 the king and Parliament tried another plan. They laid a tax on several goods—tea, paper, paint, lead, glass—brought to the colonies from England. The English thought that the colonists would not mind paying taxes if the taxes were part of the cost of the things they bought at the store. The English found out that they were wrong, however; the colonists disliked these new taxes just as they disliked the Stamp tax. The Americans refused to buy British goods until these new taxes were repealed. Most of the taxes were done away with by Parliament in 1770.

The Boston Tea Party

The Parliament kept the tax on tea, how-ever, and a law was passed in 1773 to encour-age the colonists to buy tea and pay the tax. King George thought that our people could not do without tea; therefore, several shiploads of tea were sent across the ocean to America. King George soon found, however, that the colonists had no more use for taxed tea than for stamps. They would not even let their captains bring their tea on shore, except at Charleston, and there it was packed in damp cellars where it soon rotted. A ship sent to Annapolis was set on fire and burned to the water's edge with the tea in it.

The most stirring event, however, took place at Boston. There one night, while the tea ship lay at a wharf in the harbor, a number of young men dressed like Indians rushed on board with a loud war whoop and began to break open the tea chests with their hatchets

Forty or fifty men disguised as Indians boarded the tea ships, ripped open every chest, and spilled the tea into the harbor.

and pour the tea into the harbor. This was the famous "Boston tea party." Americans liked tea, but not tea with an English tax on it. They boiled leaves and roots and made some sort of tea out of them. It was poor stuff, but it did not have any tax! Moreover, they would not buy cloth or other goods brought from England. If the king was angry and stubborn, they were angry and stubborn, too. Everyday they grew more angry, until many of them began to think that they would be better off without a king. They were not the kind of people to be made slaves of easily by King George or any other king.

When the king heard of the "Boston tea party" he was in a fury. He would make the city of Boston pay well for its tea, he said, so he sent guard ships there and gave orders that no ships should go into or out of Boston Harbor. This stopped most of the business of the town, and soon the poor people had no work to do and very little to eat. Nevertheless, they had crowded meetings at Faneuil Hall, where Samuel Adams and John Hancock and other patriots talked to them of their rights. It began to look as if war would soon come.

The time had come at last for a union of the colonies. What Franklin had failed to do at Albany in 1754 was done at Philadelphia in 1774. A meeting was held there called a "Congress," which was made up of some of the best men sent from the colonies. One of these was George Washington, who had lived on his farm at Mt. Vernon since the end of the French and Indian War.

would fight for their rights if they could not get them in peace. All around Boston, the farmers and villagers began to collect guns and powder and to drill men into soldiers. These were called "minute men," which meant that they would be ready to fight at a minute's notice, if they were asked. When people begin to get ready in this way, war is usually not far off.

The Ride of Paul Revere

One night at Boston, a man named Paul Revere stood watching a distant steeple till he saw a light suddenly flash out through the darkness. Then he leaped on his

Congress sent a letter to the king, asking him to give the people of this country the same rights that the people of England had. There was no harm in this, I am sure, but it made the king more stubborn still. I have said he was not a wise man. Most people say he was a foolish one, or he would have known that the people of the colonies

horse and rode at full speed. That light was a signal telling him that British soldiers were on the march to Concord, twenty miles away, to destroy some military supplies and guns which had been gathered there.

Away rode Revere through the night, rousing up the people and shouting to them that the British soldiers were coming. He was far ahead of the soldiers, so that when they reached the village of Lexington, ten miles from Boston, the people were wide awake and a party of minute men was drawn up on the village green. No one knows who fired the first shot, but the British soldiers fired on these men, and some of them fell dead. Those were the first shots in a great war. It was the nineteenth of April, 1775.

The British marched on to Concord, but the farmers had carried away most of the stores and buried them in the woods. Then the redcoats started back, and a terrible march they had of it. For all along the road were farmers with guns in their hands, firing on the troops from behind trees and stone walls. Some of the soldiers got back to Boston, but many of them lay dead in the road. The poor American soldiers killed at Lexington were terribly avenged.

Far and wide spread the news, and on all sides the farmers left their plows and took down their rifles, and thousands of them set out along the roads to Boston. Soon there were twenty thousand armed men surrounding the town, and the British were shut up like rats in a trap. The American people were now committed to becoming independent from the foolish King George and war had begun.

It would be a long and dreadful war, but it led to American liberty, and that was one thing well worth the fight. While the people were laying siege to Boston, Congress was in session in Philadelphia, talking about what should be done. One good thing they did was to make George Washington commander in chief of the army and sent him to Boston to fight the British there. They could not have found a better leader in all the colonies.

The Declaration of Independence

The next good thing took place a year later. This was the event which you celebrate with fireworks every fourth of July. Congress decided the country ought to be free and no longer be under the rule of an English king; therefore, a paper was written by a member from Virginia named Thomas Jefferson,

Thomas Jefferson, John Adams, Benjamin Franklin, Roger Sherman, and Robert R. Livingston were appointed to prepare the Declaration of Independence.

day for Boston. The great warships in the harbor thundered with their cannons at the men on the hills. In addition, the soldiers began to march up the hills, thinking that the colonists would run like sheep when they saw the redcoats coming near; however, the colonists—who were often called Yankees—were not there to run.

"Don't fire, boys, till you see the whites of their eyes," said brave General Prescott to the colonial soldiers.

The Yankee boys waited till the British were close at hand. Then they fired and the redcoats fell in rows, for the farmers did not waste their bullets. Those that did not fall fled in haste down the hill. It was a strange sight to see British soldiers running away from Yankee farmers.

After awhile, the British came again. They were not so sure this time. Again the Yankee muskets rattled along the earthworks, and again the British turned and ran—those who were able to.

They could never have taken the hills if the farmer-soldiers had not run out of powder. When the redcoats came a third time, the Yankees could not fire and had to fight them with the butts of their guns. Finally the British captured both hills, but they had found that the Yankee farmers were not cowards; after that time they never liked to march against American earthworks.

Washington Takes Command

Not long after the Battle of Bunker Hill, General Washington came to command the Americans, and he spent months in drilling and making soldiers out of them. He also got a good supply of powder and muskets and some cannons. One dark night in March 1776, he built a fort on Dorchester Heights that looked down on Boston.

I assure you, the British were scared when they looked up that hill the next morning and saw cannons on its top and men behind the cannons. They would have to climb that hill as they had done at the Battle of Bunker Hill, or else

A Presbyterian Rebellion

One of the groups most supportive of the patriot cause was the Presbyterians. A German captain who served with the British army in Pennsylvania once complained that the American Revolution was actually "...an Irish-Scotch Presbyterian Rebellion."

One of the most prominent examples of Presbyterian support for American independence was Rev. John Witherspoon, president of the College of New Jersey (now known as Princeton University). He was the only minister to sign the Declaration of Independence, and served in the Continental Congress from 1776 to 1782.

Staunch support was shown by George Duffield, who was the pastor of a Presbyterian church in Philadelphia and a chaplain in the Continental army. He chided his congregation for not sending more men into the army.

An interesting example of Presbyterian support for the war was seen in Rev. James Caldwell, the pastor of a Presbyterian church in New Jersey. During a skirmish near his church, Continental soldiers were running low on paper to use as wadding in their muskets. Caldwell ran into his church and brought out copies of Isaac Watts's hymnals for them to tear apart for wadding. As he did so, he told the soldiers, "Now boys, give 'em Watts!"

Christians who were supporters of the War for American Independence at times suffered at the hands of the British or the Loyalists. The almost unanimous support of Presbyterians for the patriot cause often led the British to vent their anger on Presbyterians and their property. In 1783, an official letter from the church spoke of their "...burnt and wasted churches, and our plundered dwellings, in such places as fell under the power of our adversaries."

leave Boston. They had no desire for another Bunker Hill, however, so they decided to leave. They got on their ships and sailed away, and Washington and his men marched joyfully into the town. That was a great day for America, and it was soon followed by the fourth of July and the glorious Declaration of Independence. Since that fourth of July, no earthly king has ever ruled over the United States.

Some call the War for American Independence the "American Revolution." Do you know what a revolution is? It means the doing away with an old government and replacing it with a new one. In America, however, it meant that our people were tired of the rule of tyrants in far-off England and wished to govern themselves. They had to fight hard for their freedom, it is true, but it was well worth the fight.

The war was a long and dreadful one. It went on for eight long years. At times, everything seemed lost; at other times, all grew bright and hopeful. Thus it went on, up and down, to the end. I cannot tell you all that took place, but I will give you the important points.

After the British left Boston, they sailed around for a time and then came with a large army to New York. Washington was there with his soldiers to meet them and did his best, but everything seemed to go wrong. First, the Americans were beaten in the battle and had to march out of New York and let the British march in. Then Washington and his ragged men were forced to hasten across the state of New Jersey

WASHINGTON'S RETREAT ACROSS NEW JERSEY.

with a strong British force after them. They were too weak to face the British.

When they came to the Delaware River, the Americans crossed it and took all the boats, so that the British could not follow them. It was now near winter time, and both armies went into winter quarters. They faced each other, but the wide river ran between the two armies.

You may well think that by this time the American people were getting very downhearted. Many of them thought that all was lost and they would have to submit to King George. The army dwindled away and no new soldiers came in, so it looked as if it would go to pieces. It was growing very dark for American liberty.

Washington Rallies His Troops

There was one man, however, who did not despair, and that man was George Washington. He saw that something must be done to stir up the spirits of the people, and he was just the man to do it. It was a wonderful Christmas he kept that year. All Christmas Day his ragged and hungry soldiers were marching up their side of the Delaware and crossing the river in boats—though the wind was biting cold, the air was full of falling snow, and the broken ice was floating in great blocks down the river. Nothing stopped the gallant soldiers. All Christmas night they marched down the other side of the river, though their shoes were so bad that the ground became reddened by the blood from their feet. Two poor fellows were frozen to death.

At Trenton, a number of miles below, there was a group of German soldiers. These soldiers had been hired by King George to help him fight his battles. That day they had been eating a good Christmas dinner while the hungry Americans were marching through the snow. At night they went to bed, not dreaming of danger.

They were wakened in the morning by shots and shouts. Washington and his men were in the streets of the town. They hardly

General Washington with his troops at Valley Forge

tered Philadelphia. They now held the largest cities of the country, Philadelphia and New York. While the British were living in plenty and having a very good time in the Quaker city, the poor Americans spent a wretched and terrible winter at a place called Valley Forge. The winter was a dismally cold one, and the men had not half enough food to eat or clothes to wear, and very poor huts to live in. They suffered dreadfully, and before the spring came many of them died from disease and exposure.

Victories in the North

Poor fellows! They were paying dearly for their struggle for liberty. There was, however, no such despair this winter as there had been the winter before, for news came from the north that warmed the soldiers up like a fire. Though Washington had lost a battle, a great victory had been gained by the Americans at Saratoga, in the upper part of New York state.

While British General Howe was marching on Philadelphia, another British army, under General Burgoyne, had been marching south from Canada, along the line of Lake Champlain and Lake George. Burgoyne and his men soon found themselves in a tight place. Food began to run short and a regiment of eight hundred men was sent into Vermont to seize some stores. They were met by the Green Mountain boys, led by Colonel Stark, a brave old soldier.

"There are the redcoats," said the bold colonel. "We must beat them today, or Betty Stark is a widow."

Beat them they did. Only seventy men got back to Burgoyne. All the rest were killed or captured.

had time to seize their guns before the ragged Yankees were all around them and nearly all of them were made prisoners of war.

Was not that a great and glorious deed? It filled the Americans with new hope. A few days afterwards, Washington defeated the British in another battle and then settled down with his ragged but brave men in the hills of New Jersey. He did not go behind a river this time. The British knew where he was and could come to see him if they wanted. They did not come, however. Very likely they had seen enough of him for that winter.

The next year things went wrong again for Washington. A large British army sailed from New York and landed at the head of Chesapeake Bay. Then they marched overland to Philadelphia. Washington fought a battle with them on Brandywine Creek, but his men were defeated and the British marched on and en-

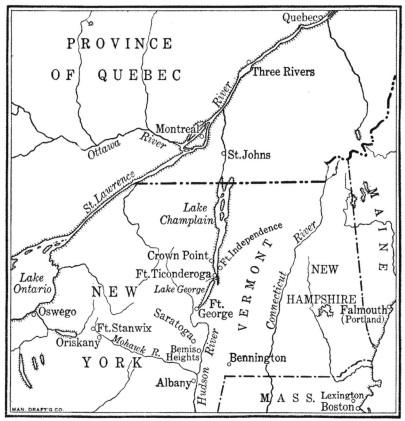

Southern Canada and New York State, location of General Burgoyne's failed campaign and the American victory at Saratoga in 1777

they fell into such a panic that they took to their heels, leaving all their tents and cannons behind them. The people in the fort did not know what it meant till Arnold came up and told them how he had won a victory without firing a shot, by a sort of clever trick.

All this was very bad for Burgoyne. The Indians he brought with him began to leave. At last he found himself in a terrible plight. His provisions were nearly gone, he was surrounded by the Americans, and after fighting two battles he retreated to Saratoga. Here he had to surrender. He and all his army became prisoners to the Americans.

We cannot wonder that this warmed up the Americans like a fire and it filled the English with despair. They began to think that they would never win back the colonies.

France Helps America

One thing the good news did was to get the French to come to the help of the Americans. Benjamin Franklin was then in Paris, and he asked the king to send ships and men and money to America. The French had no love for the British, who had taken from them all their colonies in America, so they did as Franklin wished.

There are two more things I wish to tell you in this chapter, one good and one bad. When the British in Philadelphia heard that the French were coming to help the Americans, they were afraid they might be caught in a trap, so they left in great haste and marched

Another British force, under Colonel St. Leger, marched south from Oswego on Lake Ontario. A large group of Indians was with him. This army stopped to besiege an American fort in the wilderness, and General Arnold marched to relieve the fort.

The way Arnold defeated St. Leger was a very curious one. He sent a half-witted fellow into the Indian camp with the tale that a great American force was coming. The messenger came running in among the warriors with bullet holes in his clothes. He seemed half-scared to death and told the Indians that a huge host was coming after him as thick as the leaves on the trees.

This story frightened the American Indians and they ran off in great haste through the woods. When the British soldiers saw this

General John Burgoyne

The most important result of the victory at Saratoga was France's decision to openly help the Americans.

to New York. Washington followed and fought a battle with them, but they got away. After that, Washington's men laid siege to New York, as they had formerly done to Boston. General Washington defeated the British and his army was encouraged.

That was the good thing. The bad thing that happened was that General Benedict Arnold—who had defeated St. Leger and his Indians and was one of the bravest of the American officers—turned traitor to his country. He had charge of West Point, a strong fort on the Hudson River, and tried to give this up to the British. He was found out, however, and had to flee for his life. Major Andre, a British officer, who had been sent to talk with Arnold, was caught by three American scouts on his way back to New York. They searched him for papers and found what they wanted hidden in his boot. Poor Andre was hung as a spy, but the traitor Arnold escaped. This traitor was hated by the Americans and despised by the British. Twenty years afterwards he died in shame and sorrow.

Chapter 13 Review Questions

1. Who made the statement, "Don't fire, boys, till you see the whites of their eyes?"

2. How long did the Revolutionary War last?

3. Who led the American military forces at the Battle of Trenton?

4. What crime did Benedict Arnold commit?

5. How did Benjamin Franklin help the American war effort?

John Paul Jones, the Naval Hero 14

Most Americans are very amazed at our nation's great warships with their strong steel sides and their mighty guns, each of which can hurl artillery shells miles and miles away. Such shells! Why, one of them is as heavy as a dozen of you tied together, and can bore a hole through a plate of solid steel as thick as your bodies. Modern warships now have guided missiles and nuclear power as well!

Such ships and such guns as these had not been dreamed of in the days of the War for American Independence. Then there were only small wooden vessels, moved by sails instead of engines, and a cannonball that weighed twenty-four pounds was thought very heavy. Six and twelve pound balls were common; and to hit a ship a mile away! Hardly anyone imagined that that was possible. I tell you, in those days, ships had to fight nearly side by side and men fought face to face.

There was still much hard fighting done at sea in the War for American Independence, in spite of the small ships and little guns. They fought closer together, that was all. Boast as

Commodore John Paul Jones

we may about the wonderful work done by our ships during the Persian Gulf War of 1991, we have better reason to honor the deeds of a great naval hero of the War for Independence, with his rotten old ship and poor little guns, but with his stout heart behind them all.

This hero was the sturdy John Paul Jones, one of the boldest and bravest men that ever stood on a ship's deck. His great sea fight has not been equaled in all the history of naval war. I cannot tell you the story of the War for American Independence without telling about the great ocean victory of the bold-hearted Jones.

America's First Navy

The Americans had poor ships to fight with during the War for American Independence. They had a little fleet of seven or eight small vessels whose heaviest guns threw only nine pound balls, and most of them only six pound. You could have thrown these yourself with one hand, though not very far. These were all we had at first to fight more than seventy British ships that had guns that threw eighteen pound balls, and some still heavier. Don't you think it looked like a one-sided fight?

The Americans, however, had one great advantage. They had few merchant ships and therefore little to lose upon the seas. On the other hand, the ocean swarmed with the merchant ships of England. English merchant ships brought supplies of guns and powder and food to the armies on shore and carried out important commerce with the rest of the world. Here were splendid prizes for our gallant seamen, and out of every port sailed bold privateers, sweeping the seas and bringing in many a richly-laden craft. By 1781, more than 450 private vessels had been commissioned by Congress or the states to attack British shipping.

Some of the best fighting of the war was done by these privateers.[1] While they were hunting for merchant ships they often came across warships, and you can be sure they did not always run away. No, indeed; they were usually ready to fight, and during the war, no less than sixteen war vessels were captured by our ocean rovers. On the other hand, the British privateers did not capture a single American warship. As for merchant vessels, our privateers brought them in by the dozens. One fleet of sixty vessels set out from Ireland for the West Indies, and out of these, thirty-five were gobbled up by our privateers and their rich stores brought

The privateer ship Montgomery captures an English merchant ship off the coast of Ireland.

into American ports. During the whole war, the privateers took nearly two thousand prizes. I might go on to tell you of some of their hard fights, but I think you would rather read the story of John Paul Jones, the boldest and bravest of them all. He was the terror of the seas to the British fleet.

A Brave Sea Captain

John Paul Jones was born in Scotland, but he made America his home. Since he was known to be a good sailor, he was appointed first lieutenant of the *Alfred*, the flagship of our small fleet. He had the honor to be the first man to raise a flag on an American man-of-war, and that is something to be proud of. This took place on the ship called the *Delaware*, at Philadelphia, about Christmas 1775. It was an important ceremony, for the fleet was just being put into action. At a given signal, Lieutenant Jones grasped the halyards[2] and hauled up to the topmast a great flag of yellow silk. As it unfurled into the breeze, cannons roared and crowds on shore cheered. In the center of the flag was seen the figure of a green pine tree, and under this a rattlesnake lay coiled, with the warning motto, "Don't tread on me." This was the famous rattlesnake flag. Another flag was raised on which there were thirteen stripes, alternately red and white, and in the corner the British Union Jack. Our flag then had the stripes, but not the stars. They were to come after the Declaration of Independence and the union of the states.

In August 1776, Congress made John Paul Jones captain of the sloop *Providence* and he soon showed what kind of man he was. He came across a fleet of five vessels and made up his mind to capture the largest of them, which he thought to be a fine merchant ship. He sailed pretty close to this ship before he learned his mistake. It was the British frigate *Solebay*, strong enough to make mincemeat of his little ship. There was nothing for his ship to do but run, and Captain Jones made haste to get away, followed by the *Solebay*. The Briton, however, gained on the American, and, after a four hours' run the frigate was less than a hundred yards away. It might at any minute sink the daring little *Providence* by a broadside of cannonballs.

John Paul Jones, however, was not the man to be caught. Suddenly the front of the ship was put hard up, as sailors say, and the little craft turned and dashed across the frigate's bow. As it did so, the flag of the republic was spread to the breeze, and a broadside from the ship's guns swept the frigate's deck. Then with all sails set, away dashed the *Providence* before the breeze. As soon as the British got back their senses they fired all their guns at the ship. Not a ball hit her, though, and with the best of the wind, she soon left the *Solebay* far behind.

Commodore Jones Fights Back

Now I must tell the story of John Paul Jones's greatest fight. In its way it was the greatest sea fight ever seen. It was fought with a fleet of ships which Jones sailed from a port in France. Congress had found out what a hero they had in their Scottish sailor, and now they made him commodore of a fleet.

The flagship of this fleet was a rotten old log of a ship which had sailed in the East India merchant service till its timbers were in a state of dry rot. It was a shapeless tub of a vessel, better fit to lie in port and keep rabbits in than to send out as a warship. Jones named it the *Bon Homme Richard*, which in English means "Poor Richard." This was the name first used by Benjamin Franklin for his famous almanac.

It was not until the summer of 1779 that Jones was able to set sail with his little fleet of five ships. His own ship had thirty-six guns, such as they were, and he had with him three ships commanded by French officers—the *Alliance*, the *Pallas*, and the *Vengeance*. Among his crew were a hundred American sailors who had just been set free from English prisons. His master's mate, Richard Dale, a man of his own sort, had just escaped from prison in England.

Away they went, east and west, north and south, around the British Isles, seeking for the men-of-war which should have swarmed in those seas, but finding only merchant vessels, a number of which were captured and their crews kept as prisoners. The gallant commodore, however, soon became tired of this. He had come out to fight, and he

wanted to find something worth fighting. At length, on September twenty-third, he came in view of a large fleet of merchant ships, forty-two in all, under the protection of two frigates, the *Serapis*, with forty-two guns, and the *Countess of Scarborough*, with twenty-two smaller guns.

Commodore Jones left the smaller vessel for his other ships to deal with and dashed away for the *Serapis* as fast as the tublike *Bon Homme Richard* could go. The British ship was much stronger than his in number and weight of guns, but he cared very little for that. The *Serapis* had ten eighteen-pound cannons in each battery, and the *Bon Homme Richard* only three. Jones did all his fighting with twelve and eight-pound guns; that is, with guns which fired balls of these weights.

The Battle Begins

It was night when the battle began. Soon the eighteen-pounders of the *Serapis* were playing havoc with the sides of the *Bon Homme Richard*. Many of the balls went clear through her and plunged into the sea beyond. Some struck her below the water level, and soon the rotten old craft was "leaking like a basket."

It began to look desperate for Jones and his ship. He could not return the heavy fire of the English guns, and great holes were made in the ship's side, where the eighteen-pound balls tore out the timbers between the portholes.

Captain Pearson of the *Serapis* looked at his staggering and leaking enemy, and thought it about time for the battle to end.

"Have you surrendered?" he shouted across the water to Commodore Jones.

"I have not yet begun to fight," was the famous answer of the brave Jones.

Surrender, indeed! I doubt if that word was in Paul Jones's dictionary. He would rather have let his vessel sink. The ships now drifted together, and by Jones's order the jib boom of the *Serapis* was lashed to his mizzenmast.[3] This brought the ships so close side by side that the English gunners could not open their ports, and had to fire through them and blow them off. The gunners on both sides had to thrust the handles of their rammers through the enemy's portholes, in order to load their guns.

Things were now desperate. The *Bon Homme Richard* was on fire in several places. Water was pouring into her through a dozen holes. It seemed as if she would sink or burn. Almost any man except Paul Jones would have given up the fight. I know I would, and I think most of you would have done the same. There was, however, no fear in that man's soul.

One would think that nothing could have been worse. Something worse, however, was still to come. In this crisis, the *Alliance*, one of Jones's small fleet, came up and fired two broadsides into the wounded flagship, killing a number of her crew. Whether this was done on purpose or by mistake is not known. The French captain did not like Commodore Jones, and most men think he played the traitor.

> *"Have you surrendered?" Captain Pearson shouted across the water to Commodore Jones. "I have not yet begun to fight," was the famous answer of the brave Jones.*

Then another bad thing took place. There were two or three hundred English prisoners on the *Bon Homme Richard*, taken from her prizes. One of the American officers, thinking that all was over, set these men free, and they came swarming up. At the same time, one of the crew tried to haul down the flag and cried to the British for quarter. Paul Jones knocked him down by flinging a pistol at his head. He might sink or burn—but give up the ship? Never!

The tide of the battle now began to turn. Richard Dale, the master's mate, told the English prisoners that the vessel was sinking and set them at work pumping and fighting the fire to save their lives. One of the marines who was fighting on the yardarms[4] dropped a hand grenade into an open hatch of the *Serapis*. This set fire to a heap of gun cartridges that lay below, and these exploded, killing twenty of the gunners and wounding many more, while the ship was set on fire. This ended the fight. The shooting by the marines from the tops of the mast had cleared the decks of the *Serapis* of men. Commodore Jones aided in this with the nine-pounders on his deck, loading and firing them himself. Captain Pearson stood alone, and when he heard the roar of the explosion he could bear the strain no longer. He ran and pulled down the flag which had been nailed to the mast.

Victory at Sea

"Cease firing," said Paul Jones.

The *Serapis* was his. Well and nobly had it been won.

Never had there been a victory gained at sea under such hardship. Most of the American crew was killed or injured and the *Bon Homme Richard* was fast settling down into the sea. Pump as they would, the crew could not save the ship. Inch by inch she sank deeper. Jones and his gallant crew boarded the *Serapis*. At nine o'clock the next morning the noble old craft sank beneath the ocean waves, laden with honor and with her victorious flag still flying. The *Serapis* was brought safely into port by Commodore Jones.

Captain Pearson had fought bravely, and the British ministry made him a knight for his courage.

"If I had a chance to fight him again I would make him a lord," said brave Paul Jones.

Never before or since has a victory been won under such desperate circumstances as those of Paul Jones, with his sinking and burning ship, his bursting guns, his escaped prisoners, and his treacherous fleet. It was a victory to put his name forever in the annals of fame and honor.

Chapter 14 Review Questions

1. Who was John Paul Jones? In what country was he born?

2. What was the name of the flagship of John Paul Jones's small fleet in 1779?

3. What famous statement did Jones make when he was asked to surrender by Captain Pearson of the ship *Serapis*?

4. What happened to the ship called the *Bon Homme Richard* after the sea battle?

Reference Notes for Chapter 14

1. An armed ship that is owned by a private citizen who has been given power by his government to attack and capture enemy merchant ships.

2. Ropes or tackles used for raising or lowering flags, sails, etc.

3. The mast closest to the stern of a ship with two or three masts attached to it.

4. Either end of a yard (a slender rod or spar, tapering toward the ends, and fastened at right angles across a mast) supporting a square sail, signal lights, etc.

The Swamp Fox and the General 15

Long ago back in old English history, there was a famous archer named Robin Hood, who lived in the deep woods with a bold band of outlaws like himself. He and his band were foes of the nobles and friends of the poor, and his name will never be forgotten by the people of England. No doubt you have read about the gallant archer. No man of his time could send an arrow so straight and sure as he. We, however, do not need to go back eight hundred years to find our Robin Hood. We have had a man like him in our own country who fought for us in our War of Independence. His name was Francis Marion, and he was known as the "Swamp Fox"—for he lived in the swamps of South Carolina as Robin Hood did in the forests of England. He was the stinging foe of the oppressors of the people.

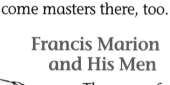

Francis Marion, the "Swamp Fox"

I have already told you about the war in the North. This is where the British, after doing all they could to overthrow Washington and conquer the country, found themselves shut up in the city of New York with Washington like a watchdog outside.

When the British generals found that the North was too hard a nut to crack, they thought they would try to fight in the South. They sent a fleet and an army down the coast, and before long they had taken the cities of Savannah and Charleston and had their soldiers marching all over Georgia and South Carolina. General Gates, the man to whom Burgoyne surrendered, came down with a mixed force of regulars and militia to fight them, but he was beaten so badly that he ran away without a soldier to follow him. You can imagine that the British were happy with their success. They thought themselves masters of the South and believed they had only to march north and become masters there, too.

Francis Marion and His Men

They soon found out, however, they were wrong. Back in the woods and the swamps were men with guns in their hands and with patriotism in their hearts. They were like wasps or hornets who kept darting out from their nests, stinging the British troops, and then darting back out of sight. These gallant bands were led by Marion, Sumter, Pickens, and other brave men; but Marion's army was the most famous of them all, so I shall tell you about the Swamp Fox and what he did.

I think all of my young friends would have laughed if they had seen Marion's army when it joined General Gates's army. Such scarecrows of soldiers they were! There were only about

Marion and his men swooping down on a British camp

twenty of them in all, some of them white and some black, some men and some boys, dressed in rags that fluttered in the wind and on horses that looked as if they had been fed on corn-cobs instead of corn.

Gates and his men did laugh at them, though they took care not to laugh when Marion was nearby. He was a small man with a thin face, and dressed not much better than his men. There was a light in his eye, how-ever, that told the soldiers he was not a safe man at which to laugh.

Marion and his men were soon on the at-tack again, and after Gates and his army had been beaten and scattered to the winds, they

went back to their hiding places in the swamps to play the hornet once more.

Along the Pee Dee River these swamps ex-tended for miles. There were islands of dry land far within, but they could only be reached by narrow paths which the British were not able to find. Only men who had spent their lives in that country could make their way safely through this broad stretch of water plants and water-soaked ground.

Marion's force kept changing in size. At one time it went down to twenty men and then up to a hundred or more. It was never large, for there was not food or shelter for many men. There were enough of them, however, to give the British plenty of trouble. They had their sentries on the outlook, and when a party of British went carelessly past, out would spring Marion's men, send their foes flying like deer, and then back they would go before a strong body of the enemy could reach them.

These brave fellows had many hiding places in the swamps and many paths out of them. Today they might strike the British in one place, and tomorrow in another many miles away. Small as their force was, they gave the enemy far more trouble than General Gates had done with all his army. Marion's headquarters was a tract of land known as Snow's Island, where a creek ran into the Pee Dee. It was high and dry, was covered with trees and thickets, and was full of animals. Moreover, all around it spread the soaking swamp, with paths known only to the patriot soldiers. Among all their hiding places, this was their chosen home.

You may be sure that the British did their best to capture Marion because he gave them so much trouble. They sent Colonel Wemyss, one of their best cavalry officers, to hunt him down. Marion was then far from his hiding place and Wemyss got on his trail. The Swamp Fox was hard to catch though. He gave the British a lively chase, and when they gave it up in despair he followed them back. He came upon a large body of Tories and struck them so suddenly that hardly a man escaped, while he lost only one man.

Tories, you should know, were Americans who fought on the British side.

Jack Davis, American Patriot

The next man who tried to capture Marion was Colonel Tarleton, a hard rider and a good soldier but a cruel and brutal man. He was hated in the South as much as Benedict Arnold was in the North. There is a good story told about how he was tricked by one of Marion's men. One day, as he and his men were riding furiously along, they came up to an old farmer who was hoeing in his field beside the road.

"Can you tell me what became of the man who galloped by here just ahead of us?" asked one of them. "I will give you fifty pounds if you put me on his track."

"Do you mean the man on a black horse with a white star in its forehead?" asked the farmer.

"Yes, that's the fellow."

"He looked to me like Jack Davis, one of Marion's men, but he went past so fast that I could not be sure."

"Never mind who he was. What we want to know is where to find him."

"Bless your heart! He was going at such a pace that he couldn't well stop under four or five miles. I'm much afraid I can't earn that fifty pounds."

On rode the troop, and back into the woods went the farmer. He had not gone far before he came to a black horse with a white star in its forehead. This he mounted and rode away. The farmer was Jack Davis himself.

A Patriotic Woman

During General Greene's campaign, he entered a tavern at Salisbury, in North Carolina. He was wet to the skin from a heavy rain. Steele, the landlord, knew him and looked at him in surprise.

"Why, General, you are not alone?" he asked.

"Yes," said the general, "here I am, all alone, very tired, hungry, and penniless."

Mrs. Steele hastened to set a smoking hot meal before the hungry traveler. Then, while he was eating, she drew from under her apron two bags of silver and laid them on the table before him.

"Take these, General," she said. "You need them and I can do without them."

Mrs. Steele's action showed that women, as well as men, did what they could to aid the cause of liberty during the War for Independence.

Those were the kind of men Tarleton had to deal with, and you may be sure that he did not catch any of them. He had his hunt, but he caught no game.

General Greene Reclaims the South

While Marion was keeping the war alive in South Carolina, an army was gathering under General Greene, who was, next to Washington, the best of the American generals. With him were Daniel Morgan, a famous leader of riflemen; William Washington, a cousin of the commander in chief; and Henry Lee, or "Lighthorse Harry," father of the famous General Lee of the War Between the States.

General Greene gathered together about two thousand men. They were half armed

General Nathanael Greene

and half supplied and knew nothing about war, so he had a poor chance of defeating the trained British soldiers. He, however, was a Marion on a larger scale and knew when to retreat and when to advance. I must tell you what he did.

In the first place, Morgan the rifleman met the bold Colonel Tarleton and soundly defeated him in battle. Tarleton hurried back to Lord Cornwallis, the British commander in the South. Cornwallis thought he would catch Morgan by surprise, but the lively rifleman was too clever for him. Morgan hurried back with the prisoners he had taken from Tarleton and crossed the Catawba River just as the British came up. That night it rained hard, and the river rose

so that it could not be crossed for three days.

General Greene now joined Morgan, and the retreat continued to the Yadkin River. This, too, was crossed by the Americans and a big rain again came up and swelled the river before the British could follow. When the British went across there was a race for the Dan River on the borders of Virginia. Greene got there first, crossed the river, and held the fords against the foe. Cornwallis by this time was ready to quit. Provisions were growing scarce, and he turned back. He soon had Greene on his track, however, and Cornwallis did not find his march a very comfortable one.

I have told you that General Greene was one of the ablest of the American leaders, and you have seen how he got the best of Cornwallis in the retreat. Several times afterwards he fought with the British. He was always defeated. His country soldiers could not face the British veterans. Each time, however, he managed to get as much good from the fight as if he had won a victory, and by the end of the year the British were shut up in Charleston and Savannah, and the South was free again.

America Wins the War

Where was Cornwallis during this time? Greene had led him so far north that he decided to march on into Virginia and get all the troops he would find there, and then come back. There was fighting going on in Virginia at this time. General Arnold, the traitor, was there, fighting against his own people. Against him was General Lafayette, a young French nobleman who

The British surrender to the Americans at Yorktown in 1781

troops. His army, however, was not yet strong enough to face Lafayette, so he marched to Yorktown, near the mouth of the York River, where he expected to get help by sea from New York. Yorktown was the trap he walked into, as you will see.

France had sent a fleet and an army to help the Americans, and just then this fleet came up from the West Indies and sailed into the Chesapeake, shutting off Yorktown from the sea. At the same time Washington, who had been closely watching what was going on, broke camp before New York and marched southward as fast as his men could go. Before Cornwallis could guess what was about to happen, the trap was closed on him. In the bay near Yorktown was the strong French fleet; before Yorktown was the army of American and French soldiers.

had come to the help of the Americans.

I suppose some of you have read stories of how a wolf or some other wild animal walked into a trap from which it could not get out again. Lord Cornwallis was not a wild animal, but he walked into just such a trap after he marched to Virginia. When he reached there, he took command of Arnold's

There was no escape. The army and the fleet bombarded the town. A week of this was enough for Lord Cornwallis. He surrendered his army, seven thousand strong, on October 19, 1781. The battle of Yorktown was the last major battle of the war. America was free because it had defeated England in its war for independence. A treaty of peace was signed between England and the United States in 1783.

Chapter 15 Review Questions

1. What was the name of the American patriot who fought against the British in the swamps of South Carolina?

2. Who were the soldiers called "Tories"?

3. Who was the man called Lord Cornwallis?

4. In what town was Lord Cornwallis trapped with his army?

5. Who was General Lafayette?

The Voyage of Our Grand Republic 16

Have any of my young readers ever been to Europe? Very likely some of you may have been, for even young folks cross the ocean nowadays. It is now an easy journey with our swift jet airplanes. In past times, however, it was a long and difficult journey in which the ships were often tossed by terrible storms and sometimes were broken to pieces on the rocks, or went to the bottom with all on board.

The American Ship of State

What I wish to say is that those people who came from Europe to this country at the time of our independence left countries that were governed by kings and came to a country that is governed by the people. In some of the countries of Europe, the people had few rights or freedoms, for they had no one to speak for them, and the person who ruled them was born to power. Even in England, which was the freest of them all at the time, the people had little opportunity to choose their leaders. The king or queen and the House of Lords were born or appointed to power, and only the wealthy and powerful were allowed to vote for the members of the House of Commons.

Of course, you all know that this is not the case in our country today. In the United States, almost everyone in power is put there by the votes of the people. As President Lincoln said many years ago, we have a government "of

The Great Seal of the United States was adopted by the Continental Congress on June 20, 1782, and by the U.S. Congress on September 15, 1789.

the people, by the people, and for the people."

We did not have such a government before the fourth of July, 1776. Our country was then governed by a king, and, what was worse, this king was on the other side of the ocean and cared nothing for the people of America except as bags of money to fill his purse. After the fourth of July, however, we governed ourselves and had no earthly king for lord and master. We have prospered very well without one ever since.

Now you can see what the Declaration of Independence and the War for American Independence meant. With the Declaration we cut loose from England. Our "Ship of State" set out on its long voyage to liberty. The Declaration cut the chain that fastened this great ship to England's shores.

The War for American Independence was like the stormy passage across the ocean waves. At times, it looked as if our Ship of State would be torn to pieces by the storms or driven back to the shores from which it set sail; but then the clouds would break, the sun would shine, and onward our good ship would speed. At length, it reached the port of liberty and came to anchor far away from the land of ungodly tyrants.

The Constitution is the rock upon which our liberty stands.

This is a sort of parable. I think every one of you will know what it means. The people of this country had enough of monarchs and their ways and of being taxed without their consent. They determined to be free to tax and govern themselves. It was for this right that they fought for freedom, and won liberty with their blood.

The Constitutional Convention

Now, before we go on with the history of our country, it will be wise to stop and ask what kind of government the Americans gave themselves. They had to make a new government for the people. I hope you do not think this was an easy task. If an architect or builder is shown a house and told to build another just like it, he finds it very easy to do. If he is shown, however, a heap of stone and bricks and wood, and is told to build out of them a strong house unlike any he has ever seen, he will find his task a very hard one.

That is what our people had to do. They could have built a king's government easily enough. They had plenty of patterns to follow for that. They had no pattern, however, for a people's government and, like the architect and his house, they might spoil it in the making.

The fact is, this is just what they did. Their first government was spoiled in the making, and they had to take it down and build it over again.

This was done by what we call a Convention, made up of delegates sent by several states. The Convention met in Philadelphia in 1787 for the purpose of forming a Constitution, that is, a plan of government under which the people should live and which the states and their citizens should have to obey.

This Convention was a wonderful body of statesmen. Its kind has not often been seen. The wisest and ablest men of all states were sent to this great meeting. They included all the great men—some we know already, Washington, Franklin, Hamilton, and Adams, and many others of fine ability. For four months these men worked in secret. It was a hard task they had to perform, for some wanted one thing and some another, and many times it looked as if they would never agree. In the end, though, all disputes were settled and their long labors were at last successful.

General Washington was the president of the Convention, and at the top of the chair on which he sat the figure of the sun was carved. When the Convention was over, Benjamin

Franklin pointed to this carving and said to those who stood near him:

"Often while we stood here, troubled by hopes and fears, I have looked towards that figure and asked myself if it was a rising or a setting sun. Now I know it is the rising sun."

The rising sun indeed it was, for when the Convention had finished its work, it had formed the noble Constitution under which we now live, the greatest state paper which man has ever formed. It is a great document because our founding fathers prayed to God for help and asked Him for wisdom to establish a just and fair government. God answered their prayers.

Right now, however, I think you want to know more about the noble framework of government built by the wise men of the Convention of 1787.

This cartoon shows the weakness of the Articles of Confederation.

The Framework of Government

After the Union was formed, there were still thirteen states, but each of these had lost some of its old powers. The powers taken from the states were given to the central government. Every state had the right to manage its own affairs, but certain things that concerned all of the people were managed by the central or federal government.

What were these things? Let's see. There was the power to coin money, to lay import taxes, to control the post office, and to make laws for the purpose of carrying out the constitutional duties of the federal government. There was the power to form an army and navy, to make treaties with other countries, and to declare war if we were attacked by other nations.

Under our country's first form of law, called the Articles of Confederation—which was formed during the War for American Independence—the states could do these things for themselves. Each state functioned in many respects as an independent nation. Under the new Constitution, however, the states would be required to give up some of their former powers to the central or federal government.

I have referred several times to the general or federal government. No doubt you wish to know what this government is like. Well, it consists of three parts: one makes laws for the people, the second considers if these laws agree with the Constitution, and the third executes these laws, or puts them in force. These three parts are known as the legislative, judicial, and executive branches of our federal government.

The Legislative Branch

The body that makes our national laws was named the Congress of the United States. It consists of two parts. One is called the Senate, which is made up of two members from each state. As we now have fifty states, the Senate at present has one hundred members. The other section is called the House of Representatives, and its four hundred thirty-five members are directly voted for by the people. The members of the Senate were voted for by the legislatures of the states, who had been elected by the people, until the year 1913 when the Constitution was amended to change the election of Senators to a direct popular vote.

The Executive Branch

All the laws are made by Congress, but not one of them can become a law until it is approved by the President. If he does not approve of any law, he vetoes it or returns it without signing his name to it; then it cannot be enforced as law until it is voted for again by two-thirds of the members of Congress.

White House

Supreme Court Building

U.S. Capitol Building

It is the duty of the President to execute the laws. He takes the place of the king in other countries. He is not born to his position like a king is, however. He has to be voted for by the people and can only stay in office for four years. Then he, or someone else, has to be voted for again. Our President's power is also very limited by the Constitution. For example, the President can not raise taxes without the direct approval of Congress, and a President cannot serve more than a total of eight years in a row.

Next to the President is the Vice-President, who is to take the President's place if he should die, resign, or be impeached. While the President is in office, the Vice-President has few vital duties to perform except to act as presiding officer of the Senate. After the Vice-President comes the Cabinet, which is made up of individuals chosen by the President to help him in his work. You must understand that it takes a great number of leading men and women to help the President complete his constitutional duties.

The Judicial Branch

The third body of our federal Government is called the Supreme Court. This court is made up of some of the ablest lawyers and judges in the country. They were not to be elected, but to be chosen by the President and approved by the members of the Senate. The duty of the Supreme Court is to consider any law brought to its notice and decide if it agrees with the Constitution. If the Court decides that a law is not constitutional, it ceases to be of any effect. This high court cannot change or make a law, but it can make it hard for a law to be enforced.

This is not so very hard to understand is it?

The President and Congress are elected by the people; the Supreme Court and Cabinet are selected by the President; the Constitution is the foundation of our government; and the laws passed by Congress provide the rules and regulations that our government needs to operate properly from day to day.

Our Constitutional Republic

Our government's great feature is that it is a constitutional republic—a republic based on law. This kind of republic is designed to protect the individual liberties of its citizens through the election of representatives who are committed to the rule of law. The United States government is not a democracy where the political desires of the majority of citizens determine how everyone must live. In a democracy, all citizens of a country meet together and make decisions and laws for themselves based on the will of the majority. In a constitutional republic, however, the citizens choose leaders to make decisions and laws based on the Constitution. These leaders are called "representatives," and it is the duty of every citizen to choose these representatives by voting for them on election day.

Ours is not the first republic. It is the greatest,

Preamble to The Constitution of the United States

We the People of the United States, in Order to form a more perfect Union, establish Justice, insure domestic Tranquility, provide for the common Defense, promote the general Welfare and secure the Blessings of Liberty to ourselves and our Posterity, do ordain and establish this Constitution for the United States of America.

however, because it is founded upon the laws of right and justice found in the Bible. It is the only one that covers half a continent and is made up of states, many of which are larger than some of the nations of Europe. For more than two hundred years the Constitution made in 1787 has been successful. Then it covered thirteen states and less than four million people, now it covers fifty states and over two hundred and fifty million people. Thank God that America has a Constitution that limits the power of government in many ways.

The U.S. Constitution is the "Supreme Law of the Land." This means that no person in government has any power outside of the power given to him in the Constitution. A wise form of government will limit the power of men because all men are sinners.

In many nations of the world today, people set up governments where the leaders are above the law. The United States Constitution makes sure that the God-given rights of a free people are not stolen by power hungry men or women. In America, only the people can change the Constitution. All American citizens have the duty to keep government leaders from destroying our God-given constitutional rights.

The celebration of the adoption of the Constitution in New York City

Chapter 16 Review Questions

1.   The Declaration of Independence stated that America was no longer under the rule of what country?

2.   What did the Convention in Philadelphia do in the year 1787?

3.   Who was the president of the Convention?

4.   What are the names of the three main parts of our federal government system?

5.   Is the American system of government set up as a republic or democracy?

6.   Are all American citizens required to live under the rules of the Constitution?

7.   Why is it so important to have every American under the same set of rules?

The End of a Noble Life 17

Every four years a great question arises in this country, and all the States and their people are disturbed until this question is settled. Even business nearly stops, for many persons can think of nothing but the answer to this question.

Who shall be President? That is the question which at the end of four years' time troubles the minds of our people. This question was asked for the first time in 1789, after the Constitution had been made and accepted by the states. During this time period the people found it a very easy question to answer.

There were many men who had taken a great part in the making of our country, and who might have been named for President. One of these was Thomas Jefferson, who wrote part of the Declaration of Independence. Another of them was Benjamin Franklin, who convinced France to come to our aid and did many other noble things for his country. None of them, however, stood so high in the respect and admiration of the people as George Washington, who had led our armies through the great war, and to whom, more than to any other man, we owed our liberty.

Our First President

This time, then, there was no real question as to who should be President. Washington was the man. All men, all parties, settled upon Washington. No one opposed him; there

Washington took the oath of office at Federal Hall in New York City on April 30, 1789. He stood for no party but was the choice of all the people. John Adams was elected Vice-President.

was no man in the country like him. He was unanimously elected the first President of the United States.

In olden times, when a victorious general came back to Rome with the splendid spoils brought from distant countries, the people gave him a glorious parade, and all Rome rose to do him honor and to gaze upon the splendor of the show. Washington had no splendid spoils to display, but he had the love of the people, which is far better than gold and silver won in war. All the way from his home at Mount Vernon to

New York, where Washington was to take the office of President, the people honored him with a triumph.

Along the whole journey, men, women, and children crowded the roadside and waited for hours to see him pass. Since that was before the day of airplanes, he had to go slowly in his carriage, and everybody had a fine chance to see and greet him as he went by. Guns were fired as he passed through the towns; arches of triumph were erected for his carriage to go under; flowers were strewn in the streets for its wheels to roll over; cheers and cries of greeting filled the air. All that the people could do to honor their great hero was done.

On the thirtieth of April, 1789, Washington took the oath of office as the first President of our country and people. He stood on the balcony of the building in which Congress met, and in the street before him was a vast crowd full of joy and hope. When he had taken the oath with his hand on the Bible, cannons roared out, bells were rung in all the neighboring steeples, and a mighty shout burst from the assembled crowd:

"Long live George Washington, President of the United States!"

This, I have said, was in New York. Philadelphia, however, was soon chosen as the seat of government, and the President and Congress moved to that city the next year. There they stayed for ten years. In the year 1800, a new city named Washington, on the banks of the Potomac, was made the capital of our country. In that city, Congress has met ever since.

Alexander Hamilton

I must say something here about another of the great men of this time period, Alexander Hamilton. He was great in financial or money matters, and this was very important at that time, for the finances of the country were in a sad state.

During the War for Independence our people had very little money, and that was one reason why they had so much suffering. Congress soon ran out of gold and silver, so it issued paper money. This did very well for a time because a great deal of paper money was printed and given out, but people soon began to get afraid of it. There was too much money of this kind for so poor a country. The value of the Continental currency, as it was called, began to go down, and the price of everything else went up. In time, the paper money lost most all its value, as it is always prone to do when it is not backed up by gold or silver.

Alexander Hamilton

Such was the money the people had at the end of the War for Independence. It was not good for much, was it? It was the only kind of money that Congress had to pay the soldiers or to pay the other debts of the government, however. The country owed much more money than it could pay, so that it was what we call "bankrupt." Nobody would trust it or take its paper in payment. What Alexander Hamilton did was to help the country pay its debts and bring back its lost credit; in that way, he won great honor.

Hamilton came to this country from the West Indies, shortly before the War for American Independence. Although only a young man, he showed himself a good soldier, and Washington made him an officer on his staff

George Washington, our first President

and became one of his friends. He often asked young Hamilton for advice, and he took it, too.

Hamilton was one of the men who helped to write the Constitution, and when Washington became President, he chose Hamilton as his Secretary of the Treasury. That is, he gave him the money affairs of the government to look after. Hamilton was not afraid of the load of debt and soon took off its weight. He asked Congress to pay not only its own debt, but the war debts of the states as well, and also to make the value of the paper money worth something again. Congress did not like to do this, but Hamilton talked to the members until he convinced them to do so.

Then he set his plan in motion. He laid a tax on whiskey and brandy and on all goods that came into the country. He had a mint and a national bank built in Philadelphia. He made the debt a government fund or loan, on which he agreed to pay interest, and to pay off the principal as fast as possible. It was not long before all the fund was taken up by those who had money, and the country restored its lost credit. After that all went well.

Washington's Final Years

Washington was President for eight years. That made two terms of four years each. Many wished to make him President for a third term, but he refused to run again. Since then our Constitution has been changed in order to limit a person from being President more than eight years.

George Washington had done enough for his country. He loved his home back in Virginia, but he had little time to live there. When he was only a young man, he had been called away to take part in the French and Indian War. Then, after spending some happy years at home, he had been called away again to lead the army in the War for American Independence. Finally, he served his country eight years as President.

He was now growing old and wanted rest, and he went back with joy to his beloved home at Mount Vernon, hoping to spend the remainder of his days there. Trouble arose with France, however, and it looked as if there would be a new war, and Washington was asked to take command of the army again. He consented, though he was somewhat tired of fighting; thankfully the war did not come, so he was not required to leave his home.

He died in December 1799, near the end of the century in which he was one of the greatest men. The news of his death filled all American hearts with grief. Not while the United States exists will the name of Washington be forgotten or left without honor. His home and tomb at Mt. Vernon are visited each year by thousands of patriotic Americans. As was said of him long ago by General Henry Lee, he was and is "first in war, first in peace, and first in the hearts of his countrymen."

Chapter 17 Review Questions

1. How often do the American people vote for their president?

2. Who was the first President of the United States?

3. How did our nation get into financial trouble when it was young?

4. What person was most responsible for helping America to overcome its money problems?

5. How many years did George Washington serve as president? When did George Washington die?

The New Nation Begins to Grow 18

I think you must now have learned a great deal about the history of your country from the time Columbus crossed the Atlantic Ocean till the year 1800. You have been told about discoveries, settlements, wars, modes of life, government, and other things, but you must bear in mind that these are not the whole of American history.

The story of our country is broad and deep enough to hold many other events and issues. For instance, there are the stories of our third President Thomas Jefferson, the preachers of the Second Great Awakening, and our great inventors, to whom we owe so much. I propose in this chapter to tell you about some of these stories that took place around the beginning of the nineteenth century.

Thomas Jefferson

A New Leader

Thomas Jefferson was born in Virginia on April 13 in the year 1743. He had learned his ABC's in a little white schoolhouse with his cousins. He had his own little library of books, which he liked to read. Jefferson also liked to draw plans for beautiful houses. When he married his lovely young wife, he built a house called Montecello for her on the top of a hill in Virginia. From there, he could look all around him to the mountains and the valleys.

When George Washington's soldiers were fighting to make America a free country, Thomas Jefferson was helping to write the Declaration of Independence. Jefferson was fighting for freedom with words instead of a gun. He was working hard and doing everything he could to help George Washington. During the later part of the war, he became governor of Virginia. Once he had to flee his home, because English soldiers marched into Virginia, and he could not run the risk of being captured by the English.

Thomas Jefferson was not around to help write the Constitution, because he was in France as America's ambassador. When he returned to the United States, he became President Washington's first secretary of state. He was responsible for our country's dealings with other nations. While in this office he had great differences with

Alexander Hamilton over the powers of the federal government. Did the Constitution give large powers to Congress and the President? Hamilton said, "Yes!" Jefferson said, "No!" From this disagreement, two political parties were formed—Hamilton's Federalist Party and Jefferson's Democratic-Republican Party. Jefferson later served as Vice-President under John Adams, the second President of the United States.

The Nation Expands

Thomas Jefferson was elected President of the United States in 1800. He went to live in the White House in Washington, D.C., although the White House was not yet finished. The national capital was a very new city at that time. The streets were knee-deep in mud when there was rain. Everywhere around the city were woods. You could ride for miles through them and not meet anyone or even see a house.

At that time, the city of New Orleans and a wide strip of land from the Mississippi River to the Rocky Mountains belonged to France. That land was called the Louisiana Territory. President Jefferson thought that the United States needed some of that land. So he sent men to France to see if they could buy New Orleans. To his surprise, France sold them all the land in 1803. They paid about fifteen million dollars for it. The Louisiana Territory was later cut up into more than ten states. Some of the richest land in America lies in those states. Do you think Jefferson got a good bargain?

Do you think Americans knew much about this territory? At the time, not much was known, so President Jefferson sent an expedition led by Meriwether Lewis and William Clark to examine the new land. They tried to find if there was a water route along the rivers between the Mississippi Valley and the Pacific Ocean. The Lewis and Clark expedition left St. Louis on May 14, 1804, and returned on September 23, 1806. Lewis and Clark did not find a water route to the Pacific but explored much of the new territory along the Missouri River, over the Rocky Mountains, and down the Columbia River to the Pacific Ocean.

Thomas Jefferson was elected President again in 1804, serving for a total of eight years. Then he went back home to his house

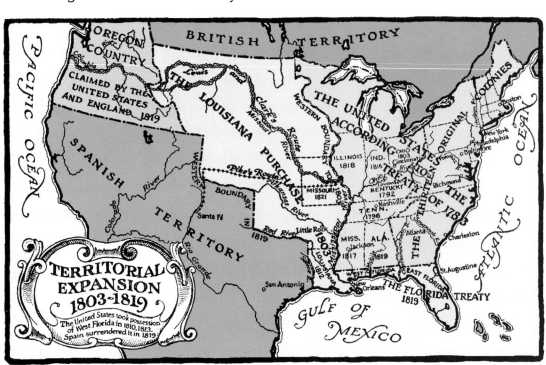

The United States almost doubled in size when it bought the Louisiana Territory from France in 1803. The most immediate benefit of the Purchase was free navigation of the Mississippi River and use of the port of New Orleans.

on the top of the hill. He then helped to plan and build the University of Virginia. Thomas Jefferson lived a long and useful life. He died on the fiftieth anniversary of the Declaration of Independence, July 4, 1826, when he was eighty-three years old.

A New Spiritual Revival

By the end of the War for American Independence, the United States was in need of a new revival. The influence of the Bible and the gospel had begun to fade away. This was especially true in the frontier, where there were few churches and organized communities.

God did not abandon America, however. In the late 1790s, revival again began to spread throughout New England. This was the beginning of the Second Great Awakening that took place in America. The Spirit of God once again moved in the churches, and church membership began to grow while new congregations were being formed. In the theological schools in New England, there was also a revival among the students.

In 1795, Timothy Dwight, Jonathan Edwards's grandson, became the president of Yale. Many of his students were following the false teachings from France which attacked the Bible and its truth. By God's grace, Dwight

---

Haystack Prayer Meeting

One day in 1802, while Samuel J. Mills, Jr., was plowing on his farm in Connecticut, he believed that God was calling him to preach the gospel. Four years later, he obeyed God's command by entering Williams College at Williamstown, Massachusetts. A group of like-minded men, called the Society of the Brethren, often met in a maple grove close to the college for prayer and discussion.

As Mills and five of his fellow students were heading for prayer one day, they were forced by a sudden thunderstorm to take cover in the shelter of a nearby haystack; there they began to talk about the untold millions living in spiritual darkness without the saving knowledge of Christ and His cross. They even pondered how they could accomplish the task and what that would mean to each of them personally. Mills proposed that they devote themselves to reaching the non-Christian world with the gospel. They prayed and then committed themselves to becoming America's first foreign missionaries. Hereafter, they became known as the "Haystack Group."

God answered their prayers in a way they could not have imagined. The Holy Spirit used their enthusiasm to prompt thousands to commit themselves to carrying the gospel overseas. Although Mills was never able to serve abroad, he used his gifts to help others.

---

was able to restore the authority of Scripture through the preaching of the gospel. In 1802, revival swept the campus and one third of the 225 students were converted. Many of these students were sent out to preach in New England, New York, and beyond, bringing the gospel throughout the country.

Even as revival was spreading in the East, God began to work on the frontier. One of the means God used to revive the West was the camp meeting—an outdoor religious service which lasted for several days. People would come from miles around to stay at a campsite and listen to the revival preachers. The camp meeting method, pioneered by Presbyterian James McGready, was used effectively by Methodist, Baptist, and other Presbyterian preachers. It has been said that in 1811 alone, four hundred such meetings were held across the frontier.

Before this great revival, God was preparing another man to come and spread the gospel. At the age of sixteen, Francis Asbury (1745–1816) began preaching in England. In 1771, he eagerly responded to John Wesley's call for volunteers to go to America. Asbury began to travel on horseback to where the gospel had not been heard. He encouraged other Methodist preachers to do the same, telling them to "go into every kitchen and shop; address all, aged and young, on the salvation of their souls."

Asbury's zeal for the gospel took him almost 300,000 miles all over America and even into Canada—mostly on horseback. He was probably known by more Americans than any other person at that time. In spite of his labors, the growth of Methodists was meager. This was due to the War of Independence and to their connections with the Church of England. After the war, God began to work through Asbury and his associates during the Second Great Awakening.

Francis Asbury

In 1787, the Methodists formed their own denomination, and from that time on the church began to grow rapidly. The greatest growth took place west of the Appalachian Mountains. In the city or in the wilderness, though, his message was the same—a call for repentance and faith. He also organized local classes, preaching circuits, and general conferences, which further helped the church to expand, especially on the frontier.

New Inventions

During this exciting time, our nation was also growing in another way. To tell you about this, I must ask you to go back with me to a kitchen in Scotland many years before 1800. On the open hearth of that kitchen a bright fire blazed. Nearby sat a thoughtful-faced boy with his eyes fixed on the teakettle which was boiling away over the fire, while its lid kept lifting to let the steam escape. His mother, who was hustling about, no doubt thought he was idle and may have

scolded him a little. He was far from idle, however; he was busy at work—not with his hands but with his brain. The brain, you know, may be hard at work while the body is doing nothing.

How many of you have seen the lid of a kettle of boiling water keeping up its clatter as the steam lifts it and puffs out into the air? What thought has this brought into your mind? Into the mind of little James Watt it brought one great thought, that of power. As he looked at it, he said to himself that the steam which comes from boiling water must have a great deal of force if a little of it could keep the kettle lid clattering up and down, and he asked himself if such a power could not be put to some good use.

Our Scottish lad was not the first one to have that thought. Others had thought the same thing, and steam had been used to move a poor sort of engine. What James Watt did when he grew up, though, was to invent a much better engine than had ever been made before. It was a great day for us all when that engine was invented. Before that time, men had done most of their daily work with their hands, and you may imagine that the work was hard and slow.

The Power of Steam

The development of the steam engine opened up a new era for American inventors. I have spoken about the steam engine because it was with this that most inventors worked. They thought that if horses could drag a wagon over the ground and the wind could drive a vessel through the water, steam might do the same thing. They tried to see in what way a carriage or a boat could be moved by a steam engine.

Very likely you have all heard about Robert Fulton and his steamboat, but you may not know that steamboats were running on American waters years before Fulton built his first boat. Why, as long ago as 1768, before the War for American Independence, Oliver Evans, one of our first inventors, had made a little boat which was moved by steam and paddle wheels. Years afterwards he made a large engine for a boat at New Orleans, but due to a dry season and low water the boat could not be used so the owners took the engine out and used it in a saw mill. It did so well there that it was never put back in the boat so that steamboat never had a chance.

Oliver Evans was the first man who labored to make a steam carriage, but there were others who thought they could move a boat by steam. Some of these were in Europe and some in America. Down in Virginia there was an inventor named Ramsey, who moved a boat at the speed of four miles an hour. In this boat, jets of water were pumped through the stern and forced the boat along. In Philadelphia there was another man named John Fitch, who was the first man to make a successful steamboat. His boat was moved with paddles like an Indian canoe. It was put on the Delaware River between Philadelphia and Trenton in 1790, and ran for several months as a passenger boat at the speed of seven or eight miles an hour.

"Fulton's Folly"

I am glad to be able to tell you a different story of the next man who tried to make a steamboat. His name was Robert Fulton. He was born in Pennsylvania, and as a boy was very fond of the water. He and some other boys had an old flatboat which they pushed along with a pole. Fulton got tired of this way of getting along and, like a natural-born inventor, set his mind to work. In the end, he made two paddle wheels which hung over the sides of the boat. These could be moved in the water by turning a crank and, thereby, forcing the boat onward. The boys found this much easier than the pole, and likely enough, young Fulton thought a large vessel might be moved in the same way.

He knew all about what others had done. He had heard how Ramsey moved his boat by pumping water through the stern and how Fitch propelled his by paddling it along. He also had seen a boat in Scotland moved by a stern paddle wheel. I think he had not forgotten the side paddle wheel he had made as a boy, for when he set out to invent his steamboat, this is the plan he tried.

Fulton made his first boat in France but had little success there. Then he came to America and built a boat in New York. While he was at work on this boat in America, James Watt, of whom I have already told you, was building him an engine in England. He wanted the best engine that he could get, and he thought the Scottish inventor was the right man to make it.

Robert Fulton

While Fulton was working, some of the people in New York were laughing. They called his boat "Fulton's Folly," and said it would not move faster than the tide would carry it. Fulton let them laugh, however, and worked on. At last, one day in 1807, the new boat, which he named the *Clermont*, was afloat in the Hudson ready for trial. Hundreds of curious people came to see it start. Some were ready to laugh again when they saw the boat with its clumsy paddle wheels hanging down in the water on both sides. They were not covered with wooden frames.

"That boat move? So will a log move if set adrift," said the local people. "It will move when the tide moves it, and not before." None of them felt like laughing, however, when they saw the wheels begin to turn and the boat to glide out into the stream, moving against the tide.

"She moves! She moves!" cried the crowd, and nobody said a word about "Fulton's Folly" again.

Move she did. Up the Hudson she went against wind and current, and reached Albany, one hundred and forty-two miles away, in thirty-two hours. This was at the rate of four and a half miles an hour. It was just a few years before steamboats were running on all our rivers.

That is all I shall say here about the steamboat, for there is another story of invention I wish to tell you before I close. This is about the cotton fiber, which you know was one of the great products of the southern states.

Eli Whitney and the Cotton Gin

The cotton plant when ripe has a white, fluffy head and a great bunch of snow white fibers in which are found the seeds. In old times, these had to be taken out by hand, and it

Eli Whitney

was a whole day's labor for a worker to get the seeds out of a pound of cotton. This made cotton so expensive that not much of it could be sold.

In the 1780s, a young man named Eli Whitney went south to teach as a private tutor. Before he arrived there, someone else had been given his job and he was left with nothing to do. Mrs. Greene, the widow of General Greene who fought so well in the War for Independence, took pity on him and gave him a home in her house. He paid her back by fixing up things around her house. She found him so handy that she asked him if he could invent a machine to take the seeds out of her cotton. Whitney said he would try, and he set himself to work. It was not long before he had a machine made which did the work wonderfully well. This machine was known as the "cotton gin," or cotton engine, for "gin" is short for "engine." On one side of it are wires so close together that the seeds cannot get through. Between them are circular saws which catch the cotton and draw it through, while the seeds pass on.

The Cotton Gin

The machine was a simple one but it acted like magic. A hundred workers could not clean as much cotton in a day as one machine. The price of cotton soon went down and a demand for it sprang up. In 1795, when the cotton gin was made, only about 500,000 pounds of cotton were produced in the United States. By 1801 this had grown to 20,000,000 pounds.

The cotton gin had a tremendous impact on the South. It made cotton "king" in the South, encouraging the spread of cotton production and the settlement of new lands. By 1845, the United States was producing 88 percent of the world's cotton.

I am sorry to say, however, that while the cotton gin helped bring more wealth to the South, it also helped revive slavery in the South. Slavery had been declining throughout the nation, but large-scale cotton production required abundant cheap labor which slaves could provide. You can say that Eli Whitney's invention changed the South's economy and contributed to the divisions which so tragically affected our nation many years later.

What made it worse was the evil actions of some of the British captains. One of them went so far as to stop an American war vessel, the *Chesapeake,* and demand four members of her crew, who, he said, were British deserters. When Captain Barron refused to give them up, the British ship, *Leopard,* fired all its guns and killed and wounded twenty-three members of the American crew. The *Chesapeake* was not ready to fire back, so her flag had to be pulled down and the men had to be given up.

You may well imagine that this insult made the American blood boil. There would have been war at that time if the British government had not apologized and offered to pay for the injury. A few years afterwards, the insult was paid for in a different way. Another proud British captain thought he could treat Americans in the same insulting fashion. The American frigate *President* met the British sloop of war, *Little Belt,* and hailed it. The captain called through his trumpet, "What ship is that?"

Instead of giving a proper reply, the British captain answered with a cannon shot. Then the *President* fired a broadside which killed eleven and wounded twenty-one men on the *Little Belt.* When the captain of the *President* hailed again, the rude Briton was glad to reply in a more honest fashion.

The United States was then a poor country and not in a condition to go to war. No nation, however, could submit to such insults as these. It is said that more than 6,000 sailors had been taken from our merchant ships. Among these were two nephews of General Washington, who were seized while they were on their way home from Europe and put to work as common seamen on a British war vessel. The British also seized ships from American seamen as well.

The War of 1812

Finally, on June 18, 1812, the United States declared war against Great Britain. It had put up with insults and injuries as long as it could bear them. It did not take long to teach the haughty British captains that American sea dogs were not to be played with. The little American fleet put to sea, and before the end of the year it had captured no less than five of the best ships in the British navy and had not lost a single ship in return. I think, for the moment, the people of England quit singing their proud song, "Britannia rules the waves."

THE WAR OF 1812
SHOWING STATES ADMITTED TO 1812

Shall I tell you the whole story of the War of 1812? I do not think that I have the time to tell you the whole story, so I will only give you a few details. The war went on for two and a half years on sea and land, but there were not many important battles, and the United States did not win much honor on land.

Most of the land battles were along the borders of Canada. Here there was a good deal of fighting, but most of it was of no great account. At first the British had the best of it, and then the Americans began to win battles, but it all came to an end about where it began. Neither side had gained anything for the men that were killed.

Captain Oliver Perry

On the sea, however, the sailors of our country covered themselves with honorable service. There was one naval battle in the north that I must tell you about. On Lake Erie, the British had a fleet of six war vessels and, for a time, had everything their own way. Then Captain Oliver Perry, a young officer, was sent to the lake to build a fleet and fight the British.

When he arrived there, his ships were growing in the woods. He had to cut down trees and build ships from their timber. He worked, however, like a young giant, and in a few weeks he had some vessels built and afloat and was sailing out to find the British ships.

They met on September 10, 1813. The Americans had the most vessels but the British had the most guns, and soon they were fighting like sea dragons. The *Lawrence*, Captain Perry's flagship, fought two of the largest British ships till it was nearly ready to sink. So many of its crew were killed and wounded that it had only eight men left fit for fighting. What do you think the brave Perry did then? He leaped into a small boat and rowed away with the American flag waving in his hand, though the British ships were firing directly at him.

When he reached the *Niagara*, another of his ships, he sprang on board and sailed right through the enemy's fleet, firing right and left into their shattered vessels. The British soon had enough of this, and after fifteen minutes they gave up the fight.

"We have met the enemy and they are ours," wrote Perry to General Harrison. He was a born hero of the waves.

Victory at Sea

Now I think we had better take a look out to sea and learn what was going on there. We did not have many ships, but they were like so many bulldogs in a flock of sheep. The whole world looked on with surprise to see our little fleet of war vessels making such havoc in the proud British navy. No country in Europe had ever been able to defeat the British on the high seas.

The British commander (left, with sword) surrendered his fleet on Lake Erie to the American commander, Captain Oliver Perry (center).

In less than two months after war was declared, the American frigate *Essex* met the British sloop *Alert* and took it in eight minutes, without losing a man. The *Essex* was too strong for the *Alert*. Six days afterwards, the *Constitution* met the *Guerriere,* and both of these vessels were nearly the same in size. In half an hour, however, the *Guerriere* was nearly cut to pieces and ready to sink, with a loss of a hundred of her men. The others were hastily taken off, and then down went the proud British frigate to the bottom of the Gulf of St. Lawrence.

All the island of Great Britain went into mourning when it learned how the Americans had destroyed this good ship. There soon were more losses for which the British mourned. The American sloop *Wasp* captured the British sloop *Frolic*. The frigate *United States* captured the frigate *Macedonia*. The *Constitution* met the *Java* and destroyed it the same way as it had done the *Guerriere*. In two hours, the *Java* was a wreck. Soon af-

ter, the sloop *Hornet* met the ship *Peacock* and handled her so severely that she sank while her crew was being taken off.

Later on, the British won two battles at sea, but that was all they gained during the whole war. On the water, the honors stayed with the Americans.

Washington, D.C. Burned

In July 1814, a strong British fleet sailed up Chesapeake Bay with an army of nearly five thousand men on board. The army landed and marched on the city of Washington, the capital of our young republic.

Their coming was a surprise, and there were few trained American soldiers to meet this army. As you probably already know, these were not the days of railroads or airplanes, so no troops could be brought in quickly. Those that gathered were nearly all new militia, and they did not stand long before the British veterans who had fought in

While being held prisoner on a British ship, Francis Scott Key could see the American flag through the smoke of battle as Fort McHenry was being attacked by the British. The fort was the city of Baltimore's first line of defense against attack from the sea.

the wars with Napoleon. They were defeated at the Battle of Bladensburg on August 24 and the British army marched into our capital city.

They set fire to the public buildings and burned most of them to the ground. The Capitol, the President's house, and other buildings were burned, and the records of the government were destroyed. The British did this in retaliation for government buidings that were burned by Americans in Canada. Then the British returned to their ships.

They had been so successful at Washington that they thought they would try the same thing with another city. This time they picked Baltimore, which was an important city close to Washington. The British thought that it would be an easy matter to capture the city so they made an attack upon Fort McHenry which guarded the city. British warships pounded Fort McHenry on the thirteenth and fourteenth of September, 1814, but the brave Americans refused to surrender. After the attack was over, the stars and stripes were still flying over the fort. A man by the name of Francis Scott Key witnessed this battle and wrote our national anthem, "The Star-Spangled Banner" to commemorate the heroic men who successfully defended Baltimore.

The Battle of New Orleans

There was a general at New Orleans who was not used to being defeated. His name was Andrew Jackson, one of our bravest soldiers. He had already won fame in the war by de-

The Star-Spangled Banner

On September 14, 1814, Francis Scott Key penned the words of "The Star-Spangled Banner" during the War of 1812. While Fort McHenry was being bombarded by a British fleet anchored in Baltimore Harbor, Francis Scott Key was inspired to write his famous anthem. He was being held prisoner on a British ship, but he could still see the U.S. flag flying in "the dawn's early light." His words quickly became very popular, but it was not until the War Between the States that it was adopted unofficially as an anthem by the Union Army. Later during World War I, "The Star-Spangled Banner" became the official anthem of the U.S. Army. It finally became the U.S. national anthem by an act of Congress, and President Herbert Hoover signed the act into law on March 3, 1931.

feating the pro-British Creek Indians in Alabama and driving the British from the Spanish settlement of Pensacola, Florida. He was a man who was always ready to fight, and this the English found out when they marched on New Orleans. There were twelve thousand British soldiers sent against New Orleans, and Jackson only had half that many. The British were trained soldiers, while the Americans were militia. They were old hunters, however, and knew how to shoot.

Some of you may have heard that Jackson's men fought behind cotton bales. That is not quite true, but he was in such a hurry in building his walls of protection that he did put in them some bales of cotton taken from the warehouses. The British, who were in as great a hurry, built a wall of sugar barrels which they found on some of the plantations. The cannonballs, however, soon set the cotton on fire and filled the air with flying sugar, so the bales and the barrels had to be pulled out. It was found that cotton and sugar, while good enough in their place, were not good things to stop cannonballs!

Soon the British army marched against the American defenses and there was a terrible fight.

"Stand to your guns, my men," said Jackson to his soldiers. "Make every shot count. Give it to them."

Many of the men were old hunters from Tennessee, some of whom could hit a squirrel in the eye, and when they fired, the British fell in rows. Not a man could cross that terrible wall of fire, and they fought on until twenty-six hundred of them lay dead or wounded on the field, while only eight Americans were killed.

That ended the battle. The British soldiers could no longer face gunfire like that. It also was the last battle of the war and the last time American and British soldiers ever fought each other. Jackson became the hero of the country, and in 1828 he was elected President of the United States. Jackson was a Christian man who honored the Bible. Andrew Jackson once said "The Bible, Sir, is the foundation upon which our republic rests."

Chapter 19 Review Questions

1. What country did the United States declare war against in June of 1812?

2. What did the British soldiers do to the city of Washington during August of 1814?

3. Who was the general responsible for defending the city of New Orleans from British attack?

4. Who wrote the statement "We have met the enemy and they are ours"?

5. What city did Fort McHenry defend?

6. Who wrote the "Star-Spangled Banner"?

The Lone Star Republic 20

I have told you the story of more than one war. I shall have to tell you now about still another in which the Americans fought the Mexicans in Texas.

I suppose you know that Texas is one of our States and the second largest of all the fifty states. In former times, it was part of Mexico and was a portion of what is called Spanish America. People kept coming there from the United States until it was much more of an American culture than a Spanish culture.

General Santa Anna, who was at the head of the Mexican government at the time, was very much a tyrant, and he tried to rule the people of Texas in a way they would not permit. He ordered them to give up all their guns to his soldiers, but instead, they took their guns and drove the Mexican soldiers away. Shortly after this battle there was war, as you might well suppose.

"Remember the Alamo!"

I will now tell you what happened to some very brave Americans. There were only one hundred and seventy-five of them, and they were attacked by General Santa Anna with an army of several thousand men. They were commanded, however, by Colonel Travis, a brave young Texan. Among them was the famous David Crockett, a great hunter, and

A little band of Texans defended themselves in the Alamo against the Mexican army. The siege lasted from February 23 to March 6, 1836.

Colonel James Bowie, who invented the terrible "bowie knife," and other bold and daring men. They had made a fort of an old Spanish building called the Alamo to protect themselves from Santa Anna.

The kind of men I have named do not easily give up. The Mexicans threw bombs and cannonballs into their fort, battering down the walls and killing many of them. Nevertheless they fought on like tigers, determined to die rather than surrender. Finally, so many of them were dead that there were not enough left to defend the walls, and the Mexican soldiers captured the Alamo. The valiant Crockett kept on fighting, and when he fell, the ground before him was covered with dead Mexicans. Then Santa Anna ordered his soldiers to shoot down all that were left. That is what is called the "Massacre of the Alamo."

It was not long before the Americans paid back the Mexican soldiers in a new battle. The principal leader of the Americans was a bold and able man named Samuel Houston. He had less than eight hundred soldiers, but he marched on the Mexicans, who then had about thirteen hundred men.

"Men, there is the enemy," said brave General Houston. "Do you wish to fight?"

"We do," they all shouted.

"Charge on them, then, for liberty or death! Remember the Alamo!"

"Remember the Alamo!" they cried, as they rushed onward with the courage of lions.

In a little time the Mexicans were in full retreat, and the daring Texans were closing in on them. Of the thirteen hundred Mexicans, all but four hundred were killed, wounded, or taken prisoner, while the Americans lost only thirty men. They had well avenged the gallant Travis and his men.

The cruel Santa Anna was taken prisoner. He had only one healthy leg, and the story was that he was caught with his wooden leg stuck firmly in the mud. Many of the Texans wanted to hang him for his murders at the Alamo, but in the end he was set free.

Texas Becomes a State

All this took place in 1836. Texas was made an independent country, the "Lone Star Republic," with General Houston as President. Its people, however, did not want to stand alone. They were American born and wished to belong to the United States, so the country of Texas asked to become a part of the United States. Nine years later Texas was added to the Union of the States.

Perhaps some of my readers may think that this story has much more to do with the history of Mexico than that of the United

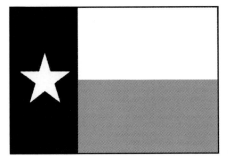

The Lone Star
Flag of Texas

States. The taking of Texas as a state, however, is United States history, and so is what followed. You know how one thing leads to another. Mexico did not feel like giving up Texas so easily, and her rulers said that the United States had no right to take it. It was not long before the soldiers of the two countries met on the border lands and blood was shed. There was a hard fight at a place called Palo Alto and a harder one at a place called Resaca de la Palma. In both of them, the Mexicans were defeated.

The Mexican War

Congress then declared war against Mexico, and very soon there was hard fighting going on elsewhere. General Zachary Taylor, a brave officer who had fought the Seminole Indians in Florida, led the American troops across the Rio Grande River into Mexico and, some time afterwards, marched to a place called Buena Vista. He had only five thousand men while Santa Anna was marching against him with twenty thousand—four to one. General Taylor's army was in great danger. Santa Anna sent him a message asking him to surrender if he did not want his army to be cut into pieces; but "Rough and Ready," as Taylor's men called him, sent word back that he was there to fight, not to surrender.

Zachary Taylor

The battle that followed was a desperate one. It took place on February 23, 1847. The Mexican cavalry rode bravely against the American lines and were driven back at the cannon's mouth. For ten long hours, the fighting went on. The Mexicans gained the high ground above the pass and put the American troops in danger. Charge after charge was made, but

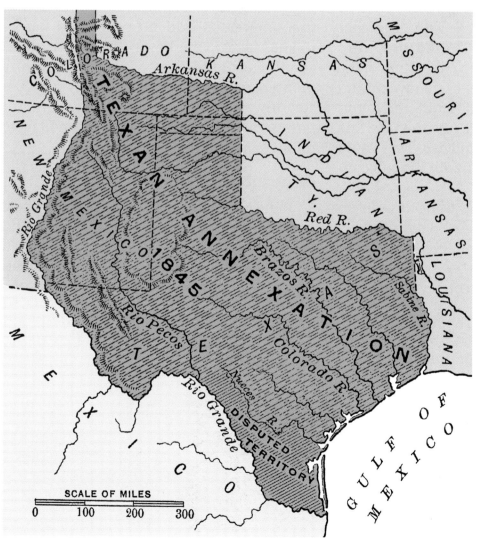

The shaded area on this map represents the territory that was added to the United States in 1845. The disputed territory is what caused the Mexican War.

like bulldogs the Yankee soldiers held their ground. On came the dashing Mexican cavalry, shouting their war cry of "God and Liberty" and charging a battery commanded by Captain Bragg. The Mexicans captured some of the guns and drove the soldiers back. Captain Bragg sent a messenger in haste to General Taylor, saying that he must have more men.

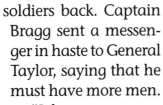

"I have no more men to send you," said Rough and Ready. "Give them a little more grapeshot, Captain Bragg."

The cannons were loaded with grapeshot and fired into the ranks of the enemy, cutting great gaps through them. Again and again

General Santa Anna

they were loaded and fired, and then the fine Mexican cavalry turned and fled. They could not stand any more of Captain Bragg's cannon shot.

That night both armies went to sleep on the field of battle. When the next day dawned, however, the Mexicans were gone. Santa Anna had led them away during the night and General Taylor had won the greatest victory of the war. He received a noble reward for it, for the following year he was elected President of the United States.

The next thing done in this war was an attempt to capture Mexico City, the capital of the country. The easiest way to get there was by sea, for it was a long journey by land from the United States. A fleet was prepared and an army sent south on the Gulf of Mexico. This army was led by General Winfield Scott, who had fought against the British in the War of 1812.

Onward they sailed till they came to the seaport city of Veracruz. This had a strong fort which was battered for four days by the American cannons, until its walls were so shattered that the Mexicans gave it up. In this way, a good starting point was gained.

I would have you all know, however, that the Americans had no easy road before them. Mexico City lies in the center of the country on land that is as high as many mountains. The way to it from the coast goes steadily upward and has many difficult passes and rough places, where a small force might stop an army.

General Scott's Campaign

If the Mexicans had known their business and had a few good generals, I am afraid the Americans might never have marched up this rugged road. The Mexicans had men enough, but they lacked good leaders. At one

General Winfield Scott's campaign in Mexico from Veracruz on the coast to Mexico City

General Sam Houston, Legendary Hero

On March 2, 1793, Samuel Houston was born near Lexington, Virginia, and was raised by his mother in Tennessee. As a youth he spent much of his time with Cherokee Indians and became their good friends. When he was twenty years old, he joined the army and served under Andrew Jackson in the Creek wars. In 1818, Houston resigned his post, was elected attorney general in Nashville, and was appointed head of the Tennessee militia. He served two terms in Congress (1823-27) and in 1827 was elected governor of Tennessee.

On January 1, 1829, Houston married Eliza Allen, but the marriage quickly came to an end. The scandal of his failed marriage forced him to resign his office. For the next six years he lived with Cherokees in the Indian Territory (now Oklahoma), where he took a Cherokee wife named Tiana Rogers. He became a Cherokee citizen and was chosen to represent the tribe to the U.S. government on several occasions.

It was as a tribal representative that he first went to Texas, which was then under Mexican rule. In 1832, he tried to secure a land grant for the tribe but failed. By 1835, Houston had moved to Texas. That same year, the Texan Revolution broke out and he was named commanding general of their army. In March 1836, Houston became a delegate to the convention which declared Texas an independent republic. Then on April 21, 1836, General Houston led the Texan army to a brilliant victory over Santa Ana in the Battle of San Jacinto.

Houston served as the first president of the new republic from 1836 to 1838. In 1840, Houston married Margaret Lea, who persuaded him to stop his drinking habit and join the Baptist church. The following year, he was elected to a second term as president. After the United States annexed Texas in 1845, he was elected to the U.S. Senate, where he served for eight years. In the Senate, Houston was known as a staunch Unionist and friend of the Indians. In 1859, he became unhappy that Texas seemed to be moving toward leaving the Union, so he successfully ran for governor as an independent Unionist. Despite his efforts, however, the people of Texas voted to leave, and he was forced out of office in March 1861. Sam Houston, one of the most interesting persons in America during the nineteenth century, died at his home in Huntsville on July 26, 1863.

terfere with the operation of state governments. Many historians call this the argument over "State's Rights."

Another troublesome issue that divided the states was that of slavery. In many respects, the problem of slavery was not a new issue, but it would not go away. When our country was founded, the issue of slavery was never

Although most farmers in the South did not own slaves, the large plantation owners found it difficult to function without slave labor.

dealt with properly. As a result, slavery continued to be a source of friction between the American people. Few Americans in the North or South were very fond of slavery. The largest industries in the South prior to 1860, however, were cotton and tobacco. Both of these crops required a large amount of inexpensive hand labor to make them profitable. For this reason, many Southern leaders and successful plantation owners were not eager to move away from the use of slave labor until a better system could be developed.

Many people in the South did not own slaves, but they knew how quickly the Southern economy and standard of living would be damaged if the Northern politicians forced Southern farmers to immediately free their slaves. Most Americans in the South

became upset because they felt that politicians in the North were using the issue of slavery as an excuse to impose further restrictions upon the Southern states. Many newspapers in the North began calling the political leaders in the South cruel and backward because they refused to promptly abandon the practice of slavery. This made many Southerners angry and, in their pride and stubbornness, less willing than ever before to work toward a solution to the problem of slavery.

Some of my readers may be curious to know why slavery was, for the most part, done away with in the Northern states by 1860. The reason is primarily that Northern businessmen did not need slave labor to operate their stores and factories because they made much greater use of the new machines that cut down the amount of hand labor that was necessary to complete a job. In other words, businesses in the North used improved tools and machines to make things for sale, instead of relying on large numbers of people to complete their tasks. It was very difficult, therefore, for leaders in the North to comprehend why it was so difficult for Southern farmers to move away from the use of slave labor on their large plantations.

In the end, most Southerners believed that the real trouble that existed between the North and South was their differing views on the proper role of the federal government in Washington, D.C. If the Southern states would not be able to have the authority to solve their own unique problems, in a manner and time that was beneficial to their people, then they thought that they were little more than slaves to the central government. The politicians in the South began to openly talk about their desire to leave the United States to form a new country where the central government would exist only for the benefit of each sovereign state.

The Election of 1860

During this time of confusion and bitterness in the Congress of the United States and throughout the nation, the time came for the American people to elect a new President. Two men from the state of Illinois were the leading candidates for the office of President. Mr. Stephen

Abraham Lincoln

Douglas was a well-known politician who represented the Democratic political party. This party stressed keeping the Union together along strict Constitutional lines while continuing to work on the problem of slavery over time. The other candidate, Mr. Abraham Lincoln, represented a new political group called the Republican Party. This party spoke much more openly about challenging the South on the issue of abolishing slavery as soon as possible. The Republicans were also more interested in expanding the role of the federal government in the future.

In November of 1860, the presidential election took place and the winner was Abraham Lincoln. The people in the South were very surprised and disappointed. Candidate Lincoln's name did not even appear on the election ballots in most of the Southern states. His election was viewed by many Southern leaders as a vote for a strong central government and

against the independence and authority of state governments. It was also widely believed that a Republican president would be unwilling to seriously consider the special economic interests that many Southern states thought were vitally important to their survival. For years, politicians from the South had been fighting the North with words in congressional meetings. Now they were determined to leave the Union and to fight if the Northern states would not let them leave in peace.

One by one, many of the Southern states passed resolutions to withdraw from the United States. Very soon, both sides began to quickly train soldiers and collect rifles and weapons of war. Most of the Southern states formed a new nation, which was called the Confederate States of America. They set up their capital at the city of Richmond, Virginia, and elected Jefferson Davis as their first President.

War Breaks Out

The leaders in the North refused to recognize the right of the Southern states to leave the Union. President Lincoln notified the Southern states that he would continue to resupply the federal forts that were located in the states that were part of the new nation known as the Confederate States of America. This decision angered the leaders in the Confederate States and they decided to stop Northern naval forces from invading their country for the purpose of resupplying the military garrison at Fort Sumter, South Carolina. The South Carolina militia fired on Ft. Sumter to ensure that their country would no longer have a foreign military power on their territory, and this act was regarded by the United States government as an act of war.

When the War Between the States broke out, we had only thirty-three states. Eleven of these states tried to leave the Union and twenty-two remained, so that the Union states outnumbered the Confederate ones. In addition, the Union states had more than twice the people and had ten times the wealth, so that,

Fort Sumter

as you will see, the war was a one-sided affair. It was nearly all fought in the South, and these people suffered greatly for their attempt to leave the Union. Many of them lost all they had and became very poor during their war for independence.

There were three areas or regions in which this war took place. One of these was a narrow region lying between Washington and Richmond, the two capital cities. Small as it was, however, the greatest battles were fought there. Both sides were fighting fiercely to save their capitals.

The second region of the war was in the West. This was a vast region, extending from Kentucky and Missouri down to the Gulf of Mexico. Here there were many long, weary marches and much hard fighting and great loss of life. The third region was on the ocean and rivers, where iron-clad ships first faced off and where some famous battles took place.

Over these three regions more than two million men struggled for years, fighting with rifle and cannon, with sword and bayonet, killing and wounding one another and causing no end of misery in all parts of the land. The people at home suffered as much as the men on the battlefield, and many mothers and sisters were heartbroken when word came to them that their dear sons or brothers had been shot down on the field of battle. War is a very terrible thing upon the earth, though men try to make it look like a pleasant show with their banners and trumpets and drums.

As soon as the news of the war came, there was a great coming and going of soldiers, beating of drums, fluttering of banners, and making of speeches. Thousands marched away, some to Washington and some to Richmond, and many more to the strongholds of the West. Mothers wept as they said good-bye to their sons whom they might never see again. Moreover, many of the soldier boys had sad hearts hidden by brave faces. Soon hundreds of these poor fellows were falling dead and wounded on fields of battle, and then their people at home had good reason to weep and mourn.

The War in the East

The first great battle of the war took place near Manassas, Virginia, just south of Washington. Here the Southern army gained the victory, and the people of the South were full of joy. Congress, however, then called for half a million men and voted half a billion dollars for war aid. Both sides saw that they had a major war before them.

The first big battle at Manassas or Bull Run was the only severe battle in 1861, but in 1862

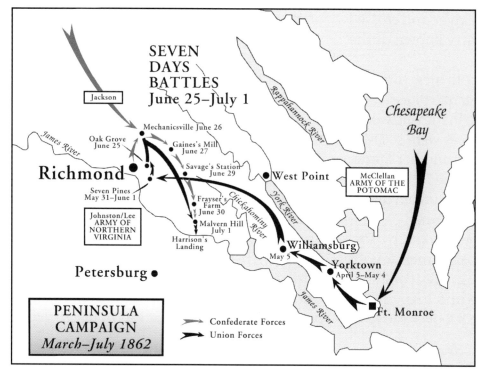

SEVEN
DAYS
BATTLES
June 25–July 1

Jackson

Mechanicsville June 26

Oak Grove
June 25

Gaines's Mill
June 27

James River

Richmond

Savage's Station
June 29

West Point

McClellan
ARMY OF THE
POTOMAC

Seven Pines
May 31–June 1

Frayser's
Farm
June 30

Chickahominy River

York River

Chesapeake
Bay

Rappahannock River

Johnston/Lee
ARMY OF
NORTHERN
VIRGINIA

Malvern Hill
July 1

Harrison's
Landing

Williamsburg
May 5

Petersburg

James River

Yorktown
April 5–May 4

Ft. Monroe

PENINSULA
CAMPAIGN
March–July 1862

→ Confederate Forces
→ Union Forces

both the North and the South had large armies, and there was hard fighting in the East and the West.

I must tell you first of the fighting in Virginia. General George B. McClellan was in command of the Union army there. In the Spring of 1862, he led it close to Richmond, which he hoped to capture. There was a sharp fight at a place called Fair Oaks, where General Joseph Johnston, the Confederate general, was wounded. General Robert E. Lee took his place. The Confederate army could not have picked out a better man, for he proved himself to be one of the greatest soldiers of all times.

The Confederates had another fine general named Thomas J. Jackson. He was called Stonewall Jackson, because, in the Battle of Bull Run, someone had said:

"Look at Jackson! There he stands like a stone wall!"

General Lee and Stonewall Jackson were not men to keep quiet. In a short time they drove McClellan back after a hard fight lasting a whole week and then made a sudden march to the north. Here was another Union

army on the old battlefield of Bull Run. A dreadful battle followed; men fell by the thousands. In the end, the Union army was defeated and forced back towards Washington.

General Lee knew that he could not take Washington, so he marched away north in September, waded his men across the Potomac River, and entered the state of Maryland. This was a slave state and he hoped many of the people would join his army. The farmers of Maryland, however, loved the union too well for that, so General Lee brought very few of them into his ranks.

Then he went west, followed by General McClellan, and at a place called Sharpsburg (Antietam) the two armies met. The bloodiest battle of the war was fought there. They kept at it all day long and neither side seemed beaten. That night, however, General Lee and his men waded back across the Potomac into Virginia, leaving McClellan master of the field. There was one more terrible battle in Virginia that year. General Burnside, who now commanded the Union army, tried to take the city of Fredericksburg in December 1862, but was defeated and his men driven back with a dreadful loss of life.

Spring of 1863

Both armies now rested until the spring of 1863 and then another desperate battle was fought. General Hooker had taken General Burnside's place and thought he also must fight a battle. He did not care, however, to try Fredericksburg as Burnside had done, so he marched up the river and crossed into a rough and wild country known as the Wilderness.

General Lee hurried there to meet him and the two armies came together at a place called Chancellorsville. They fought in the wild woods where the trees in some places were so thick that the men could not see one another. Stonewall Jackson, however, marched to the left through the woods and made a sudden attack on the right wing of the Union army.

This part of the army was taken by surprise and driven back. Hooker's men fought all that day and the next, but they could not recover from their surprise and loss, and in the end they had to cross back over the river again. General Lee had won another great victory. Stonewall Jackson, however, was wounded and soon died, but General Lee would rather have lost the battle than to have lost this hard-fighting soldier.

It would seem that the North had a right to feel very discouraged in heart by this time. The war had gone on for two years, and the Union army had been defeated in all the great battles fought in Virginia. The only victory won was at Sharpsburg (Antietam) in Maryland. They had been beaten at the two battles of Bull Run, the Seven Days' fights at Richmond, and the battles of Fredericksburg and Chancellorsville, and the Battle of Sharpsburg had been won with great loss of life.

EMANCIPATION PROCLAMATION
January 1, 1863

Whereas, on the twenty-second day of September, in the year of our Lord one thousand eight hundred and sixty-two, a proclamation was issued by the President of the United States, containing, among other things, the following, to wit:

"That on the first day of January, in the year of our Lord one thousand eight hundred and sixty-three, all persons held as slaves within any State, or designated part of a State, the people whereof shall then be in rebellion against the United States, shall be then, thenceforward, and forever free; and the Executive Government of the United States, including the military and naval authority thereof, will recognize and maintain the freedom of such persons, and will do no act or acts to repress such persons, or any of them, in any efforts they may make for their actual freedom.

"That the Executive will, on the first day of January aforesaid, by proclamation, designate the States and parts of States, if any, in which the people thereof respectively, shall then be in rebellion against the United States; and the fact that any State, or the people thereof, shall on that day be in good faith represented in the Congress of the United States by members chosen thereto at elections wherein a majority of the qualified voters of such State shall have participated, shall in the absence of strong countervailing testimony, be deemed conclusive evidence that such State, and the people thereof, are not then in rebellion against the United States."

... And I hereby enjoin upon the people so declared to be free to abstain from all violence, unless in necessary self-defence; and I recommend to them that, in all cases when allowed, they labor faithfully for reasonable wages.

And I further declare and make known, that such persons of suitable condition, will be received into the armed service of the United States to garrison forts, positions, stations, and other places, and to man vessels of all sorts in said service.

And upon this act, sincerely believed to be an act of justice, warranted by the Constitution, upon military necessity, I invoke the considerate judgment of mankind and the gracious favor of Almighty God.

In witness whereof, I have hereunto set my hand, and caused the seal of the United States to be affixed.

Done at the city of Washington, this first day of January, in the year of our Lord one thousand eight hundred and sixty-three, and of the Independence of the United States of America the eighty-seventh.

Abraham Lincoln

The War in the West

I wish to say just here that the people of the North took the defeats in Virginia better than you would think. They had good reason not to be discouraged, for while they had been losing battles in the East, they had been winning battles in the West—so one victory helped to make up for the other. If you will follow me now to the West we will see what was taking place there.

The North did not have to change its generals as often in the West as in the East, for it soon found a good one and the Union was wise enough to hold on to him. This was General Ulysses S. Grant, one of the greatest generals in the history of the world.

Grant was only a captain at first. Then he was made a colonel and was soon raised to the rank of general. He met the Confederates first at Belmont, Missouri. Here he was defeated and had to take his men aboard river boats to get them away. That was his first and nearly his last defeat.

The Confederates had built two strong forts in Kentucky which they named Fort Henry and Fort Donelson. General Grant marched against them with an army, and Commodore Foote steamed against them with a fleet of iron-clad steamboats. Fort Henry was taken by the fleet before Grant could get to it. Then he marched across country to Fort Donelson on the Cumberland River. He attacked this fort so fiercely that the Confederates tried to get out of it but did not succeed. They proposed to surrender and asked him what terms he would give them.

"No terms except an immediate and unconditional surrender," he said. "I propose to attack your fort immediately."

General Ulysses S. Grant

This settled the matter. They surrendered, fifteen thousand in all. After that, many said that U. S. Grant stood for "Unconditional Surrender" Grant.

I cannot tell you about all the fights that took place in the West, but there was one terrible battle at a place called Pittsburgh Landing (Shiloh). It lasted two days, and Grant was very nearly defeated. There was another severe battle at Murfreesboro on the last day of the year and another one three days afterwards. Grant was not there, but Bragg, the Confederate general, was defeated in these two battles.

The Confederates had an important stronghold on the Mississippi River at the city of Vicksburg, where they had many forts and a large number of cannons. General Sherman tried to capture these forts but was driven back. Then General Grant tried it and found it a very hard task.

The country was all swamp and creeks which no army could get through, so Grant at last marched south on the other side of the river, and then crossed over and marched north again. He had to fight every step of the way and live on the food his men could carry, for he was too far from the North. He soon reached the city, however, and began a long siege. The Confederates held out until all their food was gone and until they had eaten up nearly all their horses and mules. Then they surrendered their troops. Twenty-seven thousand men were taken prisoner.

This took place on the fourth of July, 1863, the same day that General Lee would march away from the battlefield at Gettysburg. The North finally had something to cheer about after these important battles.

Gettysburg

Shortly after the fight at Chancellorsville, General Lee broke camp and marched north with the greatest speed. The Union army followed as fast as it could march, for there was danger of Baltimore or even Philadelphia being taken. Both armies kept on until they reached the town of Gettysburg, in eastern Pennsylvania. Here was fought the greatest battle of the war. It lasted for three days, the first, second, and third of July, 1863.

The loss of life on both sides was dreadful. The Confederates, however, lost the most men and lost the battle besides. They tried in vain to break through the Union lines and in the end were forced to retreat. On the fourth of July, General Lee sadly began his backward march, and the telegraph wires carried all through the North the tidings of a great victory. This was the turning point in the war.

I must tell you a short story about the noble Robert E. Lee regarding his actions after the battle of Gettysburg. During the Confederate retreat from Gettysburg, General Lee and his staff came across a group of Northern soldiers who had been wounded during the fighting. One of the wounded men began to shout nasty and ungodly words at General Lee as he rode past. A few moments later, Lee climbed down from his horse and walked up to the angry soldier. In spite of the fact

The first day of fighting around Gettysburg on July 1, 1863 was fierce. Union casualties were heavy in desperate, hand-to-hand fighting.

that Lee had just lost the most important battle of his military career, he decided not to argue with this foolish man or to harm him. Lee simply put his arm on the man's shoulder and said, "Son, I hope you will soon be well, you are in my prayers."

As soon as the big-hearted General rode away, the wounded soldier became so moved by Lee's compassionate words that he began to cry. Robert E. Lee showed this man what it means to live as a Christian and how to "love your enemies."

The War Between the States would grind on for two more years before the Confederate states would admit defeat and be forced to re-enter the Union.

After the Confederate defeat at Gettysburg, General Lee comforted a wounded Union soldier in spite of the fact that the soldier had been cursing him.

General Robert E. Lee

Chapter 21 Review Questions

1. How many states were in the Union at the outbreak of the Civil War?

2. Who was the general who commanded the Confederate army at the battle of Sharpsburg (Antietam)?

3. What famous Confederate general was called "Stonewall"? Why?

4. Who was the general who commanded the Union army at the battle of Pittsburgh Landing and Vicksburg?

5. In what state was the battle of Gettysburg fought?

War on Sea and Land 22

I have told you part of the story of how our people fought each other on land. Now suppose we take a look at the water and see how they fought there. Have any of you heard of the battle between the *Monitor* and the *Merrimack*? If you have you will be sure to remember it, for it is one of the strangest stories in the history of war. In the lower part of Chesapeake Bay is an area of water named Hampton Roads, into which the James River flows. Here, in the month of March 1862, lay a fleet of Northern war vessels. These were not the kind of warships which we see today. They were wooden vessels such as were used in former wars but which would be of no more use than floating logs against the great battleships of today.

The *Monitor* vs. the *Merrimack*

Something strange was soon to happen to these ships. On the eighth of March there came into the waters of the bay a very odd

The Monitor vs. the Merrimack, the first naval battle between ironclad ships

looking craft. It was a ship, but instead of a deck it had a sloping roof made of iron. It looked something like a house gone adrift. I think the people in the wooden ships must have been a little scared when they saw it coming, for they had never seen a warship with an iron roof before.

The Northern sailors might well be scared, for they soon found that their cannons were of no more use than peashooters against this strange craft. The cannonballs bounded off her sides like so many peas. On came the iron monster and struck one of the ships, tearing a great hole in its side. Down into the waters sunk the gallant ship with all on board; and there it lay with its flag flying like a flag above a grave. Another ship, the *Congress,* was driven onto mud and had to give up the fight.

There were three more ships in the fleet, but it was now almost night time, and so the *Merrimack,* as the iron monster was called, steamed away. Her captain thought it would be an easy thing to settle with them the next morning, and very likely the sailors on them did not sleep well that night, for they could not forget what had happened to the *Congress* and the *Cumberland.*

As the old saying goes, however, "There is many a slip between cup and lip." The *Merrimack* was to learn the truth of this. For when she came grimly out the next day, expecting to sink the rest of the fleet and then steam up to the city of Washington and perhaps burn that, her captain found in front of him the strangest thing in the shape of a ship he had ever seen. It was an iron vessel that looked like "a cheese box on a raft." All that could be seen was a flat

deck that came just above the water, and above this a round tower of iron, out of which peeped two cannon monsters.

This strange vessel had come into Hampton Roads during the night, and there it lay ready to do battle for the Union. It was a new style of warship that had been built in New York and was called the *Monitor.*

The *Merrimack* soon had enough to keep herself busy and was forced to let the wooden fleet alone. For four long hours these two iron monsters battered each other with cannonballs. Such a fight had never been seen before. It was the first time two ironclad ships had met in war.

I cannot say that either ship was hurt much. The balls could not get through the iron plates and glanced off into the water. The *Merrimack,* however, got the worst of it, and in the end she turned and hurried back to Norfolk to get needed repairs. The *Monitor* waited for her, but she never came out again. Soon afterwards the Confederates left Norfolk and sunk their iron ship, and that was the last of the *Merrimack.*

Other Battles on the Sea

When the news of this wonderful sea fight reached Europe, the kings and ministers of war read it with concern. They saw they had

*The burning of a Northern ship
by the C.S.S. Alabama*

something to do. Their wooden war vessels were out of date, and they started to work in a hurry to build ironclad ships. Today all the great nations of the earth have fleets of steel warships.

All through the war there were battles of ironclads. On the western rivers steamboats were plated with iron. These ships attacked the forts on shore. Along the coast, ironclad vessels helped the wooden ships to block the ports of the South. More vessels like the *Monitor* were built in the North, and a number similar to the *Merrimack* were built in the South. I cannot say that any of them did much good either for the North or South.

One of the greatest naval battles, however, was fought in the Bay of Mobile, on the Gulf of Mexico. Strong forts and a powerful ironclad ship were here. Admiral Farragut sailed into the bay with a fleet of wooden ships and several iron vessels like the *Monitor*. When he went past the forts, he stood in the rigging of his ship with his spy glass in his hand. He did not seem to care anything for cannonballs. He took the forts and since then Farragut has been one of our great heroes.

There was one Confederate privateer, the *Alabama,* which caused terrible loss to the merchants of the North. It sunk sixty-six vessels, which were set on fire and burned. In June 1864, the *Alabama* met the frigate *Kearsarge* near the coast of France, and a furious battle took place. For two hours they fought, and then the *Alabama* sagged down into the water and sank to the bottom of the sea. She had done much harm to the North, but her career was at an end.

The Battle of Lookout Mountain

Now let us turn back to the war on land and see what was going on there. I have told you the story of the fighting up to the great fourth of July, 1863, when Vicksburg surrendered to General Grant, and General Lee marched away from Gettysburg. That is where we dropped the story which we will now take up again.

After Grant had taken Vicksburg and gained control of the Mississippi River, he set out from the town of Chattanooga, which is in Tennessee, just north of Georgia. Here there had been a great battle in which the Confederate army won the victory. The Union troops were shut up in Chattanooga with very little to eat.

Grant was not there long before an important change took place. At first, General Bragg, the Confederate commander, had his army stationed at the top of two mountains named Lookout Mountain and Missionary Ridge. These were defended by strong forts. The Union troops, however, charged up the mountain sides in the face of rifles and cannons and soon had possession of the forts. General Bragg's army was defeated with great loss. This was one of the most brilliant victories of the war. The Battle of Lookout Mountain has been called "the battle above the clouds."

Everybody now saw that General Grant was the best general on the Union side, and President Lincoln made him commander in chief of all the armies in the field. Grant at once laid his plans to have the armies all work together. General Sherman was left in command of the army of the West, and Grant came to Virginia to fight General Lee.

Union Troops Close In

In the green month of May 1864, all the armies were set in motion, and North and South came together for the last great struggle of the war.

Grant led his men into the wilderness where General Hooker and his army had been badly defeated the year before. Lee was there to meet him, and a great battle was fought in the depth of the woods and thickets. It lasted two whole days but neither side won.

Then Grant marched towards Richmond, and Lee hurried down to head him off. Several hard battles were fought, the last being at Cold Harbor, near Richmond. Here the Union army lost a battle and ten thousand men were killed and wounded, while the Confederates, who were behind strong wooden walls, lost only a thousand.

General Grant saw he could not reach Richmond that way, so he crossed the James River and began a siege of both sides, digging in-

stead of fighting till great heaps of earth were thrown up. Grant's men put hundreds of cannons on top of these small hills.

General Grant kept his men very busy, as you may see. General Sherman's men were just as busy, though. He marched south from Chattanooga and fought battle after battle until he had gone far into Georgia and captured the important city of Atlanta. General Hood, the Confederate commander, then made a rapid march to Tennessee, thinking that Sherman would follow him. Sherman, however, did not move. The brave General Thomas was there to take care of Hood and his army.

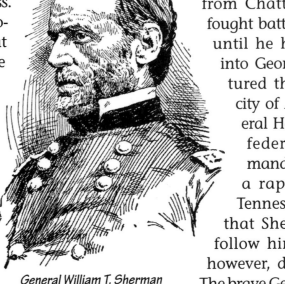
General William T. Sherman

"Let him go; he couldn't please me better," said Sherman.

What Sherman did was to cut loose from the railroads and telegraphs and march his whole army into the center of Georgia. For a whole month the people of the North heard nothing of him. His 60,000 men might be starving for food, or might all be killed, so far as they knew. It was November when they started, and it was near Christmas when they were heard of again.

They had lived off the country and destroyed railroads and farms, and at length they came to the sea at the city of Savannah. Three daring scouts made their way in a boat down the river by night and brought to the fleet the first news of Sherman's march. Perhaps you have heard the song "Marching through Georgia." That was written to describe Sherman's mission to destroy and punish Confederate civilians and their property.

Lee Surrenders

The South was now getting weaker and weaker, and most men saw that the war was near its end. It came to an end in April 1865. Grant kept moving south until he marched past the Confederate earthworks at Petersburg, and Lee was forced to leave Richmond in great haste.

The Union army followed as fast as it could march, and the cavalry rode on until it was ahead of the Confederates. Then General Lee saw that he was surrounded by an army far stronger than his own. He could fight no longer. His men were nearly starved. To fight

Christin the Camps

America, during the time of the 1860s, was a religious land. The existence of the Civil War did not change that fact. As Abraham Lincoln stated in his Second Inaugural Address, "Both [sides] read the same Bible, and pray to the same God...." During the war, Christians in both the North and South were active in ministering to the troops of the Union and Confederate armies.

Most regiments had chaplains from their home states. These chaplains would often work with the troops to organize chapel services and Sunday schools, and their preaching tended to be focused on the spiritual needs of the soldiers. Churches were also active with the troops. The Presbyterian Church (USA), for example, estimated that by the end of the war it had distributed Christian literature to more than 700,000 Union soldiers, and had worked with injured men in hospitals and with Confederate prisoners of war.

In addition to chaplains and churches, volunteer societies were active with the armies. The YMCA founded the United States Christian Commission as a ministry to the military, providing Christian literature, emergency supplies, and wholesome activities for Union soldiers and Confederate prisoners of war. Eventually, more than 5,000 volunteers, including Dwight L. Moody, worked with the Christian Commission; many worked close to the front lines in hospitals, horse-drawn food wagons, and chapels. Already existing tract and Bible societies also worked with the Union and Confederate armies, providing Bibles and tracts for the troops.

Many Union and Confederate leaders encouraged the work of the Gospel among

the armed forces. Several Confederate generals such as Robert E. Lee, J. E. B. Stuart, and Stonewall Jackson, were godly examples to their men. General Jackson was particularly active among his men, encouraging godly activities, occasionally distributing gospel tracts, and preaching the Word of God from time to time. In the Union army, General McClellan provided a good example by attending worship services and declaring that the army should observe the Sabbath as often as possible. President Lincoln endorsed the work of the Christian Commission and also sought to promote the Christian Sabbath by ordering "...that Sunday labor in the Army and Navy be reduced to the measure of strict necessity."

The work of the gospel among the troops bore much fruit. Revivals were common in both armies, and many soldiers were prepared to meet their Maker on the battlefield. Spiritual revival was particularly noticeable among the Confederate forces toward the end of the war. These conversions were so famous that Chaplain J. William Jones, who served with the Army of Northern Virginia, wrote a book entitled *Christ in the Camp*.

The murder of President Lincoln at the Ford Theater by John Wilkes Booth

would be to have them all killed, so on the ninth of April he gave up his sword to General Grant, and the long and bloody war was ended a short time later.

No one was more happy about this victory than President Lincoln, who had done so much to bring it about. His happiness, however, was not long to be enjoyed. Poor man! Five days afterwards, he was shot in a theater in Washington by an actor named John Wilkes Booth.

Booth was pursued and killed, but his death could not bring back to life the murdered President. It was a terrible crime, and it turned the joy which the Northern people felt at the end of the war into the deepest sorrow and grief.

Chapter 22 Review Questions

1. What were the names of the two iron-plated ships that faced each other in March 1862?

2. How many vessels did the *Alabama* sink?

3. Who did Lincoln appoint as commander-in-chief of the Union armies?

4. Which army won the War Between the States?

5. What happened to President Lincoln at the end of the war?

The Wealth of Peace 23

Let us suppose that the history of the whole world is spread out before us like a picture and that we are looking down on it. What do we see? Well, we see places where God has dealt like a terrible storm that has swept over the nations in judgment leaving only darkness and ruin in its track. We also see other places where God has poured out His mercy and blessing on the peoples of the earth and they have prospered. Some of the dark places represent war; some of the bright places stand for peace. All throughout history there have been times when men have gone out to kill and burn and do all the harm they could; there have been other times when they have stayed at home to work and build up what war had cast down. It is only by the grace of God, however, that meaning and happiness has been granted to the nations through the gospel.

In the picture of our own history, we see such dark and bright places. One of the darkest of them all was the terrible War Between the States, the story of which you have just read. In this war, our people fought against and killed one another. All the harm was done at home instead of in foreign lands. The war was a dreadful one. Hundreds of thousands of our people were killed or wounded. Houses, barns, and factories were burned, railroads were torn up,

ships were sunk, growing crops were trampled into the earth. As Robert E. Lee so properly stated, "It is a good thing that war is such horrible business, or we would grow to like it too much."

The Reign of Peace

Now, if we look again at the picture of our history, we shall see a great, bright space of peace following the dark space of war. That is what I wish to tell you about now—the reign of peace, when everybody was busy at work building up what had been torn down by the cruel hand of war. Our country grew faster than it had ever grown before.

When the war was done, the soldiers marched back to their homes. Their old battle flags, twisted and torn by bullets, were put away as valued treasures. Their rusty rifles, which had killed thousands of men, were now used for hunting. They took up their axes and they went into the fields with their plows. They entered the workshops with their tools, and soon they were all at work again as if they had never seen a field of battle.

During your short lives there has been no war which has come near to us in our homes. By the grace of God, plenty and prosperity have been the rule. None of our young folks have known what it is like for an army of soldiers to march past their homes, destroying and burning and leaving ashes and ruins where there had been happy homes and fertile fields. In our past history, however, this happened to many as young as you, and they were glad that their lives were not lost after everything else was gone.

Let us put the thought of war out of our minds and go on to see what took place under the blessed reign of peace. The first thing of which I shall tell you was one of the most wonderful of all. Have I told you the story of

Professor Morse and the first telegraph line? Perhaps you know how the telegraph wires spread over the country until they were many thousands of miles in length. In the year 1866, a still greater thing was done. A telegraph cable was laid under the ocean from Europe to America. This had been done before, but it had been a failure. The new cable was a success, and at that time a man in London was able to talk with a man in New York as if he were a hundred yards away. Of course, I do not mean with his voice, but with the click of the telegraph instrument. Now we have the telephone which is many times more amazing, for with it we can talk to people far away with our voices.

America Grows Up

During the year 1867, a great addition was made to the United States. There was a large region in the north, known as Russian America, which Russia offered to sell to this country for seven million dollars. Many people talked about this as their forefathers had done about the Louisiana Purchase. They said that it was a land of ice and snow, that Russia wanted to get rid of it, and that it would be of no use to anybody. It was bought, however, for all that money, and it has proven to be a very good bargain.

This country we now call Alaska. In 1959, Alaska became our nation's forty-ninth state. We get fresh and canned salmon from Alaska, which some of you think is very good food. We also get some of our country's oil supply from Alaska. That country is rich in furs, fish, and timber; and that is not all, for it is rich in gold. Millions of dollars in gold are obtained there every year. It has been something like California, whose gold was not found until Americans traveled there to dig in the mid-nineteenth century.

These are not the only things that took place in the years after the War Between the States. Railroads were built in all directions. East and west, north and south they went. Therefore travel became easier than it had been before. The greatest thing done at this time was the building of a railroad across the plains and mountains to San Francisco, on the far Pacific coast, three thousand miles from the Atlantic shores. Before that time men who wanted to go to California had to drag along over thousands of miles in slow wagon trains and spend weeks and months on the road. Now they could go there in less than a week. It was the longest railroad that the world had ever seen up to that time. Now we can cross our continent in hours instead of days with the invention of the airplane. We will talk about the airplane and the automobile in later chapters.

While all this was going on, people were coming to the United States in great multitudes, crossing the ocean to find new homes in our happy land. They did not have to come in slow sailing ships, as in former times, but were brought here in swift steamships that crossed the seas as fast as the iron locomotive crossed the land. All these new people went to work, some in cities and some in the country, and they all helped to make our nation rich and powerful.

Great Disasters

You must not think, however, that everything went well and that we had no dark days. Every country has its troubles, even in times of peace. War is not the only trouble. Great fires break out, storms sweep over the land, earthquakes shake down cities, and many

The Great Chicago Fire of 1871

other disasters take place. Of all these things, fire, when it gets beyond control, is the most terrible. In fact, we will now learn about a frightful fire.

About the year 1831, a small fort stood near the shore of Lake Michigan, and around this a few pioneer families had built their homes which were only rude log houses. In 1871, forty years later, the fort and the huts were gone and a large city stood at that place. Its growth had been wonderful. When this city was only forty years old it was already one of the great cities in the country. This was the famous city of Chicago.

One night in October, a dreadful thing took place in this city. According to many accounts, a cow kicked over a lamp in a stable. The straw on the floor took fire, and in a minute, the blaze shot up into the air. The people ran for water, but they were too slow, and in a few minutes, the whole stable was in flames. You may think that this was not so bad, but there happened to be a gale of wind, and soon great blazing fragments were flying through the air and falling on roofs blocks away. It was not long before there was a terrible fire.

Chicago at that time was mostly built of wood, and the fire spread until it looked as if the whole great city would be burnt to ashes. For two days it kept on burning until the richest part of the city had gone up in smoke and flame. Many people were burned to death in the streets and two hundred million dollars worth of property was destroyed. It was one of the most frightful fires in American history. Americans, however, do not stop because of fire or water. The city was built up again far larger than before; and it is now one of the greatest cities not only of this country but of the world.

This was not the only disaster which came upon the country. In 1886, there was a frightful earthquake in South Carolina that shook down a large part of the city of Charleston. Also in 1889, there was a terrible flood that swept away the city of Johnstown, in Pennsylvania, drowning more than two thousand people. There were tornadoes in the west that blew down whole towns as you might blow down a house of cardboard with your breath. Moreover, there were great strikes and riots that were almost like war—not to mention various other troubles. All these, however, could not stop the growth of the country. Every year it became richer. New people came, new factories were built, and new fields were farmed. The United States seemed like a beehive of industry and its people like bees, working away, day by day, and gathering wealth as bees gather honey. Love of God and hard work made America strong.

One of America's Great Inventors

No country ever had so many inventors, and never were there more wonderful inventions. I have told you about some of our inventors; I shall have to speak of some more of them. There were hundreds of men busily at work inventing new machines and tools—new things to help everybody including the farmer, the merchant, the workman in the factory, and

Thomas Alva Edison, one of the greatest inventors who ever lived

the cook in the kitchen. Soon there was very little work done by hand, as in old times, but nearly everything was done by machine.

Some of these inventions were very wonderful. There was the telephone which was not used before 1876, but now people wonder how they ever got along without them. It is certainly very nice when you have to talk with someone far away. The telephone, as I suppose you know, works by electricity. It is only another form of the telegraph. Nearly all the remarkable inventions of recent times have had something to do with electricity. The greatest of the electrical inventors was Thomas A. Edison, a man who has been talked about so much that I really think people once knew his name more than that of the President of the United States.

Edison began inventing as a mere boy, and received most of his schooling from his mother at home. He was an American full of energy and genius. Edison went into business when he was only twelve years old, selling newspapers and other things on the railway cars. He was so smart and did so well that he was able to send his parents five hundred dollars a year. That was a considerable sum in those days. When he was sixteen, he saved the child of a railroad station master from being run over by a locomotive, and the father was so grateful that he taught him how to operate a telegraph. He was very quick and smart, and he soon became one of the best telegraph operators in the United States.

After he grew up, Edison began to invent. He worked out a plan by which he could send two messages at once over one wire. He kept at this until he could send sixteen messages over a wire, eight one way and eight the other. As you probably know, it was a Mr. Bell who invented the telephone, but Edison was the one who made great improvements in it. He also worked and worked for years on making a better electric light, which someone else had invented. He not only made inventions of his own, but he improved those of others. The most wonderful of all Edison's inventions is the phonograph, or "talking-box," by which people could listen to recorded music and the human voice.

The telegraph was used to send messages across America.

Booker T. Washington

Although Booker T. Washington (1856-1915), a lifelong Baptist, was born into slavery, he became known as an educational pioneer and a black leader. As a child, he had to work in the coal mines most of the year and was only allowed to go to school for three months. When he grew older, he diligently worked his way through Hampton Normal and Agricultural Institute, graduating in 1875. Hampton was the first school founded by the American Missionary Association. All throughout his life, Washington was a Christian man who demonstrated Christ-likeness in all that he did.

He is well-known as the founder of the Tuskegee Institute, an Alabama trade school for black Americans. In 1881, he was appointed as its first president. Tuskegee opened with only one teacher, nearly fifty students, and $2,000 a year from the state of Alabama. Twenty-five years later, the school had more than 1,500 students being trained in thirty-seven areas of learning. All this was accomplished under Washington's leadership.

Washington lived during a time when his people were treated very badly, so he encouraged blacks to go to school and learn a trade. In this way, he believed, his people could find good jobs, get established, and then fight for their God-given rights. At the Atlanta Exposition in 1895, he gave a powerful speech which summed up his convictions. He urged blacks to succeed in a white society through self-discipline, a godly lifestyle, and hard work in farming and the mechanical trades. He was asking his people to suffer for a little while as they patiently proceeded along the path toward gaining their full rights. His willingness to work within the limits set by white society has been praised as brilliant by some and condemned as naive by others.

Washington, however, did help his people by raising funds for black causes and in getting blacks appointed to federal jobs. Later, he became an advisor on racial matters to Presidents Theodore Roosevelt and William Howard Taft. He also was a learned author, who wrote, among other books, an autobiography called *Up from Slavery*, which was published in 1901. Washington ended his years as a widely respected Christian educator and leader.

Other Important Inventors

Frank Sprague

Do you know some of the other things which have been done by the aid of electricity? Steel rails were laid, and train cars moved smoothly and swiftly along on them, propelled by something that nobody can see—unless the train's wheel should happen to slip; then one could see something like a little lightning flash on the wire overhead. That was the flash of the electricity in the wire. Can you guess what this invention was called? It was the old-fashioned streetcar, or trolley car, that once was used, like buses are today, in all the big cities of the world.

If I should attempt to tell you about all our inventors I am afraid there would be no end to the story. There is a long line of them, and many of them invented wonderful machines. I might tell you, for instance, about Frank Sprague who built the first modern trolley in the United States in Richmond, Virginia.

Cyrus McCormick

Then there was Cyrus McCormick, who invented the reaping machine. When he showed his reaper at the London World's Fair in 1851, the newspapers made fun of it. *The London Times* said it was a cross between a chariot, a wheelbarrow, and a flying-machine. When it was put in a wheat field, however, and gathered in the wheat far faster than reaping by hand, they changed their tune; in fact, the *Times* said it was worth more than all the rest of the exhibition. This was the first of the great agricultural machines. Since then hundreds have been made, and the old-fashioned, slow, hand work in the fields is over. McCormick made a fortune out of his machine.

I cannot say that of all inventors, for many of them had to go through hard times. For example, both Charles Goodyear and Elias Howe experienced difficulties with their inventions just like Samuel F. B. Morse with his telegraph.

Charles Goodyear

All the rubber goods we have today we owe to Charles Goodyear. Before his time India rubber was of very little use. It would grow stiff in the winter and sticky in the summer, and people said it was a nuisance. What was needed was a rubber that would stand heat and cold, and this Goodyear decided to make.

He tried mixing sulphur with the gum, and by accident touched a red-hot stove with the mixture. To his delight the gum did not melt. Here was the secret. Rubber mixed with sulphur and exposed to heat would stand heat and cold alike. He had made his discovery, but it took him six years more to make it a success. Charles Goodyear never made much money from it, yet everyone honors him today as a great inventor.

Elias Howe

Elias Howe had as hard a time with the sewing machine. For years he worked on it, and when he finished it nobody would buy it or use it. He went to London and had to overcome some serious problems. He had to pawn the model and patent papers of his sewing machine to raise enough money to get home again. His wife was very sick, and he reached home only in time to see her die.

Poor fellow! Life was very dark to him then. His invention had been stolen by others who were making fortunes out of it while he was in need of bread. Friends lent him money and he brought suit against these robbers, but it took six years to win his rights in the courts. In the end he grew rich and gained great honor from his invention.

Henry Ford

Transportation has changed a great deal in just a few years. A man named Henry Ford was the first man to build large numbers of automobiles. In 1910, very few Americans could know the pleasure of driving down the street in a car. Very soon, however, Henry Ford was making thousands of "Model T" automobiles and Americans were able to travel faster and farther than ever before.

In modern times, the automobile has been improved a great deal. Cars today are more sturdy and comfortable than the old "Model T" Fords. Modern automobiles can also travel faster and further than in the days of Henry Ford.

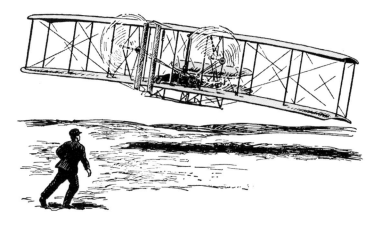

Orville and Wilbur Wright

In addition to the automobile, America gave the world the first practical flying machine. The first successful flying machine, or airplane, was invented by Orville and Wilbur Wright around 1902. The Wright brothers flew their motor-powered plane successfully for the first time at a field called Kitty Hawk. Since then, other inventors have perfected the airplane by making it faster and bigger. Modern airplanes are known as jets and can travel several hundred miles per hour while carrying hundreds of people.

In every way this was a wonderful age of invention. Steam was the most powerful thing which man knew a century ago. Electricity and atomic energy have taken its place as the most powerful and marvelous thing we know today.

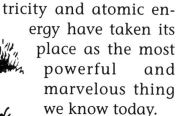

Chapter 23 Review Questions

1. What country sold the land area known as Alaska to the United States?

2. What did we discover in the land of Alaska?

3. What happened to the great city of Chicago in 1871?

4. Who invented the telephone?

5. Who invented the "reaping machine" that was so helpful to farmers?

6. Who invented the mixture that permitted rubber to stay steady and usable in extreme heat and cold?

7. Who invented the phonograph?

8. Who invented the airplane?

How the 19th Century Ended 24

Very likely many of my young readers remember the city of Philadelphia, which was founded by William Penn more than three hundred years ago on the banks of the broad Delaware River, and where now over one and a half million people make their homes. Many of you who do not live there but who love your country and are proud of its history, are likely to go there sometime during your lives, to visit the birthplace of your noble nation.

Have you ever thought that the United States, as an independent nation, was born in Philadelphia? In that city stands the stately Independence Hall, in which the Declaration of Independence was made and signed. You may see there the famous old bell which rang out "Liberty throughout the land!" You may also stand in the room in which our grand Constitution was formed. Philadelphia, therefore, should be a place of interest to all true-hearted Americans, who wish to see where their country was born.

It was such a place of pilgrimage in the year 1876. Then, from every part of our country, from the north, the south, the west and the east, our people made their way in thou-

Centennial Exposition of 1876
Fairmount Park, Philadelphia

sands towards that great city, which was then the center of all American thought. A hundred years had passed from the time the famous Declaration was signed, and the centennial anniversary of this great event was being celebrated in the city which may be called the cradle of liberty.

Great Celebrations

A grand exhibition was held. It was called a World's Fair, for splendid objects were sent to it from all parts of the world, and our own country sent the best of everything it had to show, from Maine to California. On the broad lawns of Fairmount Park, many handsome buildings were erected—all filled with objects of use or beauty. More than ten million people passed through the gates, glad to see what America and the world had to show.

If you wish to know what our own country displayed, I may say that the most striking things were its inventions, machines that could do almost everything which the world wants done. The newest and most wonderful of all these things was the telephone. This magical invention was shown there to the people for the first time, and the first voice shouted "Hello!" over the talking wire.

In the years that followed, centennial

celebrations became common. In 1881, the centennial anniversary of the surrender of Cornwallis was celebrated at Yorktown. In 1882 the bicentennial (the two hundredth anniversary) of the landing of William Penn was celebrated at Philadelphia. A vessel that stood for the old ship *Welcome* sailed up the stream, and a man dressed like the famous old Quaker landed and was greeted by a number of men who took the part of Indian chiefs.

In 1887 Philadelphia had another grand anniversary, that of the signing of the Constitution of the United States, which was celebrated by magnificent parades and processions while the whole city was dressed in red, white, and blue. In 1889 New York celebrated the next grand event in the history of the nation—the taking of the oath by Washington, our first President.

The next great anniversary celebrated the discovery of America by Columbus, four hundred years before 1892. As we learned at the beginning of our story, this event featured a wonderful exposition at Chicago, one of the most beautiful that the world had ever seen. Columbus landed in October 1492, and the buildings were dedicated in October 1892, but the exposition did not take place until the next year. Those who saw this exposition will never forget it. Its buildings were like kings' palaces, so white and grand and beautiful, and at night, when it was lit up by thousands of electric lights, the whole place looked wonderful. The world would not soon see anything more beautiful for many years to come.

I cannot tell of all the expositions. There were others at New Orleans, Atlanta, and other cities, but I think you will be interested in hearing about the large ones. The Centennial at Philadelphia set the pace. After that, cities all over the country wanted to have their great fairs, and many of the little towns had their centennial celebrations, with music and parades, speeches, and fireworks.

America Grows

During all this time, the country kept growing. People crossed the ocean in the millions. Our population went up, not like a tree growing, but like a deer jumping. In 1880, we had 50,000,000 people. In 1900, we had half as many more. Just think of that! Over 25,000,000 people added in twenty years! In 1998, the population was estimated to be 270,900,000. How many people do you think we will have when the youngest readers of this book get to be old men and women? It is a good thing that America is a large country.

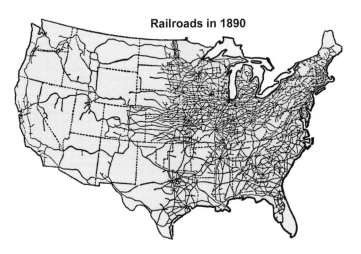

Railroads in 1890

As people increased in number, they spread more widely over the country. Railroads were built everywhere; steamboats ran on all the major rivers; telegraphs and telephones came near to every man's front door; and the post offices spread until letters, newspapers, and packages were carried to the smallest village in the land. The automobile and airplane soon made it possible for people to travel long distances as well. People thought nothing of a journey across the continent or the ocean. Wherever they were, they could talk with their friends by letter, telegraph, or telephone, and they could go anywhere that the newspaper could follow them.

Because of these changes, the wilderness areas of the country began to rapidly fill up. If you have ever seen an old map of our country, you may have noticed places in the

West marked "great desert" or "unknown territory" or by some such name. People made their way into these unknown regions, however, and filled them up. First they went with their families and household goods in great wagons. Then they went far more swiftly in railroad trains. There they settled down and began farming; farther on, where there was not rain enough to farm, they raised cattle and sheep on the rich grasslands; still farther, in the mountain regions, they set to work mining—getting gold, silver, copper, iron, and coal from the hard rocks.

Cities grew up where the Native Americans and the buffalo had roamed. The factory followed the farmer, and the engine began to puff its steam into the air—helping wheels to turn, machines to work, and goods of all kinds to be made. The whole country became like a great hive of industry, where everybody was busy and thousands of people grew rich.

All this great western country, however, was not given up to the farmer, the miner, or the lumberman. There are places which God has made beautiful or grand, and these are kept as places for all the people to visit. One of these is the beautiful Yosemite Valley in California; another is the wonderful Yellowstone Park, with its marvelous springs and geysers; others are the groves of giant trees; still others are great forests, which the

Yellowstone Falls and the Painted Canyon in Yellowstone National Park, Wyoming

government told the lumbermen not to use—all of which have been set aside for the pleasure of all the people of the land. These places are known as national parks.

Some of you may ask, what became of the American Indians, who were spread all over the west? There were hundreds of tribes, and many of these people were bold and brave. When they saw the white men pushing into their country, they fought fiercely for their homeland. They could not stand, however, before the guns of the pioneers and the cannons of the soldiers. In time, they were all forced to submit. Then places were set aside for them, and they were made to live in them. The Native Americans were not always treated well. They were robbed and cheated in a hundred ways, but that, I hope, is all over for now. During the twentieth century, the American Indians were treated with a greater degree of fairness.

The Spanish-American War

Now I have another story to tell. The War Between the States, which you have read about, ended in 1865. For thirty-three years after that, one-third of a century, we were at peace at home and abroad. During this time, our country had the wonderful growth of which you have just read. Then, in 1898, almost at the end of the century, war came again. By God's grace, it was not a big war this time, and it was one I can tell you about in a few words.

It was pity and charity that brought us into this war. South of Florida is the large and fertile island of Cuba which had long belonged to Spain, and whose people had been very badly treated. At length, they said they could stand it no longer, so they took their guns, left their homes, and went to war with the soldiers of Spain. For two years they fought bravely. Their old men and their women and children, who had stayed at home, helped them all they could. Having no pity, the Spaniards drove these people from their homes into the cities and left them there with hardly anything to eat. Thousands of these poor Cubans starved to death.

You may be sure that our people thought this was very wicked. The United States government told the Spanish soldiers to stop their unkind acts. The Spanish, however, would not do what the Americans wished. Then the Americans tried to send food to the starving people. Some of it got to them and some of it was used by others. Everybody in our country felt very badly to see this terrible thing going on at our very doors, and the American government decided that it ought to take some action. What the government did was to send one of its war vessels, the *Maine*, to the harbor of Havana, the capital of Cuba.

Then something took place that would have made almost any country go to war. One dark night, while the *Maine* floated on the waters of the harbor—and nearly all her crew were fast asleep in their berths, a terrible explosion was heard under her, and the good vessel was torn nearly in half. In a minute, she sank into the muddy bottom of the harbor, and hundreds of her sleeping crew were drowned. Only the captain and some of the officers and men escaped alive.

I believe all of you must know how angry our people felt when they heard of this dreadful event. I do not think there were many Americans who did not feel sorry for our poor, dead sailors. Although no one could prove that the Spanish blew up the *Maine*, many American leaders were ready to believe the worst regarding Spain's involvement in the sinking.

War soon came. In April 1898, the Congress declared war against Spain and a strong fleet of warships was sent to Cuba. An army was gathered as quickly as possible, and the soldiers were put on board ship and sailed away to the south. There was a Spanish fleet in the harbor of Santiago de Cuba, and an American fleet outside the harbor kept the ships of Spain inside like prisoners. The soldiers were sent to that place, and it was not long before an

The USS Maine, which had been sent to Havana to protect American interests, blew up at night on February 15, 1898.

army was landed and was marching towards the city of Santiago. I am glad to say that the fighting did not last very long. There was a bold charge up hill by the Rough Riders and others in the face of the Spanish guns, and the Spanish army was driven back to the city. Here they were shut up until they surrendered on July 17, and the fighting in Cuba had come to an end.

The attack on San Juan Hill, an important point near Santiago

The ships in the harbor, however, would not give up—not them; they would go down before that. On the third of July, they made a brave dash to escape destruction, coming out at full speed where the great American ships lay waiting. Soon there was one of the strangest fights that had ever been seen. The Spanish ships rushed through the waters near the coast, firing as they fled. After them came the American ships at full speed, firing as they followed. Not many of the Spanish shells touched the American ships, however, while the great guns of the Americans raked the Spaniards fore and aft.

Soon some of their ships were on fire and had to be run ashore. In an hour or two, the chase was at an end, and the fine Spanish fleet was either sunk or burning—with hundreds of its crew killed. Thankfully, only one man had been killed on the American ships. It was a daring flight and fight, which reminds me of another story of the same kind to relate.

The Battle of Manila Bay

Far away from Cuba on the other side of the world, in the broad Pacific Ocean near the coast of China, is a great group of islands called the Philippines, which had long belonged to Spain. Here, in the harbor of Manila, the capital of the islands, was a Spanish fleet. There was an American fleet in the harbor of the former British colony of Hong Kong along the coast of China, under the command of Commodore George Dewey. As soon as war had been declared, Dewey was ordered to go to Manila and sink or take the Spanish fleet.

Dewey was a man who thought it his duty to obey orders. He had been told to sink or take the Spanish fleet, and that was what he meant to try his best to do. Over the waters sped his ships, as swiftly as steam could carry them, and into the harbor of Manila they went at midnight while deep darkness lay upon the waters. It was early morning of the first of May when the American ships rounded up in front of the city and came in sight of the Spanish fleet. This fleet lay across the

Commodore George Dewey received a cable ordering him to go at once to the Philippine Islands to capture or destroy the Spanish fleet stationed there. On May 1, 1898, the astonished Spaniards saw Dewey's ships in Manila Bay, getting ready for action. The Spanish had more vessels but were no match for the Americans. That May morning Dewey destroyed the Spanish fleet without the loss of a vessel or a man.

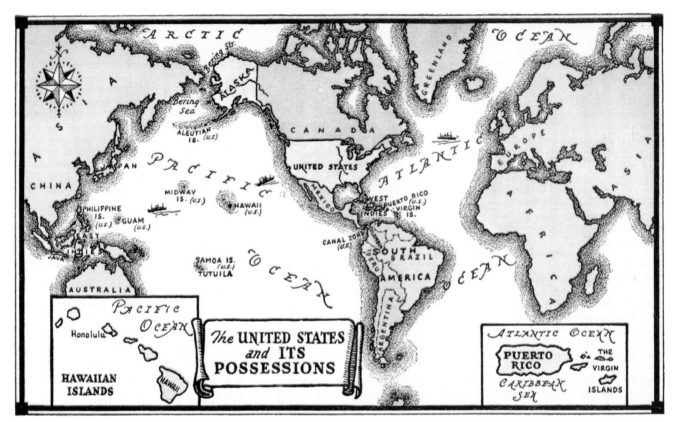

This map of the world shows the United States and its possessions in the early 1900s.

mouth of a little bay, with forts to guard it on the land at each side.

It was a great danger which Commodore Dewey and his bold followers faced. Before them lay the Spanish ships and forts. There were torpedo boats which might rush out and sink them. There were mines under the waters which might send the flagship itself to the bottom. Some men would have stopped and considered what to do, but George Dewey was not that kind of man. Without stopping for a minute after his long journey from China, he dashed on with the fleet and ordered his men to fire. Soon the great guns were roaring and the air was full of smoke and fire.

Round and round went the American ships, firing as they passed. Every shot seemed a direct hit. It was not long before some of the Spanish ships were blazing, while hardly a shell had touched an American hull. After an hour or two of this hot work, Dewey drew out and gave his men their breakfast. Then back

he came and finished the job. When he was done, the whole Spanish fleet was either sunk or burning, with hundreds of its men dead and wounded, while not one American ship was badly hurt and not one American sailor was killed. There had hardly been so one-sided a battle since the world began.

There, I have, as I promised, told you in few words the story of the war. Soon after, a treaty of peace was signed and all was at an end. The brave Dewey was made an admiral and was greatly honored by the American people.

The End of the Nineteenth Century

If you should ask me what we gained from the war, I would answer that we first of all gained freedom for Cuba from the cruel rule of Spain. We, however, did not come out of it without something for ourselves. We obtained the fertile islands of the Philippines in the East Indies. During the war with Spain we obtained another fine group of islands, known as Hawaii, in the Pacific Ocean as well as the islands of Guam and Puerto Rico. In the year 1959, Hawaii became America's fiftieth state. You can see from this that our country spread widely over the Pacific Ocean at the end of the nineteenth century. The winning of all these islands was an event of the greatest importance to the United States. It gave this country a broad foothold on the seas and a new outlook over the earth. Some of the proud nations of Europe had looked on this country as only a local national power with no voice in world affairs. When Uncle Sam, however, set his left foot on the Hawaiian Islands in the Central Pacific, and his right foot on the Philippine Islands near the coast of Asia, these powers of Europe opened their eyes and began to get new ideas about this great republic in the New World. It was plain that the United States was becoming a world power.

This was soon seen to be the case when China began to murder missionaries and try to drive all foreigners from its soil. Thankfully America wants to keep out of war, but sometimes war is impossible to stop, for as long as men are sinners there will be war. Putting down the Boxer Rebellion in China was such a time when war was necessary. For the first time in history, the United States joined with Europe in an Old World quarrel. Peace was restored, the Boxers put down, and China was forced to pay for the damage that had been done. It was clear that the world could not be cut up and divided among the powers without asking permission from Uncle Sam, too.

The Front Porch Campaign

The 1896 presidential election between Republican William McKinley and Democrat William Jennings Bryan was one of great contrasts. Bryan waged a modern campaign, crisscrossing the country traveling 18,000 miles. He was considered one of the world's greatest speakers, giving over 600 speeches during his bid for the presidency. McKinley, on the other hand, conducted a campaign of a different sort. Due to his wife's illness, McKinley spent most of his time campaigning from his front porch in Canton, Ohio. Special trains brought groups of people to Canton to meet McKinley and hear him speak. Over the course of the campaign, he spoke to approximately 750,000 people from his front porch. McKinley's "front porch campaign" eventually proved to be the winner in 1896.

Campaign style was not the only difference between McKinley and Bryan. The Republicans and Democrats differed over the key issue of the day—gold vs. silver money. The Republicans favored using gold as the standard for American money, while the Democrats supported using silver. Bryan was so opposed to the use of gold that, in one of his speeches, he told supporters of the gold standard: "You shall not crucify mankind upon the cross of gold."

In spite of the political differences between these candidates, they shared a common faith in Jesus Christ. William Jennings Bryan was a Bible-believing Presbyterian, who ran for President two more times, served as secretary of state for a while, and finished his life defending the Christian view of man's origin (the truth of creation vs. the theory of evolution) in the Scopes trial of 1925. William McKinley was a faithful Methodist, who served as President during the Spanish-American War. He was reelected in 1900, but was murdered in 1901 and was succeeded by Vice-President Theodore Roosevelt.

Chapter 24 Review Questions

1. In what city did our nation have the major centennial anniversary celebration?

2. What was the population of the United States in the year 1900?

3. List the names of two of our nation's greatest national parks.

4. What nation did the United States go to war against in 1898?

5. In what year, did the islands called Hawaii become one of the United States?

The Wars for World Freedom 25

The United States was fast becoming a world power in the years after 1900. This new role of world leadership resulted in the United States becoming involved in two big wars.

How did the United States become a world power? Was it because of her quick and decisive defeat of Spain in the Spanish-American War? Was it because the United States now had colonies on both sides of the globe? Whatever the reason, the rest of the world was sitting up and taking notice. When President Theodore Roosevelt proudly sent the United States Navy on a spectacular round-the-world cruise in 1907, there were few doubts that the United States had become a world power.

creased. Ships from the United States traded with China, Japan, and India. They also traded in Europe. Many people from the United States toured Europe. They wanted to see the homelands of their ancestors who had come to America.

The U.S Navy's "Great White Fleet" left the United States in late 1907 and returned in early 1909, after touring the world.

America Trades with the World

American businessmen wanted to sell American-made products all over the world. Markets in the continental United States were not enough. New places were needed to sell goods. The strong navy could protect the nation's great merchant fleets, so American business was on the move everywhere in the world.

Trade with countries all over the world in-

The increased trade was profitable, but it presented many problems. Before the year 1900, the United States had consistently tried to keep out of European affairs. In the early days of American independence, Presidents Washington and Jefferson urged the nation to keep out of European wars. Times had changed, however, and the United States could not be a world power and not take part. After 1900, representatives from the United States attended a number of meetings of European

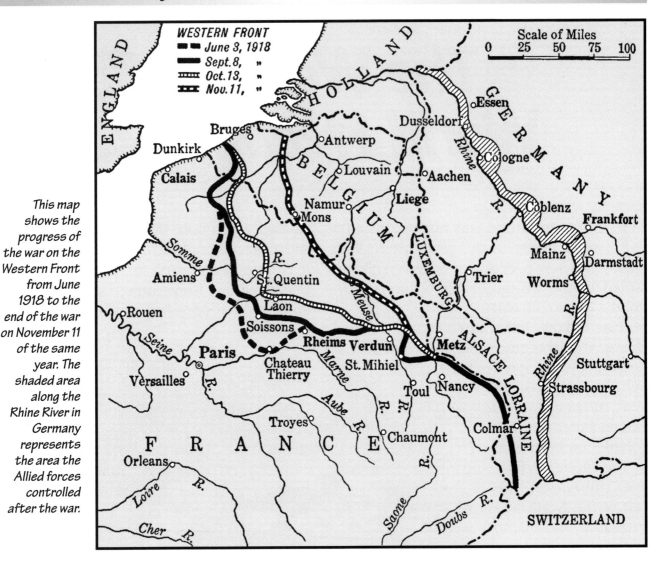

WESTERN FRONT
- - June 3, 1918
—— Sept. 8, „
▥▥ Oct. 13, „
▤▤ Nov. 11, „

Scale of Miles
0   25   50   75   100

This map shows the progress of the war on the Western Front from June 1918 to the end of the war on November 11 of the same year. The shaded area along the Rhine River in Germany represents the area the Allied forces controlled after the war.

powers. Some of these meetings were called "peace conferences," but the world was actually approaching war.

Keeping the peace in Europe was not easy. Too many countries were jealous of one another. No one wanted any nation to become too powerful. To prevent the rise to power of any single nation, alliances were made between countries to balance the power of any country which was becoming too strong.

World War I

Have you ever heard of the "Great War" or the "War to end all Wars"? That is what your great-grandparents might have called World War I when they were young. Well, with all of the wars in the twentieth century,

we know that World War I did not end all wars. And I do not know about you, but I would not call a war that started from the murder of two people, and resulted in the deaths of millions of people particularly great. This war became known as World War I because it eventually involved all of the great powers in the world, and many of the smaller countries as well. Almost every country in Europe participated in the war, with fighting in Europe, Africa, and Asia.

By 1914, many of the world's most powerful countries had separated themselves into one of two groups. On one side were Germany, Austria-Hungary, and Italy—the Triple Alliance. On the other side were Britain, France, and Russia—the Triple Entente.

As I have already mentioned, this terrible war began with the murder of two people—Archduke Franz Ferdinand of Austria-Hungary and his wife—by a Serbian terrorist in the city of Sarajevo. Austria accused the Serbian government of organizing this crime and sought revenge. Austria-Hungary declared war on Serbia on July 28, 1914, beginning a chain reaction that no one seemed able to stop, as each country tried to help its allies. Within days, Britain, France, and Russia, along with a few smaller countries, were at war with Germany and Austria. Italy stayed on the sidelines at first, but switched to the support of Britain and France in 1915, who had become known as the Allies. Later in 1914, Turkey joined Germany and Austria-Hungary—which were by then called the Central Powers.

The SPAD was one of the most successful French fighters in World War I. It was also used by British, Italian, Belgian, and American air units.

lion soldiers and civilians dying during the war. The war was very expensive, costing more than $280 billion dollars in terms of destroyed property and war expenditures. World War I also saw more new weapons invented or developed than any other war in history. Such things as submarines, machine guns, tanks, airplanes, poison gas, high explosives, and quick-firing field artillery came into common use during this destructive war.

America Enters The War

Some of you might be wondering what America did during World War I. At first, the United States remained neutral; we did not fight on either side. Many people in the United States, however, favored Britain and France. They felt that Kaiser Wilhelm II of Germany was trying to set up a world empire. Many people in the United States, therefore, felt that we should help the Allies, who were fighting against the Central Powers. For nearly three years, however, the United States stayed out of the fighting.

The United States was the strongest neutral country in the world. The countries at war wanted food, guns, clothing, and other supplies from America. They

The Fokker Triplane was used by German pilots near the end of the war.

Did you know that World War I was the most terrible war the world had ever seen up to that time? More than 65 million men served in the armed forces of the various countries during the war, with over 14 mil-

borrowed money in this country and purchased supplies.

The British bought more goods and borrowed more money than the Germans and Austrians did. Meanwhile, German submarines were sinking merchant ships bringing supplies to Britain and France. American ships were also sunk and American sailors were killed. Time after time, President Woodrow Wilson warned the Germans that America would go to war if more ships were sunk.

For a time, the sub-marines stopped sinking merchant and passenger vessels. Finally in 1917, however, Germany decided that she had to stop goods from going to her enemies or she would lose the war. After Germany began using its sub-marines to attack American ships again, the United States declared war on April 6.

The United States was unprepared to immediately send troops to fight in France, but quickly began to get ready for war. Training

camps were established, and ships were built. Many soldiers volunteered, and the government also drafted men for military service. Eventually, about two million American soldiers were sent to Europe to help the French and British push the German army out of France. More than a century before, France had helped the United States to win her independence. Now the United States was helping France. When the first United States troops arrived in France, the cry was, "Lafayette, we are here!"

In addition to sending armies to France, the United States sent millions of tons of goods to Europe. American factories produced more than those of any other country in the world. From the United States came guns, tanks, airplanes, and ships, as well as shoes, clothes, and food. Finally on November 11, 1918, the war ended. By the time the war ended, the United States was the strongest nation in the world. Her farms and factories were producing tremendous quantities of goods. Many loans were made to European governments to help rebuild destroyed cities and buildings. Millions of dollars worth of food and clothing were also given to needy people in Europe.

President Wilson had hoped that this war would be the last one. He called it a "war to end all wars." At his suggestion, a new organization was formed called the League of Nations which brought together leaders from many nations. Their representatives met at Geneva, Switzerland, to discuss and settle world problems. The League held many meetings in Geneva, but only had limited success in preserving the peace. In spite of President Wilson's support of the League of Nations, the United States never joined. Many United States senators were afraid that the League of Nations would get the United States involved in unwanted foreign alliances.

Good Times and Bad

A few years after World War I, a young man by the name of Charles Lindbergh made history. Lindbergh was the first person to fly an airplane from the United States to Europe. This wonderful event opened up a new era in world travel. Lindbergh showed the people of the world that the airplane could permit people to travel around the world faster than ever before. The name of the airplane used by Lindbergh in 1927 was the *Spirit of St. Louis*. The *Spirit of St. Louis* is now hanging in a large museum called the Smithsonian Institute located in Washington, D.C.

One day in May 1927, the world was thrilled by the news that Charles A. Lindbergh had flown his monoplane, The Spirit of St. Louis, from New York to Paris without a stop.

The good times lasted for more than ten years after the war. Wages and salaries were high. People bought refrigerators, automobiles, and a new gadget called the radio. Roads were paved and bridges were built as the United States grew and developed.

Many farmers, however, were not doing well. The boll weevil, which had become a menace shortly after 1900, destroyed much of the cotton in the South. In many other parts of the country, the farmers' problems resulted from increased governmental controls. So much wheat, corn, meat, eggs, and milk were produced that the price dropped. The farmers could not sell enough goods to pay for things they needed.

People in the cities did not worry about the problems which the farmers were having. Then in 1929, the prosperity of the United States suddenly collapsed. Overnight, the good times of the 1920s changed to bad times. Factories closed, and workers were without jobs. Stores could not sell the goods which they had on hand. Millions of people were soon without jobs. Banks failed and closed. Many people lost their savings. Soon thousands of families had to be provided with food and clothing. This period is called the Great Depression.

In 1933, when the economic depression was at its worst, Franklin D. Roosevelt became President. He offered the country a "New Deal." The government made jobs for people. Americans were paid to do things like rake leaves or build playgrounds in their towns and cities. Many public buildings were constructed with federal money. The government regulations on banks protected people's savings. These federal government programs and regulations, however, often violated the United States Constitution and undermined the freedoms of individuals and private businesses.

The government did much to help farmers, businessmen, and laborers. Prices were increased on farm products. Money was loaned to companies to build factories. Wages of working people were raised, and working hours were reduced. These efforts gave a temporary lift to our sagging economy.

Confidence, or belief that prosperity would return, now became stronger and stronger. Factories employed more workers. The people bought automobiles, built houses, and purchased other things which they wanted. Young men and women again had funds to go to college. By the end of the 1930s, the United States was recovering from the depression.

Although the government spent a lot of time and money trying to solve the nation's money problems, they also set in motion a dangerous policy in our government. This policy, that encouraged our federal government to spend great sums of money that were not backed up with gold and silver, began the growth of inflation. Inflation is the direct result of government spending more money than it takes in taxes. Inflation robs the people because it makes the money that each citizen earns worth less in terms of buying power. Government spending can never give a nation long-term economic growth because governments must always take from the people more than it can give away.

The Rise of Tyranny

The United States was not the only country which suffered from a depression. European countries also had many problems. In some countries, dictators (powerful oppressive leaders) came into control during this period.

In Germany, Adolph Hitler blamed the Jewish people for Germany's defeat in World War I and her hard times after the war. Eventually, he became dictator of Germany. Hitler's followers, the Nazis, made great promises to the people but provided only war and death. In Italy, a dictator by the name of Benito Mussolini had taken over even before Hitler came to power in Germany. Mussolini's followers were known as Fascists. The two dictators became friends and allies during the 1930s.

In 1917, the Russians had stopped fighting in World War I because their country was in the midst of a revolution. Communists had overthrown the new Russian Republic after Tsar Nicholas II was deposed. The idea of communism was not new. The Russians, however, were the first people to try to organize a communist government for their country. The leaders of the Russian movement said that all farms and factories should be run for the benefit of the workers. The government would own all of the means of production and control all education.

Communist officials explained, however, that there would be some time before the people could actually control the farms and factories. Until all the problems were worked out, the leaders of the Communist Party would have many powers. As a result, Russians—like Germans and Italians—lived under a dictatorship.

During the 1930s, Hitler organized large rallies and made emotional speeches that stirred the patriotic feelings of Germans.

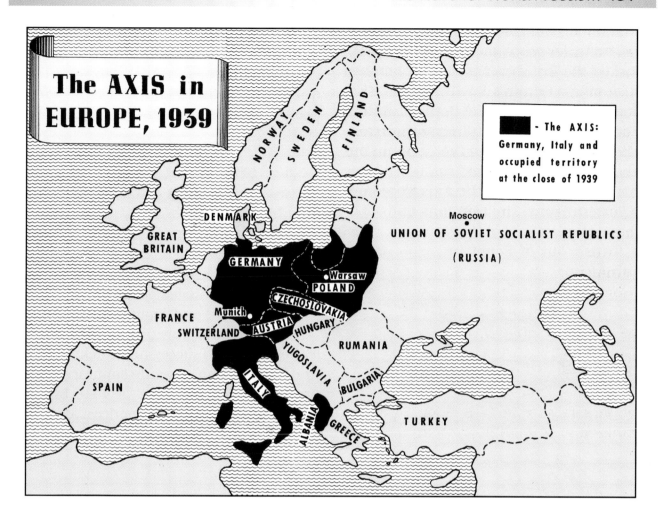

The AXIS in EUROPE, 1939

■ - The AXIS: Germany, Italy and occupied territory at the close of 1939

Germany started building a powerful army. The German people were good workers. Their factories produced more than most countries except for the United States and Russia. The Italians also built up their military forces. To protect themselves from Germany and Italy, other nations in Europe spent large sums of money for their armies and navies. In Asia, Japan invaded China. Japan became an ally of Germany and Italy. The three allies came to be known as the Rome-Berlin-Tokyo Axis.

World War II

As I said earlier, World War I was not the "war to end all wars." The three Axis powers wanted to grab territory. The world went to war again on September 1, 1939, when Germany invaded Poland; Russia joined in the attack on Poland a few days later by capturing eastern Poland in accord with a se-cret treaty with Germany. Germany fired the first shot in the new world war, but other countries quickly followed.

Britain, France, and China opposed the attacks by the Axis nations, but without much success at first. Germany defeated and occupied several countries in Europe, including France, by using new tactics and improved tanks and airplanes. German submarines also sank many ships which were bringing supplies to Britain. In June 1941, Germany and its allies launched a surprise attack on Russia, capturing much of its territory. Things were looking good for Germany in 1941. Look at the map above and you can see what I mean; with the exception of the neutral countries of Sweden and Switzerland, Germany and its allies controlled everything on the continent of Europe from just west of Moscow in Russia to France.

Yet not all was lost. Since Britain refused Hitler's offer for peace, the Germans, in 1940, attacked the British air force and bombed British cities. Britain's Royal Air Force defeated the Germans in the Battle of Britain by destroying over 1,700 German aircraft. In 1941, the Russians kept the Germans out of their capital Moscow and still had a large army that was fighting the Axis troops on the Eastern Front. The Germans and Italians also were not able to force the British out of Egypt in North Africa.

The R.A.F.'s Spitfire fighter was key to winning the Battle of Britain.

America Is Forced to Fight

At first, the United States stayed out of the war. The American people, however, favored Britain, France, and China. Many supplies were sent to help these countries, and the United States declared she would not recognize the Japanese conquests and stopped selling Japan the supplies it would need to continue its war in Asia.

Representatives from Japan came to Washington, but negotiations for peace were unsuccessful. Without warning, Japanese planes bombed Pearl Harbor in the Hawaiian Islands on December 7, 1941. The United States was once more involved in a world war. Our allies were Britain, France, China, and Russia. Our opponents were Germany, Japan, and Italy.

In 1942, things at first were going badly for the United States and its allies. For six months, the Japanese army and navy could not be stopped. They conquered several European and American

The German ME-109 single-seat fighter aircraft was used throughout World War II.

can colonies in Asia and the Pacific Ocean. The Japanese defeated American and Filipino troops and captured the Philippine Islands. German armies and their allies launched successful attacks in Russia and North Africa. German submarines sank many American ships that were bringing needed war supplies to American forces and to our allies.

General Dwight D. Eisenhower, commander of U.S. forces in Europe and commander of the Allied invasions of North Africa and France

Gradually the United States and its allies caught up. Thousands of ships and airplanes were built. Armies were enlarged and strengthened. The American and British navies were able to defeat the German submarines. Allied armies forced the Germans and Italians to surrender in North Africa and invaded Italy. The

Russians also began to recapture their territory. The important job, of course, was to defeat Germany. In 1944, soldiers of the Allied forces led by General Dwight D. Eisenhower landed on the northern coast of France. After many battles, they pushed the Germans out of France and Belgium. In 1945, Germany was invaded from the west by Canadian, British, American, and French armies, and from the east by the Russian army. Germany was

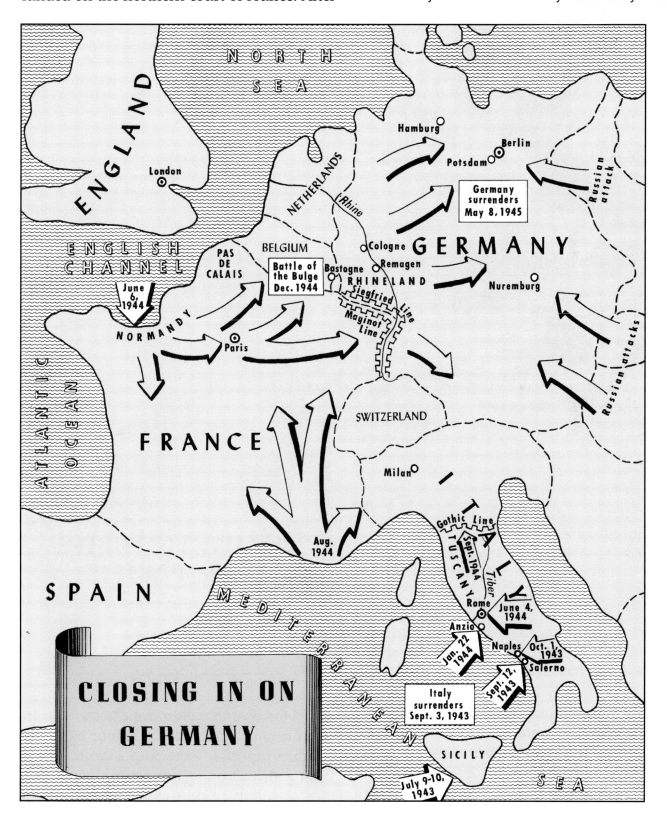

CLOSING IN ON GERMANY

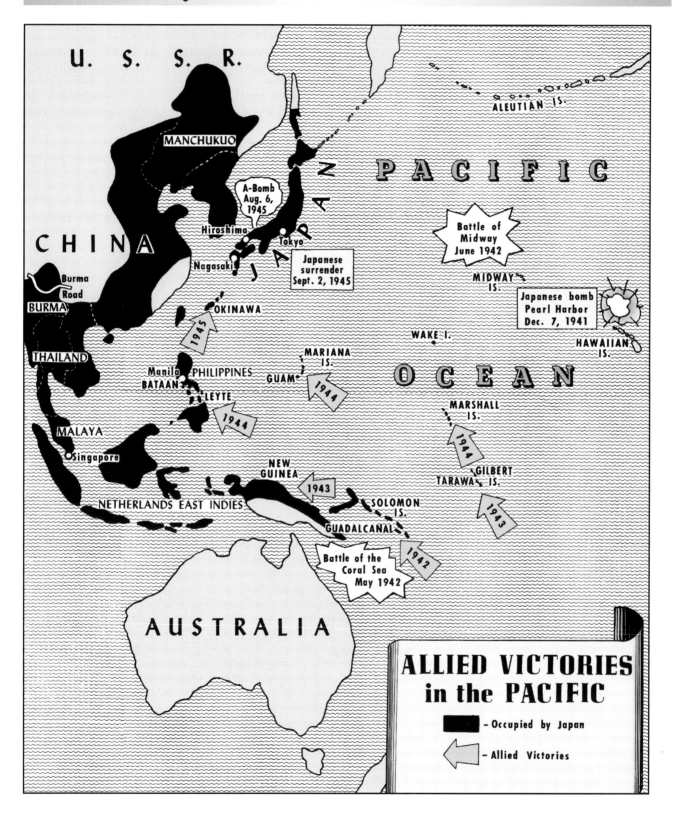

ALLIED VICTORIES in the PACIFIC

- Occupied by Japan

- Allied Victories

defeated after several months of fighting; the German army surrendered in May 1945.

In the Pacific the Japanese were having their own trouble. After stopping the Japanese in an important naval battle, the United States forces under Admiral Chester Nimitz and General Douglas MacArthur began to capture Japanese occupied islands in the Pacific. British and Chinese armies also began to advance against the Japanese in

Burma and China. Eventually, shortly before the end of the war, the Russians attacked the Japanese in China and Korea.

American bombers began to drop bombs on Japan and American submarines sank many Japanese supply ships, but Japan refused to surrender. Finally, in August 1945, the United States dropped a new kind of bomb on Japan. Atomic bombs were dropped on the Japanese cities of Hiroshima and Nagasaki. These bombs were far more powerful than any military weapon ever used before, destroying most of each of these cities. Shortly after the second bomb was dropped, the Japanese surrendered. The age of atomic energy had begun in a sad way.

The Cost of World War II

World War II was worse than World War I. More countries were involved in World War II than any other war. Fighting occurred throughout large areas of Europe, Asia, Africa, and the Pacific. All of the new weapons of World War I—except for poison gas which was never used—were made more deadly. World War II also saw some new weapons—aircraft carriers, missiles and rockets, jet aircraft, and atomic weapons, the most destructive of all.

World War II was the costliest war in all of history. The nations of the world spent at least $1.154 trillion for war materials and weapons. Probably between 15 and 20 mil-

"Praise the Lord and Pass the Ammunition"

The Japanese air attack on the United States naval base at Pearl Harbor in Hawaii on December 7, 1941, was a complete surprise. Without declaring war, the Japanese bombed American ships and airfields, killing 2,400 people, sinking or disabling eighteen ships, and destroying 200 airplanes. In spite of being caught by surprise, American sailors and soldiers fought back as best as they could, shooting down twenty-nine enemy airplanes and sinking five Japanese midget submarines. As President Franklin D. Roosevelt put it, December 7 became a "date which would live in infamy."

Chaplain Howell Forgy of the heavy cruiser *New Orleans* was an example of both surprise and resistance. When the alarm of the Japanese air attack first came early Sunday, this Presbyterian chaplain was busy reviewing his sermon for the morning service. At first, he thought that the alarm was just a practice drill, but soon realized that the attack was real once he saw the burning ships, the firing guns, and the attacking Japanese airplanes.

As a chaplain, Lieutenant Commander Forgy was not allowed to participate in the fighting, or even help carry ammunition to the guns firing at the Japanese planes. He could, however, encourage those involved in the fighting. At first, he was with the doctor in sickbay, but when he was not needed there, he went to bolster the spirits of the men who were carrying the heavy shells by shouting "Praise the Lord and pass the ammunition." Forgy's conduct during the Japanese attack went on to inspire the popular war song, "Praise the Lord and pass the ammunition."

lion military personnel were killed and civilian dead numbered approximately 25 million. All sides attacked cities with bombers, killing many civilians. Of particular horror was the Nazi system of concentration camps, where many captives worked as slaves and died from mistreatment. Some camps even had places specifically designed to put people to death. Christians who opposed Nazi policies were often imprisoned in the camps, where many of them died. No one knows for sure how many died from overwork and intentional killing, but it has been estimated that more than six million Jews, gypsies, Slavs, and others the Nazis did not like were killed in what many call the "Holocaust."

German ME-262 jet fighter

Millions of American men either volunteered or were drafted to serve in the army, navy, marines, and air force, 292,000 of whom were killed during the war. Young women volunteered to serve as nurses, office workers, and car drivers. Food, gasoline, tires, and other goods were so scarce that they were hard to get. To keep prices down during the period of shortages, prices on some goods were fixed by the government.

During the war, leaders of the world powers had begun to plan a new organization similar in purpose to the old League of Nations. The new organization was to be known as the United Nations. Headquarters were established in New York City. The United Nations has failed to stop nations from fighting with one another, and in many respects has proved to advance the cause of communist countries. Many of the communist countries of the world send spies to the United Nations' building in New York in an attempt to undermine our nation's security.

Chapter 25 Review Questions

1. In what year did World War I begin?

2. In what year did the United States declare war on Germany during World War I?

3. Who called World War I "the war to end all wars"?

4. What happened during the Great Depression of 1929?

5. What American President offered the American people a "New Deal" during the Great Depression?

6. In what year did World War II begin?

7. Why did America finally decide to enter World War II?

Two Decades of Change 26

Communist Expansion

After World War II was over, a new threat to the freedom-loving nations of the world was coming into view. A kind of war—called a "Cold War"—developed between communist countries and non-communist countries. A cold war is mostly a war of words between countries who do not agree with each other, although actual fighting may occasionally occur.

The armed forces of the communist Soviet Union had taken over much of Eastern Europe during World War II. The Soviet Union forced communist governments on the countries of Poland, Czechoslovakia, Hungary, Romania, Bulgaria, and eastern Germany. Local communist movements also took over Yugoslavia and Albania. The only country in Eastern Europe to be saved from communist control was Greece. The Greeks were able, with the help of the United States and Great Britain, to defeat a communist rebellion.

Joseph Stalin was the absolute ruler of the former Soviet Union from 1929 to 1953. During his ruthless rule, he killed over 25 million people. His policies in Eastern Europe helped create the Cold War.

The Cold War expanded from Europe, as communists sought to takeover several countries in Asia. After winning a long civil war, communists took over mainland China in 1949—forcing the government and military of the Republic of China to flee to the island of Taiwan where they established their own independent government. Communist-led revolts also occurred in the Philippines and Vietnam.

Communism came to Korea as it did in much of Eastern Europe, through the power of the Soviet army. At the end of World War II, the Americans and Russians freed Korea from Japanese control, with the Russians in northern Korea and the Americans in southern Korea. The hope was that Korea could become a free and democratic nation. Therefore, in 1947, the United States asked the United Nations—a new organization developed near the end of World War II to help the nations of the world meet together and solve their problems without war—to unify the two halves of Korea. The United

Nations agreed to supervise nationwide elections but were not allowed to go into North Korea. Free elections were held in South Korea in August 1948 and the Republic of Korea was established. A month later, the communist-controlled Democratic Republic of Korea was proclaimed in North Korea.

The Korean War

General
Douglas MacArthur

The communists, however, were not satisfied with North Korea alone; they wanted all of Korea. On June 25, 1950, the North Koreans invaded South Korea and by August had almost captured the entire country. The United States soon began to help the South Koreans and asked the United Nations for assistance. Once it became clear that the North Koreans would ignore the United Nations's request to stop their invasion, the United Nations asked its member countries to help South Korea defeat the invasion. Eventually, a total of seventeen countries sent soldiers to fight against the communist invasion of South Korea, under the flag of United Nations, with South Korea and the United States providing most of the troops.

General Douglas MacArthur was the first commander of this United Nations army. He developed the plan that forced the North Koreans to remove their soldiers from the south. By October, the United Nations army began to liberate North Korea from the communists as well. Before North Korea could be freed, however, Communist Chinese troops joined the fighting to save the North Korean com-

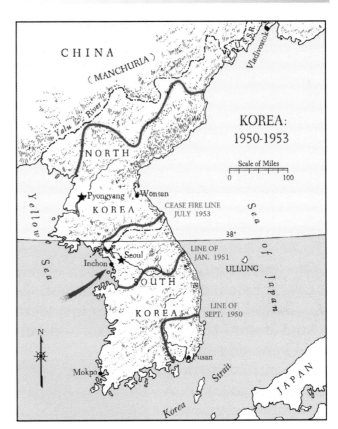

Map showing the progression of the Korean War

munists from total defeat. The war eventually lasted until July 1953, when the nations decided to stop fighting, although a final peace treaty has never been signed. South Korea was saved, but North Korea remained under communist control.

Shortly before the close of the Korean War, the American people elected Dwight D. Eisenhower as President of the United States. Eisenhower held the office of President for two terms, or eight years. During this period, the Cold War between communist and free nations was stable enough that American soldiers did not have to fight in a war. It was a period of relative peace, and the American people turned their attention to solving problems within their own land.

Our Nation Grows

One of the greatest problems in our land, at this time, was racial bigotry. Many people in America who had black, brown, yellow, or red skin were denied the basic rights granted

An interstate highway going through Downtown Los Angeles, California

space. The Russians sent a satellite into orbit around the earth, which they called *Sputnik*. This event encouraged the United States to begin developing its own spacecraft and satellites. It would take until the late 1960s before the United States could send a manned spaceship to the moon and back.

One of the major programs started by President Eisenhower in 1956 was the Federal Highway Act. This act was responsible for starting the largest road building project in American history. These new roads were called interstate highways. The federal government felt that this was a good project for it would help to unite the entire country and would provide jobs for many Americans.

Our federal government, therefore, continued to grow at a slow but steady rate under President Eisenhower. Gradually, our government began to spend great sums of money in

to all Americans under the Bill of Rights. President Eisenhower, along with the United States Congress and the Supreme Court, began to deal with this problem during the late 1950s. It would take, however, several more years before the constitutional rights of all American citizens would be clearly protected.

During the late 1950s, scientists in America and other nations began to experiment with rockets that could travel into outer

---

Let Justice Roll Down

John Perkins was born in New Hebron, Mississippi, in 1930. His family members were sharecroppers and he grew up in crushing poverty. At the age of seventeen, Perkins decided to leave Mississippi for a better life in California where he found a good job. In 1951, he married Vera Mae Buckley and settled in southern California. During this time, Perkins began a spiritual journey which led to his conversion at the age of twenty-seven. From that moment on, he and Vera Mae began to work with Child Evangelism Fellowship and other ministries.

His faith ultimately brought him back to Mississippi where he began to share the gospel and help his own people find fair treatment under the law and good paying jobs. God opened doors for Perkins and his family to minister to the needy of rural Mississippi. God blessed his labors and out of this work grew the Voice of Calvary ministry.

By the mid-1960s, the Civil Rights movement began to affect the entire nation. Perkins understood though "that integration, equal opportunity, welfare, charity, and all other such programs would in themselves fail to deal with the deep-seated values which had left [the] black communities spiritually bankrupt. Revolution—spiritual revolution, not reform or welfare—is the only solution to spiritual bankruptcy. And that is why the gospel of Jesus Christ, with its power to 'transform people by the renewing of their minds' (Rom.12:2) is of primary importance to the black community."

Through much injustice Perkins learned the triumph of God's transforming love. Out of violence and poverty, he came to the deep conviction that "only the power of Christ's crucifixion on the cross and the glory of His resurrection can heal the deep racial wounds in both black and white people in America." In 1976, Perkins wrote a book about his life and ministry called *Let Justice Roll Down*.

an effort to provide jobs, food, clothing, education, and housing for millions of people. The federal government's main role, however, under the United States Constitution, is to protect the American people. The federal government was never supposed to be spending great sums of money to provide for the social needs of the American people. Nevertheless, since the 1930s, American Presidents like Franklin D. Roosevelt, Harry S. Truman, and Dwight D.

President John F. Kennedy

Eisenhower greatly expanded the role and power of the federal government. This situation has become so bad in recent years that our government had to spent billions of dollars—that it did not own—trying to meet the needs of various groups of people. By the late 1990s, the American government was facing a six trillion dollar debt! In short, the socialistic policies in our federal government have greatly weakened the United States economy. Once, our country was the richest country in the world; now we are a debtor nation and are forced to borrow money from international bankers.

The federal government must get out of the business of social welfare before America is destroyed financially. The job of providing for the needs of the poor and needy should be done privately by churches and private charitable organizations like the Salvation Army, American Red Cross, and World Vision. Christians must lead the American people by actions and statements to see their duty to serve the poor and the needy.

Despite problems, the United States con-

tinued to grow. In 1959, our country added a new state called Alaska into the union of states. The same year, our country added another new state called Hawaii into our union. Our nation now has a total of fifty states.

Communism Spreads Further

In 1960, the American people elected John F. Kennedy as their new President. The major problem that President Kennedy faced in the early 1960s was with the island of Cuba. This nation was taken over by the communists in 1959, and a violent dictator named Fidel Castro came to power. The Russians were secretly sending weapons of war to Cuba in 1962. Since Cuba is located just a few miles from the state of Florida, many people in America became concerned. Late in 1962, it was confirmed that the Russians had put nuclear missiles in Cuba that could destroy American cities. President Kennedy told the Russians and the Cubans that all missiles and nuclear weapons must be removed from Cuba. They agreed to remove the missiles provided that America would not invade Cuba with American soldiers. The problem was settled without a war being fought.

In November 1963, President Kennedy was murdered by a man named Lee Harvey Oswald. Vice-President Lyndon Johnson was then responsible for taking over the duties of former President Kennedy.

Before President Kennedy was shot, another conflict in Asia began to develop. Vietnam, a former French colony in Southeast Asia, became independent in 1954, with communists in the north and non-communists in the south. South Vietnam came under attack by communist forces. For this reason, Presidents Eisenhower and Kennedy sent a few American advisors to this nation to see how we could help the South Vietnamese government and military. This conflict slowly developed into a war between the communists in North Vietnam along with their supporters in South Vietnam and the free people of South Vietnam.

Our nation's new president, Lyndon B. Johnson, decided to send large numbers of American combat soldiers to Vietnam during 1965-1968. At the start of this conflict, many Americans were in favor of sending troops to Vietnam. As the 1960s began to develop, however, the war became bigger and more bloody. The fed-

Airborne Ranger, as used in the Vietnam War

The Huey helicopter was used to airlift troops in Vietnam.

eral government was so afraid of starting another world war that it often would not let its soldiers wage full scale war against the North Vietnamese. American soldiers were being killed every day, but it seemed as though the government did not want to win this conflict; therefore, by 1969, thousands of American people began to march in the streets and demand that we pull our soldiers out of Vietnam. The United States' people became divided on this issue, and our country no longer had the will to support the Vietnam War in a unified way.

This was a sad time in American history. The enemies of freedom had managed to damage the noble spirit of America. Many people in the United States began to doubt their government leaders and question if our great country should stop trying to save the world from communism. By 1973, the American government finally realized that it was foolish to keep our men in Vietnam if we did not have the will to win. Our army was removed from Vietnam in 1973, and our people came home. The Vietnam War finally ended in 1975 as the communist forces in North Vietnam and local communists in South Vietnam took over the nation of South Vietnam. All of Vietnam became united under a communist government. It took many years for the American people to regain the spirit of patriotism that they lost during the Vietnam War.

The Supreme Court Defies God

The Vietnam War was not the only problem that our nation had in the 1960s. A movement began to develop in our country that started to try to remove God from our society and destroy our nation's Christian heritage. Sadly, our country's Supreme Court ruled in 1962 that it was illegal for children to pray in the public schools. The Bible could no longer be taught in the public schools and the Ten Commandments could not be read in the classroom. In addition, in 1973, our Supreme Court ruled in the case known as *Roe vs. Wade* that it was no longer illegal for a mother to kill her unborn child. This ungodly ruling has encouraged the women of America to murder their own unborn babies in violation of God's Law that says, "Thou shalt not kill."

When our courts and government leaders permitted God and the Bible to be removed from our society, they opened the way for many evil forces to gain power in our land. As a result, America is staggering under a heavy load of sin. Our land is losing its greatness, because it is losing its moral goodness. Our nation's only hope is to turn away from lawlessness and immorality, and return to God and His Word. It is true that righteousness exalts a nation and that blessed is the nation whose God is the Lord.

Astronaut Neil Armstrong

A Man on the Moon

Perhaps the brightest and best achievement of our nation in the late 1960s was our success in landing a man on the moon. In 1969, millions of Americans watched astronauts Neil Armstrong and Edwin Aldrin walk on the moon for the first time. No other nation has ever been able to send men to the moon and return them safely to earth. America's space program has continued to grow over the years. In 1981, the United States developed a special reusable spacecraft known as a space shuttle. This craft can carry several astronauts into outer space and return to earth in the same manner as a regular airplane. Therefore, the space shuttle can be used over and over again.

Chapter 26 Review Questions

1. Which President was murdered in 1963, and by whom?
2. Why did America enter the Vietnam War?
3. During what year was Alaska added to the United States?
4. Who took over as dictator of Cuba in 1959?
5. During what year did the Vietnam War end?
6. Why is the United States losing its greatness?

America's Recent Past 27

Have you ever seen your parents go vote? In time, you will be able to vote yourself. In fact, a wonderful event took place in 1971 that helped young adults to become more involved with American government. A special addition or "amendment" to our beloved Constitution was passed by our Congress in Washington, D.C. This amendment, known as the Twenty-sixth Amendment, said that anyone who was a citizen of the United States of age eighteen or older could vote in all of our country's elections. It is a great privilege and duty to help vote good and godly people into public office. All patriotic Americans who are old enough to vote should be responsible enough to vote as often as possible.

President Richard M. Nixon

The Discouraging '70s

In 1972, shortly before the close of the Vietnam War, President Richard Nixon was reelected as our nation's president. Nixon was under constant pressure from the American people to pull our soldiers out of Vietnam. Violent protests were common during the late 1960s and early 1970s, as Americans demanded an end to the war. Other citizens were marching in the streets to protest the fact that black Americans were not being given fair treatment. Adding to this confusion, was the fact that the United States was going through a mild economic recession.

President Nixon became involved in an immoral "cover-up" of crimes that were committed by a few of his staff. This cover-up led to a long and ugly investigation of Richard Nixon in 1973. Sadly, Mr. Nixon lied to the American people regarding the actions of his staff. Several months later, in 1974, Nixon decided to resign as President of the United States. Vice President Gerald Ford took over the office of President in 1974 and became America's thirty-eighth President.

In 1976, it was time for the American people to elect a new president. Mr. James Carter became our nation's 39th President. President Carter was unable to move our nation in a positive, forward direction. America's image as a world power suffered greatly during the late 1970s. Many nations around the world lost respect for the United States. President Carter made the mistake of establishing normal relations with Communist China while insulting our friends in the free nation of Taiwan. Carter gave away our nation's rights in the Panama Canal Zone, which many Americans believe has compromised our nation's security. Also, a large group of American citizens were kidnapped by Islamist terrorists in the country of Iran and President Carter provided poor leadership during this crisis. In short, our country had sunk to new lows during the Carter years. Our nation was humbled by Almighty God.

President Ronald Reagan

The Reagan-Bush Years

The American people began to look for a new president in 1980. Thankfully, our nation decided to elect a president who could motivate the American people to return to the values that made our country great. The people chose Ronald Reagan as their new president. Ronald Reagan told the American people that they should not look to big government to save them; they were told to look to God for help and strength.

In just a few short years, the people of America began to wake up and realize that they had to change their thinking. President Reagan helped to remind people that it was love of God, hard work, and a compassion toward our fellow citizens that made America great. Our country's military was strengthened

during the 1980s as new threats to our nation began to develop. A stronger economy and a stronger military have helped the United States regain respect around the world. These changes helped the "Cold War" to fade away as the leaders of several communist countries were forced to give up their power and stop causing military confrontations with the free nations of the world.

The American people elected Mr. George H. W. Bush to be their nation's forty-first president in 1988. President Bush struggled during

President George H. W. Bush

his first two years in office trying to solve America's difficult budget and economic problems, and dealing with a major military conflict that had developed in the Middle East country of Kuwait. By God's grace, American soldiers helped the country of Kuwait regain its freedom during 1991 from the cruel occupation of the Iraqi army. This military conflict was called "Operation Desert Storm." Mr. Bush was also our nation's leader during the historic breakup of the communist controlled Soviet Union in 1991. Communist leaders in the former Soviet Union (Russia) and Eastern Europe were forced by their people to give up much of their power and control over their nations in recent years. Sadly, however, civil war has occurred in a few countries in Eastern Europe as the people of these countries tried to reestablish their own national identities.

George Bush was unable to convince the American people that he had a workable plan for the U.S. economy during his four years as President. Consequently, he was defeated in his bid for reelection by the governor of Arkansas, Mr. Bill Clinton.

The Clinton Legacy

Mr. William Jefferson Clinton was elected as the forty-second President of the United States in 1992. During his first term in office, President Clinton tried to increase the role of the federal government in many areas of our economy and nation. In 1993, for example, he introduced a proposal aimed at putting the federal government in charge of a program that would guarantee all Americans full health coverage. This program would have increased the size and scope of federal government power far beyond the limits or intentions of the Constitution of the United States. He also proposed increasing the role of the federal government in areas such as education, child welfare, and in the promotion or protection of the so-called right of pregnant women to kill their unborn babies.

By God's grace, very few programs recommended by President Clinton received the approval of the American people or the Congress of the United States. As a result, our nation was kept from the path of socialism—a mild form of communism—which President

President Bill Clinton

Clinton was determined to promote. Bill Clinton also spent time promoting and defending those Americans who have chosen to live in an ungodly homosexual life-style. He ordered our nation's military leaders to change their rules so that homosexual soldiers could continue to stay in our armed forces without penalty. Mr. Clinton was the first President in all of our nation's history to publicly promote and endorse the anti-God and anti-family life-style known as "gay" or "lesbian."

Thanks to the efforts of many of the conservative leaders in the Congress of the United States during the 1990s, our nation was able to begin to cut the growth of federal government programs. Our Congress pressured President Clinton to begin to dismantle major government welfare programs and other unconstitutional activities that the leaders in Washington, D.C. have been promoting for years. This effort was supported by many pa-

The United Nations has sent peace-keeping forces around the world in recent years.

triotic Americans and resulted in many positive economic and political blessings for our country at the end of the twentieth century.

In 1996, the American people decided to reelect Bill Clinton as President. A great deal of effort was expended by the Clinton Administration during its second term to keep wars from growing in various parts of the world. In a manner inconsistent with our nation's Constitution, President Clinton sent United States soldiers to serve in foreign lands while being placed under the control and direction of leaders from the United Nations. United States troops were sent to Bosnia in Eastern Europe in 1994 to engage in peace keeping services. Our nation's soldiers were also sent to Africa as well as to the Middle East to work under the United Nations military leaders in so-called peace keeping efforts. The Lord alone knows how long our nation can continue to send

troops to trouble nations in an effort to keep conflicts around the world from turning into big wars.

During 1998, Bill Clinton brought great shame and disgrace upon the office of the President, as he committed immoral sexual acts with a woman who worked at the White House. To make matters worse, President Clinton chose to lie directly to the American people and in a federal court regarding his adulterous affair, as he attempted to cover-up his guilt. Mr. Clinton, however, decided not to resign in the wake of the scandal. As a result of this attempted cover-up, the House of Representatives voted on December 19, 1998, to impeach the President. This was only the second time in the history of the United States that a President had been impeached. This affair weakened the presidency and greatly tarnished President Clinton's legacy.

Impeachment
According to the Constitution

Impeachment is the presentation of formal charges against a public official which results in that official being removed from office. The Constitution of the United States provides for the removal of the President, Vice-president, or any other government official based upon a conviction of "treason, bribery, or other high crimes and misdemeanors"—impeachment being the first step in this process. "The sole power of impeachment" lies with the House of Representatives. This means the House has the power to bring such charges as treason, bribery, perjury (the willful telling of a lie while under lawful oath), and so forth, against a government official. The Senate, on the other hand, has "the sole power to try all impeachments." This means that after the House impeaches an official, the Senate has the responsibility to try the case set before them. The Senate needs a two-thirds vote for a conviction.

The chief justice of the United States presides over the Senate hearings if the President has been impeached. If a conviction results during this process, the President is removed from office and disqualified to hold "any office of honor,

Andrew Johnson

trust, or profit under the United States." The Senate only has the power to remove him from office, but he may still be open to further "indictment, trial, judgment, and punishment according to Law."

Although the framers of the U. S. Constitution wanted to maintain the independence of the three branches of government (the executive, legislative, and judicial), they believed that a way must be made to remove high government officials that are found guilty of breaking the law. Consequently, they placed the requirement that the Senate must have a two-thirds majority to convict an official, so the process would not be taken lightly. Moreover, they limited the charges of impeachment to "treason, bribery, and other high crimes and misdemeanors."

Only two Presidents, Andrew Johnson and Bill Clinton, have been brought to trial in the Senate on charges voted by the House, but neither were convicted. In Andrew Johnson's case, the Senate failed to convict Johnson by one vote; the charges were purely based on partisan politics. In 1974, the House Judiciary Committee voted three charges of impeachment against President Richard M. Nixon for his cover-up in the Watergate scandal. He resigned, however, before the charges could be voted upon by the House.

President George W. Bush

In 2000, George W. Bush was elected as the forty-third President of the United States. The election between George W. Bush and Vice President Albert Gore was very close. It took a few weeks after the election was over before a large number of votes could be recounted and

George W. Bush

the winner officially announced. Having won the political battle for the White House, Bush would soon face other, more significant battles that would threaten the very fabric of our society.

Early on in his presidency, George W. Bush earned the respect of many God-fearing citizens of the United States. He has performed his duties as President in a very capable and honorable fashion and has helped to guide our country through a difficult period in its history. President Bush has also shown the moral courage to select federal judges who will rule in a manner that is in keeping with the U.S. Constitution and who will protect the life and liberty of all Americans, born and unborn. Moreover, he has refused to lend his support to homosexual groups who are seeking to undermine the God-ordained institution of the family by demanding that the government recognize so-called "same-sex marriage."

In addition to fighting for biblical moral values, George W. Bush continued to try to find ways to improve the lives and security of American citizens. He led the fight for tax cuts for the American people, helping them work their way out of hard economic times. President Bush also had the courage to defy the United Nations when it refused to follow through with its commitment to disarm the military in Iraq that was controlled by Saddam Hussein. All Americans should be thankful to God for blessing them with a President that is willing to put the security needs of the United States above the fickle policies of the United Nations.

One of the few cases in which President Bush failed to provided proper moral leadership was when he did not support the efforts of Alabama Supreme Court Justice Ray Moore, who courageously refused to remove a statue of the Ten Commandments from an Alabama courthouse. In the summer of 2003, a federal court ruled that it was illegal for Judge Moore to display the Ten Commandments in a state court building, even though he paid for the statue with his own money. This situation merely highlights the ongoing battle between those who wish to weaken our biblical heritage and those who desire to turn our nation and its laws back to the sure foundation of God's Word.

The statue of the Ten Commandments at the Alabama Supreme Court building

The Battle Against Terrorism

On September 11, 2001, President Bush and all loyal Americans were shocked and angered by an attack upon two major U.S. cities by radical Islamist terrorists. These attackers hijacked four American planes and managed to fly three of them into large buildings in New York City and Washington, D.C. Shortly after the attack, which was the worst single act of terrorism in U.S. history,

to approve the use of military force against Iraq in October of 2002. After months of failed negotiations through the United Nations, George W. Bush sent U.S. and British troops into Iraq to remove the Iraqi leader, Saddam Hussein, and to destroy any weapons or training camps that could be used by terrorist groups. This military action, called "Operation Iraqi Freedom" lasted from March 19 to May 1, 2003, though scattered resistance continued for an extended period of time at the cost of hundreds of lives.

The United States military forces succeeded in removing Saddam from power and freed the oppressed people of Iraq; however, U.S. forces now have the difficult task of rebuilding the nation and establishing a new stable government. President Bush and other government leaders acknowledge that it will take several years to transform Iraq into a peaceful nation capable of governing itself.

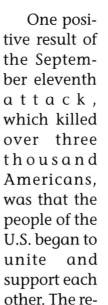

Courageous firemen worked to save lives after the attack on the World Trade Center in New York City.

President Bush declared war on any nation who supports or protects terrorist groups. American armed forces, along with those from other countries friendly to the United States, began to attack terrorist strongholds in Afghanistan in October 2001, overthrowing its pro-terrorist government.

President Bush warned the American people that the military effort against terrorist strongholds would be long, hard, and costly. Prior to the terrorist attack, President Bush had hoped to help the American economy to recover from a minor recession. In the months following the attack, however, it became more clear that the American economy would slip further into economic recession as the cost of fighting terrorism began to rise.

As the struggle against terrorism became more serious, President Bush asked Congress

One positive result of the September eleventh attack, which killed over three thousand Americans, was that the people of the U.S. began to unite and support each other. The re-

U.S. Marines helped Iraqi civilians topple a massive statue of Saddam in Firdos Square in the heart of Baghdad.

ality of terrorism simply underscores the truth of Scripture regarding the total depravity of man as well as man's need for salvation through the Prince of Peace.

Space Age Technology

Our country was the first country on earth to send a spaceship to the moon. In the year 1969, America used electricity to guide a spaceship to just the right spot on the moon's surface. It was wonderful to see America's spacemen putting the American flag on the moon! By God's grace these men returned to earth safely.

Some of the inventions which have been made in recent times are the space satellite, television, the word processor, the computer, the space shuttle, and a hundred others. There are, however, too many for me to say anything about, so I shall have to stop right here.

As wonderful as all these inventions are we must remember who is the one that makes it possible. The great Creator, Jesus Christ, gave us all of these gifted inventors capable of in-

Spacewalks are used to repair equipment or perform scientific experiments.

telligent thought and genius. When we think about all the wonderful accomplishments of mankind, let us never forget who makes all of this possible! Glory to God in the highest.

The space program of United States reached new heights in 1997 as it successfully landed a satellite on the planet Mars. This satellite took soil samples and beamed back a number of wonderful pictures of this far away planet. During this same year, the United States space program was committed to helping establish a permanent international space station that would stay in orbit high above the earth. This new space station should be launched sometime after the year 2003.

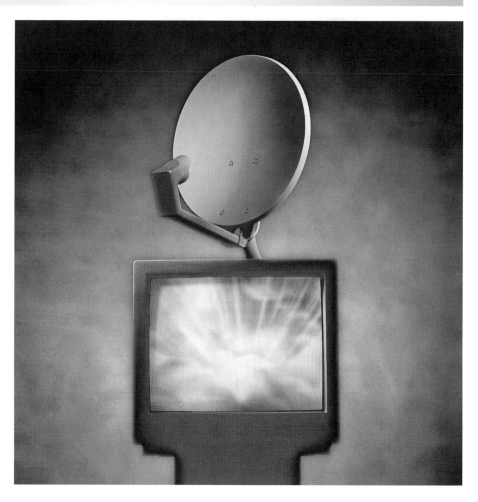

Satellite technology brings the world's events into our homes as they happen. Communication satellites are used to transmit these events from one geographic location to another. These new communication systems provide Christians with wonderful opportunities to spread the gospel and a Christian world view to the nations.

One of the most important contributions of the space program has been the development of new technology. Improvements in computers, communication systems, and solar energy have often been born out of efforts to enhance the successfulness of the United States space program. The influence of computer technology, in general, continues to impact ordinary people more and more. During the early 1990s, the "Internet" was expanded to permit people from all over the world to communicate with each other by way of a network or series of very powerful computer sites. Even youngsters in many parts of the United States enjoy "surfing" the Internet sites on their personal computers to obtain interesting information or to send electronic mail or fax letters to friends far and near.

The end of the twentieth century presented the people of the United States with many challenges and a number of confusing choices that were mingled with an aspect of excitement and fear. Much of the Western world is living in something of a spiritual fog while great Christian revivals are breaking out in many parts of Africa and Asia where people have a genuine hunger for the Word of God. The prayer of every true Christian must surely be that Christian reformation might unfold in the near future. Only then, will countries like the United States be truly prepared to summon the courage and wisdom to face the challenges of the twenty-first century.

I sincerely hope that each young reader will remember many of the things that took place in the United States during the twentieth century. As our country begins a new century, it is only right and proper that we should try to learn the lessons that God was seeking to teach us during the century that has recently ended.

John H. Glenn

John Herschel Glenn, Jr., (1921–) was born forty years before the idea of man landing on the Moon was a possibility. He grew up in Cambridge, Ohio, where he became an honor student and outstanding athlete in high school. His interest in aviation began when he was a child. One year, when he was bed-ridden due to scarlet fever, Glenn built model airplanes out of wood and then test flew them. If they crashed, he would repair the planes and fly them again. His dream of flying finally became a reality in college, where he learned how to fly in a civilian program sponsored by the Navy. After graduating, he joined the U.S. Marine Corps and became a naval aviator.

During World War II, Glenn flew fifty-nine missions and was promoted to captain in July of 1945. He also served in the Korean War (1950–1953), where he flew ninety combat missions. Later, he became a test pilot for the Navy and, on July 16, 1957, was the first man to fly faster than the speed of sound in an F8U Crusader, a supersonic jet. As his career was advancing, however, something happened that would change the course of his life. On October 4, 1957, the Russians launched *Sputnik 1*, the first artificial satellite. The next year, the U.S. government decided to form the National Aeronautics and Space Administration (NASA). NASA immediately requested men from all branches of the armed forces to join the program, and John Glenn was one of seven chosen to become an astronaut in the Mercury Program.

NASA chose John Glenn as the backup pilot for the first two Mercury flights, but he was finally selected to make the first manned flight that would orbit Earth. On February 20, 1962, astronaut John Glenn lifted off into space as millions of people watched on television. This historic flight lasted less than five hours, but he successfully guided the Mercury spacecraft, *Friendship 7*, around the earth three times. Glenn was honored in many parades throughout the country and received several medals to commemorate this remarkable event.

Glenn went on to serve his country as a senator from the state of Ohio. He won reelection three times, before he decided not to run again in 1998. Since his days as an astronaut, he had always wanted to return to space—only if it could be justified through scientific experiments. His desire was realized on October 29, 1998, when John Glenn returned to space on flight STS-95, becoming the oldest person to fly in space at the age of seventy-seven. During the flight he said, "To look out at this kind of creation out here and not believe in God is, to me, impossible. It just strengthens my faith."

A Historic Presidential Election

The 2000 election campaign between George W. Bush and Al Gore showed the unique nature of America's method of electing presidents. It is the person who gets a majority of the electoral votes, not necessarily the person who gets the most popular votes nationwide, who becomes President. Usually, of course, the winning presidential candidate gets both a majority of the electoral votes and the most popular votes, but the 2000 election showed that that is not always the case. A candidate wins electoral votes by getting the most popular votes in a state or the District of Columbia. The fifty states and the District of Columbia have a total of 538 votes—divided among the states according to their population—with the victor required to win at least 270 electoral votes.

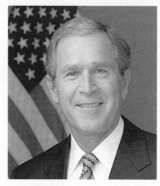

George W. Bush

The 2000 presidential election was one of the closest in American history. For the first time since 1888, the person who won the popular vote lost the election. Al Gore narrowly won the national popular vote by a little over 500,000 votes, while losing the election to George W. Bush by five electoral votes. It was not until the middle of December that the winner of the presidential election was eventually decided. The key state in the election was Florida; it took several recounts and court cases before it was determined that George W. Bush had won by 537 votes, giving him Florida's 25 electoral votes. Bush's eventual victory in Florida gave him a total of 271 electoral votes, allowing him to become the 43rd President of the United States.

In addition, George W. Bush became only the second person to have been elected President after his father held that office. The first father-son presidential combination was John Adams (second President) and John Quincy Adams (sixth President). George W. Bush became the forty-third President, twelve years after his father, George H.W. Bush, had been elected the forty-first President.

On November 2, 2004, President George W. Bush was re-elected to a second term, defeating his opponent, Senator John Kerry. One of the most encouraging aspects of the 2004 election was that a significant number of voters chose their candidate largely upon moral and religious considerations.

Chapter 27 Review Questions

1. What wonderful event took place in 1971 that helped young adults to become more involved with American government?

2. Who took over the office of President after Richard Nixon resigned in 1974?

3. Who gave away the right of the United States government to control the Panama Canal Zone?

4. What did President Ronald Reagan tell the American people regarding how our nation could regain its greatness?

5. What was the name of the war in the Middle East that involved the freeing of the country of Kuwait from the Iraqi army's control?

6. Who was elected as the forty-second President of the United States?

7. In what year did the United States space program land a satellite on the planet Mars?

The American System 28

Americans have never stood still. The first restless colonists who landed at Jamestown had a forward look in their eyes. From the colonies along the Atlantic Ocean, they moved across the Appalachian Mountains, Mississippi River, Great Plains, and Rocky Mountains. Even after they reached the Pacific Ocean, the Americans did not stand still. They soon became involved with other countries of the world—both in the Old World and the New. They even managed, by the grace of God, to put a man on the moon in 1969.

Since 1900, the United States has grown increasingly important as a world power. Since World War II, the United States' government has tried to help people in other countries of the world to maintain democratic forms of government. At the present time, billions of dollars are being spent to help the free nations protect themselves from the spread of dictatorships.

In the early 1990s, several countries in Europe and Asia were able to change their governments from communist dictatorships to free republics. The Central European country of

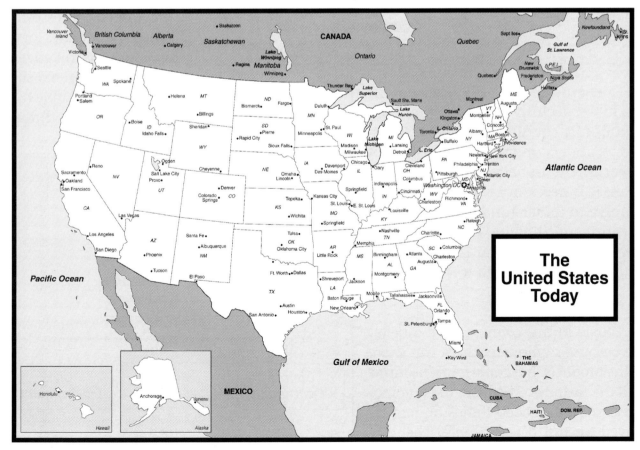

The United States Today

East Germany, for example, was reunited with West Germany in 1990 to form one free nation. Germany had been divided by the communists for many years. The old communist state of the Soviet Union, which President Reagan called an "evil empire," broke up in 1991. Russia, the main "republic" of the former Soviet Union, is now a true republic with the freedom to elect their own leaders.

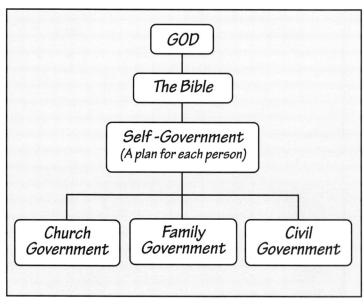

Communism is still a threat in the world—especially in Asia where several communist countries still exist. In order to understand why our system of government is better than communism, it is necessary for people in this country to understand their system of government. Studying how our form of government developed is one way of learning to understand it.

Our God-given Rights

People in this country have a better life because so many of them can share in the products that come from the farms and the factories. The food, the automobiles, and other good things are not reserved for just a few people. They are available to almost everyone who is willing to work hard. People in the United States have believed that each man should benefit from his work. We have, therefore, developed the idea that every individual has certain rights. Every individual has certain rights, but no one has the right to take away the freedom of other people. The government does not give people rights, it merely secures their God-given rights.

Americans live in groups. Each individual has certain rights, but almost everyone is a part of a group of people. As adults, Americans help decide what the groups do. The smallest units of government are cities and counties. The medium-sized units are states. The largest is the national or federal government.

The Constitution of the United States established special rules for the operation of the government. In the years since the Constitution was written, the people have added new rules or changed old ones through

Constitutional amendments (additions to the Constitution).

The fundamental principle that underscores our nation's system is the belief in the inalienable right of each citizen to life and liberty. The American people believe in free enterprise. The free enterprise system guarantees the right of a person to own property and to run his own business without burdensome government controls.

People who live under the Constitution of the United States have many important inalienable rights. They elect the officials who make the laws and who decide what kind of taxes should be collected. They have the right to a trial if they are accused of a crime, and they enjoy the right to own guns and use them in a lawful way. These are just three of the many freedoms which people in the United States enjoy.

Using Our Resources Wisely

As the population of the United States has increased, the government has faced new problems. One of these is conservation of natural resources. At first, there seemed to be more land, timber, and minerals than people would ever want or use. The country was covered with millions of acres of forest. There seemed to be plenty of coal, copper, iron ore, and other minerals beneath the ground. There was plenty of water in most areas.

The United States is still rich in natural resources, but people realize that these resources can be used up. Small trees are being planted to replace large ones which have been cut down. Land which is no longer suitable for growing crops is being planted with trees. Rivers are dammed to form lakes. Water in these lakes can be used for irrigation of crops or for city water supplies. Electricity is also created at the dams. Rules are made for the mining and the use of minerals. Wise farmers show people how to restore fertility to the soil. Terraces and ditches prevent soil from being washed away by erosion. By using our resources wisely, we can make them last for thousands of years.

Government services cost money. The people pay for all the services performed by their federal, state, and local governments. The representatives of the people decide how much money is needed. Then they levy taxes to pay the bills. The citizens really tax themselves. They can raise or lower their taxes. They control the governments which work for them. It is every American's duty to take part in the process of controlling their government. In short, the government is the hired servant of the people under God.

People in the United States believe in the private ownership of property. Every person in this country owns something—even if it is only the clothes he wears.

Farmers own their farms. Shopkeepers own their stores. Large factories may belong to a few people or they may belong to many people. For example, the American Telephone and Telegraph Company belongs to more than 2,250,000 people who own stock in the company. In many cases, people own shares in the company for which they work.

Our economic system gives freedom of opportunity to all people. They may work where they wish. Our system permits people to spend their money as they think is best.

Another way in which people in this country help other individuals is through giving money. Churches and private schools are among the institutions that are supported by gifts. Money is also collected to help families who are in need and to aid in medical research. The majority of Americans believe that God loves and blesses a cheerful giver.

Our Modern Work Force

People in the United States take pride in their mechanical gadgets. Many of these work-saving devices make it possible for Americans to complete their jobs in a short time. During the 1800s, Americans began to use a larger number of machines which made work easier. Since the end of World War II, many of the machines in factories have been improved to the point that they almost operate themselves. Changing methods in the manufacturing of cloth provides a good example of how these advances have taken place. Weaving cloth on a hand loom was a slow process. The machine-operated looms increased production tremendously, but many people were still required for the production of cloth. In recent years, machines have taken over the work which was done by many of the people in mills that produce cloth.

Various kinds of automatic equipment run by computers do many of the jobs which were formerly done by unskilled workers. For this reason, people today need to attend school longer so they will be able to do work which cannot be done by machines.

During the 1800s, people took it for granted that most workers worked from sun-

rise to sunset. Even children sometimes worked for long hours each week. During the latter part of the 1800s and the early part of the 1900s, many people began to feel that women and children should not work for long hours in factories.

More recently, the length of the work week for many workers has been cut. Most people today work about forty hours a week. The shorter work week makes it possible for workers to take part in many recreational activities. People who live near lakes have time to fish and enjoy boating. Some people enjoy playing games such as golf or tennis. Others like to attend football or baseball games.

The most important effect of the new work-saving machines, however, has been the fact that they make it possible for children to attend school much longer than they could before. By attending school, young people learn how to do more skilled work. The also learn to enjoy the books, music, and art that are being produced throughout our land.

The shorter work week has also increased educational opportunities for adults. Many people are reading books, listening to music, and visiting art galleries. People in the United States are not only enjoying those things; they are also producing them. Writers, musicians, and artists from this country are being recognized as outstanding by people in other countries. Radio, television, and numerous inexpensive books and magazines have made it possible for almost everyone in the United States to continue his education throughout life. In recent years, more parents have been taking advantage of their right to privately educate their children at home. Many of our country's great leaders have been educated at home.

Preserving Our Freedom

People in the United States know that their country is not perfect. They realize, however, that it is a good place to live. They also realize that our form of government makes it possible for them to do their part in making it a better place in which to live. Through free elections they decide how their government is to be operated.

The murder or impeachment of a President is a tragic event. The American government, however, is set up in such a way that Presidents can change without affecting the operation of the government. Because the power of the President is limited by the Constitution, no one person ever controls the government of the United States.

Control of the government by a large group of people, chosen in free elections, is a basic principle of the government of the United States. The people of the United States, working through their government, are dedicated to the idea of helping other countries to maintain free governments, too. One of the best ways of helping to maintain freedom is by setting a good example. Our society should prove to other nations that a republican form of government based on the rule of constitutional law can work effectively.

Indeed, of all the threats that America is facing today, the greatest threat is ungodliness and lawlessness. The basic need of a free society is for its people to be self-governed under God's law. True liberty is not the freedom to live as we please, but the power to live as we know God requires. A corrupt and rebellious people cannot and will not remain free, for the simple reason that such people require a powerful government to pass laws so they can be protected from one another! People will ultimately be ruled voluntarily by God's laws (i.e., the Ten Commandments), or they will be ruled forcibly by tyrants.

As you may remember, the twentieth century was filled with many changes and more than a little conflict. This century contained two world wars and numerous other smaller wars. It also changed the way that people live more than any other previous century. Prior to the twentieth century, the people of America had never seen an airplane, automobile, or space shuttle. In fact, people in the nineteenth century would have laughed at anyone who seriously thought that men could fly to the moon and back safely. At the end of the twentieth century, however, even children take for granted that men can fly a spacecraft to the moon anytime they wish.

As if this is not enough, what about the thousands of amazing inventions that have blessed the people of America and much of the civilized world? The twentieth century, for example, brought us the cordless telephone and fax machine, the television and motion pictures, the personal computer and internet technology, microwave ovens, nuclear power, submarines, and jet airplanes. All of these inventions, and many more besides, were created during the twentieth century. If you really want to have fun, just try to imagine what new inventions and changes you will see during the twenty-first century!

Chapter 28 Review Questions

1. What does the term "free enterprise" mean when people describe a country's economy?

2. Does each American receive his rights from the government? Where do our rights come from, and what is our government's true job?

3. Additions or changes to our national Constitution are known as what?

4. Do most people in the United States believe in private ownership of property or government ownership of property?

5. What types of important institutions are supported by the voluntary gifts of American people?

6. Are most Americans working longer hours today than people in the 1800s?

7. Is the power of the President of the United States limited by the Constitution?

Calling America Back to God 29

During our study of American history, we have looked at the lives of many great heroes and patriots from the past. As we prepare to close our study of the story of America, however, we must take one last look at a true American hero who lived during the twentieth century. Sit back then and read about the life of someone who made a real difference for God and country during the past century.

Schaeffer's Early Years

The snow fell on the sleepy town of Germantown, Pennsylvania, during the winter of 1912. Like most small towns in America at this time, all was peaceful and bright. The people of the United States had been blessed by Almighty God with freedom, just laws based on the Bible, good food, and happy homes. The Lord had truly shed his grace upon the American people.

It was into this peaceful setting that God sent a new baby boy into the home of Francis and Bessie Schaeffer on January 30, 1912. This new baby was named Francis, just like his father. Both parents were excited to see what would become of their son in the years ahead. As all heroes do, the man known as Francis A. Schaeffer began as a tiny baby.

Almost no one who knew little Francis would ever dream that he would grow up to be a famous Christian missionary and writer. In the first place, Francis did not seem to be in

any hurry to know God well as a young boy. Secondly, this young man did not have a strong interest in studying the Bible.

As time passed, however, God began to work in the heart of Francis Schaeffer. Just before his eighteenth birthday, he began to read and study the Bible very carefully. A short time later, this young man was brought to the place where he began to trust in Christ as Lord and Savior.

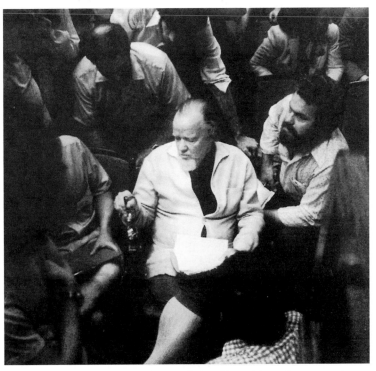

Francis Schaeffer ministering to students

During the time that Francis was drawing close to God, many people in America were moving away from faith in God and His Word. The Lord had blessed our nation with so many wonderful things that people began to think that they no longer needed God. Even church leaders began to turn away from the truths of the Bible. They taught people that they could love God any way that they felt like, even if it broke God's commandments. Americans in many parts of the country had foolishly forgotten that "Blessed is the nation whose God is the Lord."

It was at this time that Francis decided to go to Hampton-Sydney College in Virginia to further his education. He understood that he needed more skills if he was to serve God well in the days ahead. He studied very hard and graduated from this college with honors after just three years.

While in college, he became friends with a Christian girl named Edith Seville. Francis first met this young lady at his home church —the First Presbyterian Church of Germantown. Three years later they were married.

Preparing to Serve God

Francis had made an important decision to become a preacher of the gospel while at college. In 1935, he decided to go to a special Bible school for men who felt called into preaching God's Word and leading God's people.

This new school, called Westminster Theological Seminary, was led by a faithful and gifted teacher named John Gresham Machen. This man of God was forced to leave his first teaching job at Princeton Seminary because that Bible school was teaching things that went against the Word of God. After leaving Princeton, Dr. Machen

---

J. Gresham Machen

The best-known and most out-spoken leader of the early Fundamentalists (Bible-believing Christians), was Presbyterian Bible teacher J. Gresham Machen. After studying at Princeton Seminary in New Jersey, he went to Germany to study. There Machen began to wrestle with the problems of "modern thought" (or man-made ideas applied to the Bible and Christian teaching). As he struggled with the ideas of modern thought, he was supported by the prayers of his mother and his daily study of Scripture. Arriving at a solid conviction that the Bible was truthful in every way, Machen became one of the most powerful defenders of true Christianity in the early 1900s. He was committed to the teachings of the Bible as summarized in the Westminster Confession of Faith. He taught the New Testament at Princeton Theological Seminary in 1915. In 1923, his book *Christianity and Liberalism* showed that modern thought on the one hand and true Christianity on the other are not two varieties of the same religion, but two very different religions that came from two very different roots. His book was read and praised by thousands and is still widely read by serious students of the Bible today.

In 1929, Machen left Princeton Seminary after supporters of modern thought gained control of that school. He was convinced that the biblical teaching of Princeton's founding fathers should be maintained and that Bible students should not be misled with false doctrines. Machen, therefore, joined in starting a new school called Westminster Theological Seminary, in Philadelphia, Pennsylvania, during the fall of that year.

Machen and other Bible-believing Christians supported faithful independent missionaries and opposed sending out missionaries who did not believe or obey the Word of God. These men later formed the Orthodox Presbyterian Church which, to this day, stands by the Bible and in opposition to modern thought. According to God's providence, Machen died on New Year's Day, 1937. Humanly speaking, his death was a great loss to the church, but his words of godly wisdom still speak to us today.

helped start Westminster seminary, and it was here that Francis Schaeffer became involved in their program.

A type of war was going on within the Bible schools and churches of America in the 1930s and 1940s. It was not a war fought with bullets or guns, though. It was a war of words. On one side of the battle were men like Dr. Machen and Francis Schaeffer, men who believed that the Bible was true and right. On the other side of this war of words were men who said that the Bible was not really the Word of God. These men tried to lead the Christian Church in America away from the Bible and God's Law. This was why many American Christians began to get confused about what they should believe.

After seminary was over, Francis began to lead or pastor a new church group in western Pennsylvania. A few years later, Pastor Schaeffer served a new group of Christians in St. Louis, Missouri. As pastor, he taught his church families about God and His Word. He helped to lead many people to faith in the Savior, Jesus Christ.

During this time, God blessed Pastor Schaeffer and his wife with three children. This man of God worked hard to be a faithful preacher and a godly father. Several years later, God would bless the Schaeffer home with a baby boy named Franky.

Missionary to the World

In 1947, however, after the Second World War was over, Francis Schaeffer became interested in serving God overseas. A missionary organization chose Pastor Schaeffer to travel to Europe to preach the truths of the Bible. After a short time, this preacher decided to set up his missionary work in Switzerland.

It was during these early years in Switzerland that God began to bless the Bible teaching of Francis Schaeffer. Many young people began to ask good questions as they spoke to this missionary about the Bible and how to live for Christ. These questions, plus further study, helped this godly man to learn how to relate the teachings of the Bible to life in the twentieth century.

During the mid-1950s, Francis Schaeffer moved away from his duties as a traditional missionary. He believed that God was calling him to begin a special study center in Switzerland for those who were seeking a closer walk with God. This place was called *L'Abri*. This French word means *shelter*. Indeed, L'Abri was to become a wonderful shelter for those who needed a peaceful and encouraging place to explore the truths of Christianity. By 1970, the work of Francis Schaeffer began to grow, and more and more Christian study centers were set up in many countries in Europe and even in the United States. People who were hungry for the truth began to find help and hope as they turned to the Word of God. Francis Schaeffer began to write more and more books and speak at conferences and colleges around the world. This faithful man of God called the people of all nations to trust in the God of the Bible.

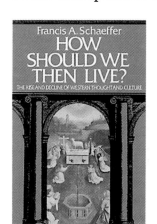

Godly Voice to America

Many Americans were filled with spiritual food for living as they read the book and watched the film series that Francis Schaeffer and his son produced entitled, *How Should We Then Live?* This encouraged the Christian church to stop running away from the problems of life in modern western society. He called Christians of all ages to live out the truths of Scripture in every area of life: in education, family life, politics, the church, and personal relationships.

This was exactly the message that the American people needed to hear at the end of the twentieth century. They needed to know that only the truth of Scripture sets people free and gives them joy and peace. The message of Mr. Schaeffer was used by Almighty God to stir a spiritual revival in the United States and parts of Europe.

In the early 1980s, Francis Schaeffer became very sick with cancer. He still continued, however, to speak and write as the Lord gave him strength. During his final years on earth, Mr. Schaeffer spent a great deal of time talking about the sin of killing unborn children and old people who are sick. He reminded the Christian church of its duty to stand up for the weak and helpless people of the world. In 1984,

Francis Schaeffer died of cancer at his home in Rochester, Minnesota.

If America is to remain a free and happy nation, its people need to return to the truths of Scripture that Francis Schaeffer so faithfully preached for over fifty years. It is not money and military power that holds a country together. Only the love of God and the truth of Scripture can preserve a free people.

Former President Ronald Reagan said of Mr. Schaeffer, "He will long be remembered as one of the great Christian thinkers of our century. It can rarely be said of an individual that his life touched many others and affected them for the better; it will be said of Dr. Francis Schaeffer that his life touched millions of souls and brought them to the truth of their Creator."

Chapter 29 Review Questions

1. Where was Francis A. Schaeffer born?

2. What type of war began to develop in the Bible schools and churches of America in the 1930s?

3. Who was John Gresham Machen?

4. Where did Mr. Schaeffer set up his overseas missionary work?

5. What does the word *L'Abri* mean?

6. What did former President Reagan say about Francis A. Schaeffer after this man of God died?

Epilogue

A teacher once asked her students this question: "If you were given a choice between being poor in a country where people are free, or being rich in a country where people have no freedoms, which would you choose?" At first, several pupils made the choice to be rich without freedom. As they continued to discuss the question, however, they changed their minds.

One girl summed up the ideas of the class when she said, "What good would a fine car, beautiful clothes, and a large home be if we didn't dare to speak our thoughts, travel where we wish, or worship God at our own church? Money would not make up for the loss of personal freedoms that we enjoy as citizens in a free country."

Our Christian Heritage

She was right. All American citizens have something that money cannot buy. We sometimes call it our American heritage, because it is passed on to every American child as his birthright. What is our American heritage? In many respects, our heritage as a free people is tied to the Christian heritage of early Americans like the Pilgrims and Puritans.

American freedoms have always flowed from the fountain of faith in Almighty God as King. Our nation has chosen to build upon the foundation of God's Word, the Holy Bible. For this reason, American laws respect individual rights and freedoms because all men are created in the image of God and have dignity. True Christianity promotes the principle that government leaders are servants of the people, not their divine masters. Furthermore, the teachings of the Bible regarding justice, love, and the duty of each person to earn an honest living through hard work form our nation's laws and traditions.

In short, freedom and liberty in America rests upon the unchanging will of God, rather than the ever-changing standards of sinful men.

Our Declaration of Independence states very clearly that all men have been blessed by their Creator with unalienable rights to life, liberty, and the pursuit of happiness. It further declares that our nation began with a firm reliance upon Divine Providence for its support and protection. The vast majority of the early charters, declarations, and constitutions of our beloved nation spoke of our people's high regard for the Bible and the Christian faith.

The Year of the Bible

In October 1982, the United States Congress asked President Ronald Reagan to declare the year 1983 as "The Year of the Bible." Thankfully, Congress passed this Declaration and President Reagan signed what became known as Public Law 97-280.

Our American heritage is a gift from God and is supported by His Holy Word. We all have the duty to honor our American heritage by supporting the Christian virtues that made our nation great.

The heritage of our beloved nation also includes things like songs that stir our hearts, our great flag with its Stars and Stripes, and the brave deeds of gallant citizens. Our nation's past is filled with stories about people who gave their lives for the holy cause of freedom. Some day, the boys and girls of America will grow up to be the leaders of America's tomorrow. With God's help, our nation will always shine forth with the pure light of liberty and justice. Blessed is that nation whose God is the Lord!

Public Law 97-280 states:

Authorizing and requesting the President to proclaim 1983 as the "Year of the Bible."

- Whereas the Bible, the Word of God, been made unique a contribution in shaping the United States as a distinctive and blessed nation and people;

- Whereas deeply held religious convictions springing from the Holy Scriptures led to the early settlement of our Nation;

- Whereas Biblical teachings inspired concepts of civil government that are contained in our Declaration of Independence and the Constitution of the United States;

- Whereas many of our great national leaders—among them Presidents Washington, Jackson, Lincoln, and Wilson—paid tribute to the surpassing influence of the Bible in our country's development, as in the words of President Jackson that the Bible is "the rock on which our Republic rests";

- Whereas the history of our Nation clearly illustrates the value of voluntarily applying the teachings of the Scriptures in the lives of individuals, families, and societies;

- Whereas this Nation now faces great challenges that will test this Nation as it has never been tested before; and

- Whereas that renewing our knowledge of and faith in God through Holy Scripture can strengthen us as a nation and a people:

Now, therefore, be it Resolved by the Senate and House of Representatives of the United States of America in Congress assembled, That the President is authorized and requested to designate 1983 as a national "Year of the Bible" in recognition of both the formative influence the Bible has been for our Nation, and our national need to study and apply the teachings of the Holy Scriptures.

Index